Charles MacCarthy Collins

The history, law, and practice of banking

With an appendix of statutes

Charles MacCarthy Collins

The history, law, and practice of banking
With an appendix of statutes

ISBN/EAN: 9783337113094

Printed in Europe, USA, Canada, Australia, Japan

Cover: Foto ©Suzi / pixelio.de

More available books at **www.hansebooks.com**

THE

HISTORY, LAW, AND PRACTICE

OF

BANKING.

WITH

An Appendix of Statutes.

BY

CHARLES M. COLLINS,

BARRISTER-AT-LAW,
FELLOW OF THE INSTITUTE OF BANKERS.

LONDON:
JAMES CORNISH & SONS, 297, HIGH HOLBORN, W.C.
LIVERPOOL: 37, LORD STREET & 42, NORTH JOHN STREET.
DUBLIN: 18, GRAFTON STREET.
1881.

PREFACE.

MANY works on the important subject of Banking have been published, and are before the Public,—Theoretical works of much interest to Economists, and Legal works written and compiled for the Legal Profession: but generally speaking, these are rather too abstruse, or too expensive to attract the ordinary reader or the Bank Official.

The aim of the accompanying volume is to supply an acknowledged deficiency, and to provide—in a form, simple, concise and inexpensive, and divested as far as possible of technicalities of expression—information of a practical and interesting description, useful and necessary, not only to Officers of Banks, but to the public in general.

That the work may commend itself to junior officials, explanatory details, otherwise unnecessary, have been incorporated with the text.

LONDON, *Nov.*, 1881.

CONTENTS.

PREFACE - - - - - - - - iii

PART I.
THE HISTORY AND PROGRESS OF BANKING.

CHAPTER
- I. THE EARLIEST RECORDS OF BANKING AND COINAGE — 11
- II. EARLY EUROPEAN BANKS - - - - - 29
- III. EARLY ENGLISH COINAGE - - - - - 34
- IV. EARLY LONDON BANKERS - - - - - 39
- V. THE BANK OF ENGLAND - - - - - 59
- VI. ENGLISH PRIVATE AND JOINT STOCK BANKS - 67
- VII. BANKING IN SCOTLAND - - - - - 70
- VIII. EARLY IRISH AND SCOTCH COINAGES - - 77
- IX. BANKING IN IRELAND—EARLY DUBLIN BANKERS - 84
- X. IRISH JOINT STOCK BANKS - - - - 102
- XI. CONCLUSION - - - - - - 114

PART II.
THE LAW AND PRACTICE OF BANKING.

- I. THE RELATIONS BETWEEN THE BANKER AND HIS CUSTOMER - - - - - - 123
- II. DEPOSIT RECEIPTS - - - - - - 127
- III. CURRENT ACCOUNT—CHEQUES - - - 135
- IV. CROSSED CHEQUES - - - - - 151
- V. PRESENTATION, PAYMENT, AND DISHONOUR OF CHEQUES - - - - - - 161
- VI. PASS BOOK—OVERDRAWN CURRENT ACCOUNT—RIGHT TO SUE ON CHEQUES - - - - 175
- VII. BILLS OF EXCHANGE AND PROMISSORY NOTES - 181

CHAPTER	PAGE
VIII. PERSONS INCAPACITATED TO BE PARTIES TO A BILL OF EXCHANGE	197
IX. THE STAMP DUTIES	202
X. THE TRANSFER OF BILLS	213
XI. PRESENTATION OF BILLS	216
XII. NOTING AND PROTESTING	221
XIII. DISCOUNT — REBATE — BILLS FOR COLLECTION — FOREIGN BILLS, ETC.	229
XIV. BANKERS' DRAFTS AND POST BILLS—LIEN—CONFIDENTIAL REPORTS, ETC.	238
XV. DEPOSITS AGAINST ADVANCES, AND FOR SAFE CUSTODY	246
XVI. BANK NOTES—I. O. U.	253
XVII. SHARES AND SHAREHOLDERS	271
XVIII. THE BANKING ACT OF 1879—DIRECTORS' DUTIES	280
XIX. THE STOCK EXCHANGE AND STOCK-BROKING	285

APPENDIX.

APPENDIX	
I. PRINCIPAL JOINT STOCK BANKS OF ENGLAND, NUMBER OF THEIR BRANCHES, SUBSCRIBED CAPITAL, PAID-UP CAPITAL, AND AUTHORISED ISSUE	303
II. A TABLE OF THE NUMBER OF DAYS FROM ANY DAY IN ONE MONTH TO THE SAME IN ANOTHER	307
III. MARRIED WOMAN'S ACCOUNT—FORM OF LETTER OF AUTHORITY TO BANKER—FORM OF INDEMNITY ON REPAYMENT OF LOST DEPOSIT RECEIPT, DRAFT, ETC.	309
IV. TABLE IN TEN LANGUAGES OF CARDINAL NUMBERS AND COMMERCIAL TERMS USED IN BILLS OF EXCHANGE	310
V. STATUTES	312
INDEX	357

PART I.

THE HISTORY AND PROGRESS OF BANKING.

HISTORY AND PROGRESS OF BANKING.

I.

THE EARLIEST RECORDS OF BANKING AND COINAGE.

THE trade of Banking is one of immemorial antiquity, and its origin is beyond the range of authentic history. It was the natural and necessary outgrowth of the commerce which arose from, and grew with, civilization. Commerce is no more than an exchanging of commodities; and exchange created the necessity for standards of value that would be generally recognised. These were, at length, found in the precious metals, which combined value with facility of carriage and transit. The system of Bills of Exchange grew out of the exigencies of trade. When a commercial community was founded, the inevitable conditions of society being that some members of it were rich and others poor, a trade in money was necessarily established, the richer lent to the poorer for interest—the poorer hired money and paid a wage for the use of it; and thus arose promises to pay and bonds. Commerce demanded a coinage, and various countries having varying coinages, the trade of money-changing was developed. It was requisite that a dealer in money should have a safe and strong place to protect his monies and securities against the predatory bands that flourished with comparative impunity of old, when government was unsettled and many held but a precarious tenure of wealth, land, and even life. To those strongly-built places people brought their gold and jewels and valuables and deposited them for better security, paying a fee for the safe custody. Thus originated the system of deposits of money, which has so far altered that the depositor is now paid for his deposit, instead of paying for the privilege of depositing; and from the custom of depositing money grew the means of drawing it out; hence our modern Cheques and Banker's Drafts.

But the trade of Banking in its various phases—not only in a primitive fashion, but even on a well-developed system and advanced principles—can boast of an extraordinary antiquity. **The Jews** in the infancy of the nation were a pastoral and not a commercial people, though during Christian centuries the greatest and the least of them have been addicted notoriously to money-trading.

The early Biblical references to "pieces of silver" in Genesis, do not, in the original, convey the idea of coins, but of weights (shekels). The Mosaic "oblation to God" was half a shekel, and a shekel is explained by Josephus as equal to four Athenian drachmæ, or of a value of two shillings and threepence of our money. A coinage with the Jews, as with the Egyptians and Assyrians, was a late institution, preceded by the long-retained custom of treating the metals like other merchandise, exchangeable by weight. The first Jewish coinage under authority was, it is believed, struck by Simon the Maccabee, about the year 140 B.C.* It consisted of shekels and half shekels and had the

---

* "The earliest known genuine Hebrew coin is a unique specimen in "copper, in the Cabinet du Roi, Paris, bearing on the obverse the sacred "seven-branched palm-tree, and the letters forming 'Eliashib,' the name

pot of manna and Aaron's rod as devices. This coinage, moreover, had its value signified upon it—"schekel Israel"—in Samaritan characters. Simon's successors placed their own profiles upon the coins they issued.

But long anterior to the time when there were coins, lending at interest, which seems—notwithstanding the agricultural and pastoral life the nation led—to have been an instinct of the race, was carried on to such a degree that it grew to be an evil, against which Moses had to hurl Divine enactments. These were to the effect that the Hebrew was not to lay " usury upon " the poor ;" " and if thy Brother become poor, thou shalt not " give him thy money upon usury," and so on—"because it is not " just to make advantage of the misfortunes of one of thy own " countrymen : it is thy gain if thou obtainest their gratitude."*
The application of these commands seems to have been confined to loans given to relieve distress rather than to loans for the purposes of trade, or by way of capital. The trade of money-lending on usury was, however, recognised in the early Jewish community; and though it was forbidden to be practised on " thy " brothers who were poor," it was, nevertheless, permitted against a stranger. "Unto a *foreigner*," runs the Divine command, "thou mayest lend upon usury ;" and Jeremiah (445 B.C.) therefore rebukes "the nobles and the rulers because they exacted

---

" of the high priest. This name furnishes no definite clue to the date, nor " does that of Eleasar, on another coin of the same archaic type. Under " the Seleucidæ there is a copious sequence of Jewish coins, especially " of those bearing the name of Simon. Many pieces have figured on their " face the vessels and instruments of the sanctuary, the candlesticks, the " trumpets, or the golden cup. The list here given closes with the tiny " copper coin weighing about 25 grains, which most probably represents the " widow's mite (*lepton*, Mark xii. 41). It bears on the face an anchor, and " on the reverse the Greek word CHALKOUS."—*Conder's Handbook to the Bible.*

* Josephus.

"usury every one from his brother." But though the trade of money-lending was general, and partly permitted by the Mosaic law, it seems to have fallen into disrepute. David condemns it; and Jeremiah significantly says—"I have neither lent on "usury, nor have men lent to me: *yet every one of them doth curse me.*" From the New Testament, however, it seems that transactions corresponding to our deposits were usual, and that interest was allowed on money deposited. In the parable of the Talents, in Matthew, the "wicked and slothful slave" is denounced, his lord saying to him, "Thou oughtest therefore to "have put my money to the Bankers, and at my coming I should "have received my own *with usury*" (Matt. xxv. 26); and in Luke, "Why then gavest not thou my silver into the bank, that "at my coming I might have received it with usury" (Luke xix. 23). But beyond this we have little certain knowledge regarding the money dealings of the chosen people.

Amongst the ancient **Brahmans*** the law of loans and interest was fair and equitable, and regulated and settled by recognised rules. A creditor was to be paid back in full, and the debtors were to pay "as much interest as has been promised by "themselves"; but some idea of the rates of interest is afforded by the provision that the creditor "shall take in the direct order "of the castes two, three, four or five in the hundred by the "month (if no pledge has been given)." The rates here mentioned are very high; but there was a limitation to the total amount. The interest on gold was not to rise higher than double the debt; on grain, to threefold, etc. There is on this subject an inexplicable provision that "on substances from "which spirituous liquor is extracted, on cotton, thread, leather, "weapons, bricks, and charcoal, the interest is unlimited."

* See *The Institutes of Vishnu.* Vol. VII. of "The Sacred Books of "the East." Edited by Max Müller.

Double the debt was the ordinary increase, and was to be exacted on all objects unspecified.

Coins were made in **China**, so long ago, it is said, as the year 2250 B.C., but they cannot have been other than portions of metal cast into a portable shape—squares, bars, spikes, or rings—such as were all the earliest monies. Bank Notes, or what would correspond to our Bank Notes, are said to have originated also there, about 120 B.C. But there can be little doubt that notes were issued in China about 1000 A.D., first by a private person and soon after by a duly constituted Joint Stock Bank of Issue. Paper money, it is recorded, was in existence in the dominions of the Mongol Prince, Mangu Khan, in the year 1252, and—according to that unreliable historian, Sir John Mandeville—the Emperor of Tartary, in 1322, manufactured paper and leather money to such an extent that gold and silver fell into disuse. The inexpensiveness and the facility of manufacturing the new circulating medium were such that it was issued profusely, and the Emperor was enabled thereby to spend "enow and outrageously." But, as was to be expected, this reckless and unbounded circulation of an intrinsically worthless and irredeemable mock money, led to the evils naturally consequent on its depreciation to such an extent that it was valueless. The paper and leather money got into just discredit and disrepute, and seem to have disappeared altogether, so that in 1668 a traveller could not find even a "recollection" of them. The issue can scarcely be regarded in its late stages in any other light than the act of an autocrat to enable him to "despende outrageously."

The Chinese have, in Banking as in everything else, made little or no progress for thousands of years. Though in the world's infancy they were more advanced in the arts and sciences than the white races, their exclusiveness and conservatism have been such, that the Chinese of to-day possess no better system of Banking than their ancestors possessed centuries ago; indeed, their system at present seems to consist solely of issuing Bills and redeeming them; and the Japanese are even still more backward and primitive in Banking and Finance.

Abraham is said to have been "rich in silver and gold;" but as this statement refers to a period subsequent to his return from Egypt, it has been surmised that he obtained his knowledge of the values of these metals from the Egyptians, but strange to say, in **Egypt**, the cradle of civilization and commerce, there was no imperial coinage. Copper and silver and gold were used, as elsewhere, to indicate values, but they were manufactured into lumps, shaped sometimes like bricks, and, in the case of gold and silver, generally in rings like the ancient Irish money of ten centuries ago; and they were valued by weight like any other commodity of commercial merchandise. It appears, to use the words of Sir John Lubbock, "almost "inconceivable that a people who created the Sphynx and the "Pyramids, the Temples of Ipsamboul and Karnac, should have "been entirely ignorant of coins. Yet it is certain from the state-"ments of Herodotus and the evidence from the monuments "themselves that such was really the case." The first coinage of money in Egypt with which we are acquainted was struck, not to assist the Egyptians themselves in their commercial dealings, but rather because the foreign merchants with whom they traded, the Greeks and Phœnicians, demanded some value-medium which would have a guarantee of its value apparent on it, and would circulate for that value; and the satrap Aryandis yielded to the pressure, and thus the honour is with him of having been the first who "struck" the precious metals into circulating authorised coin.

Turning to the great and ancient empires of **Assyria** and **Babylonia**, we find that though they, equally with the Egyptians, adhered for ages to the primitive blocks of copper and ingots of silver and gold, and did not evolve an imperial coinage, nevertheless they were possessed of a system of Banking unexpectedly complete and well-developed. Indeed, their Banking practice was so complete, and affords such conclusive evidence of the high stage of commercial knowledge to which they had attained, that while we wonder at their advancement, we wonder also at the fact that their neighbours were so backward and primitive in their Banking. Before a coinage was known, the great Banking House of Egibi and Company flourished as State Bankers, it is said, for a period of 150 years at least. Founded presumably in the reign of Sennacherib [B.C. 712], we trace it through five generations down to the reign of Darius, and we are informed that it was the Great National Bank of Babylon when Babylon was the greatest city on the earth. From the clay tablets unearthed of late years in and near Nineveh and Babylon, we obtain an insight into the social life of those wonderful peoples, and gather revelations of an astonishing progress from the records of their financial doings and commercial arrangements. The excavations in this old world have given us the originals of many most interesting documents—if that word can be permitted as applied to baked tablets. We have contracts of sales of slaves; of sale and transfer of lands, with maps and plans attached. We have records of loans on lands and on house property. We have evidences of loans of silver at fixed rates of interest on personal guaranty. We have receipts and contracts of various kinds.

The people among whom, 2,500 years ago, such usages were common, must have been possessed of the highest aptitude for commercial science; and a classification of the Banking Instruments in vogue with them—for which we are indebted to M. Le Normant—reads rather as a description of Banking extracted from a treatise written in the 19th century, than a recital of the veritable contracts made and prepared by the subjects of Sennacherib and of Darius the King. M. Le Normant thus classifies these contracts.—1. Simple obligations. 2. Obligations with a penal clause in case of default (he quotes one that had 79 days currency). 3. Obligations with a guaranty of a third party. 4. Obligations payable to a third party. 5. Drafts drawn upon one place and payable at another.—Of the latter he quotes the following, which dates between 500 B.C. and 600 B.C. :—" Four minas fifteen shekels of silver (credit) of " Ardu-Nana son of Yakin, upon Mardukabalussur son of " Mardukbalatirib in the town of Orchoe. Mardukbalatirib will " pay in the month of tibil, four minas fifteen shekels of silver " to Belabaliddin, son of Sennaidour, the 14 arakh-samma in " the 2nd year of Nabonidus, King of Babylon." This is a perfect instrument. The date, the time of payment, the payee, the amount, the drawer, and the drawee are specified, and further, the parties are identified. These Drafts or Letters of Credit were drawn on the fresh tablet, which was then baked and thus became enduring and negotiable. Frequently the payee's designation was omitted, whereby they became as drafts payable to bearer and freely transferable, for it is evident that being hard and solid they could not be transferred by endorsement. It is said that those Drafts must, when drawn, have been notified to the drawee, and this step, being a precautionary device, seems to be a natural development. Thus it will be seen that in the time of " Nabonidus, King of Babylon," and, extraordinary to contemplate, in a time when there was no such thing as current coin, there were Letters of Credit, Letters of Guaranty, Mortgages, and penal obligations.*

The following is a translation, by Mr. T. G. Pinches, of one of these tablets; it seems to be a bond for money advanced for twelve months by a member of the house of Egibi & Son.

"12½ manas of silver from *Iddin-Marduku* son of *Basa*, "son of *Nur-Sini*, unto *Itti-baladhi-Marduku* and *Nabu-musetig-* "*udda*, sons of *Ziri-ya*, son of the priest of *Gula*. For a month, "to (the amount of) 1 maneh 1 shekel of silver it increases unto "them; from the first day of the month Tebet the interest unto "them increases. (In) the month Tisri the silver and its interest "they give (back), their receipt they ask, and afterwards the bond "(?). (Agreed in) the dwelling of *Iddin-Marduku*, the owner (of "the money lent). Whoever, for the completion of the agree-"ment, unto *Iddin-Marduku* his silver and his interest will pay, "notice (?) the two (men) shall send up. Witnessing: *Marduku-* "*irba*, son of *Basa*, son of *Sinu-niqi-magir*. *Gimillu*, son of "*Nabu-iddina*, son of the priest of *Gula*. *Itti-Nabibaluadu*, "the scribe, son of *Marduku-banai-suma*, son of *Belu-edheru*, "Babylon, month Kislev, day 25th, year 1st [or 11th] Kambyses. "King of Babylon; in this day also Kyrus his father, King of "Countries."

To the **Lydians**, the invention of coining gold and silver is attributed, and the year 862 B.C. is fixed as the era of the invention, and a poetic comment on the circumstance is found in the fact that some 300 years after this period Crœsus was King of Lydia. But the coins of the period are not very elegant, and beyond the coinage we have no record of any operations of a banking nature.

But in **Greece**—the most illustrious portion of the Western

---

* A recent writer says, however, that these records may not be of a commercial character.

world—Banking was undoubtedly carried on to a considerable extent. Homer speaks of brass money (1184 B.C.), but the term was applied to weights and not coins. The art of coining, invented by the neighbouring Lydians, was soon acquired by the Greeks—the first mint was that of Ægina—and was perfected to such a degree, that the ancient Greek coins far surpassed any modern coinage. The original method of coining consisted in placing a given weight of metal, when softened, over a die upon which a national symbol or sacred emblem was engraved, and hammering it into the die till a good impression was obtained. The early coins are therefore rude and battered, and show a die impression on one side only, the other bearing the rough irregular marks of the hammer. The earliest Greek coins are of silver, whereas those of Lydia were of gold. The earliest impressions are of a sacred character,—symbols and emblems. These were succeeded by representations of the deities. The oldest Athenian coins bear an owl, the type of Athene, and this was followed by a design of the head of the goddess. The earlier Greek coins bore a letter, the initial of the town where they were struck: monograms came later: the first coin upon which a king's name is discernible is one of Alexander I. of Macedon. In the reign of Philip of Macedon the coinage had attained perfection. The reverse was now equally artistic as the obverse. The Medal of Syracuse with its head of Proserpine is one of the oldest specimens of this perfect coining, and is remarkably complete. This rapid development is not to be wondered at. The nation who strove after the beautiful in all things, who elevated beauty into a religion, and made human beauty perfect in idealism, manufactured coins on the principles of the highest art. On them we see the most lovely faces and the most perfect models of beauty in the entire range of art. Gods and goddesses, kings and heroes, lions and horses, mice, bees, roses and ears of wheat, in supreme excellence of design, find places on the old Hellenic coins. The Greeks developed rapidly also their system of Banking; they changed foreign money, they received money on deposit at interest; they granted loans. We learn this from Demosthenes, who himself kept a banking account. The rate charged on loans is said to have usually been 36 per cent., but this statement is doubtful.

Though those who engaged in the pursuit of Banking in ancient Greece were generally of low origin, being freedmen or aliens, yet they frequently rose to positions of great eminence, and became wealthy members of the State. They therefore enjoyed good credit and repute. One of the most eminent Bankers in Ancient Greece was one Pasion, who, from being a manumitted slave, became the greatest Banker of his time. Demosthenes and contemporary orators frequently make mention of him; we even get a glance at his business. He is said to have had £2,681 in deposit from his customers : to have lent £12,187 out at interest, and to have owned land worth £4,875. If this be so we are surprised at the statement that the business was worth only £400 sterling a year. The state was more than once indebted to Pasion's financial support, and he was a man of undoubted integrity, well known and trusted throughout Greece, and enjoying the friendship of the great. So eminent was his reputation and so undoubted his credit that his son Apollodorus boasted that he could obtain money wherever he pleased, because he was the son of Pasion.

The Greek Bankers were called Trapezitæ from TRAPEZA, *a table* (as the Roman were called Mensarii from *mensa*), because they conducted their business at tables in the public streets and in the temples. The Greeks were acquainted with letters of credit, and knew a method of endorsement, for one Iccratus drew in Athens a bill on his father in Pontus, which was guaranteed by Pasion the great Banker, and then bought by Stratocles. They seem to have had an instrument corresponding to our cheque, and the Athenian Bankers were the inventors of *discounts*, *i.e.*, of the system of deducting the interest at the time of making the advance or loan. The Greek Bankers also acted as public notaries and public drawers and witnesses of contracts. Even bottomry bonds were used in their commercial dealings.*

The Greeks carried their Banking practices with them in their conquests, and thus Banking in a matured fashion was introduced into **Rome**. This is proved by the fact that all the expressions bearing on finance used by the early Latin authors are of Greek extraction. In Rome, Servius Tullius stamped copper pieces (*as*) as early as about 550 B.C., with the image of a sheep (*pecus*), and hence, the word *pecunia*, the Latin for money. Brass money was in use previous to 269 B.C., when Fabius Pictor coined silver; and gold was coined 206 B.C. There are three series of early Roman coins: the Republican, the Family, and the Imperial. The *Republican* was the earliest, and circulated from the time of Servius Tullius till about 80 B.C. The metal used was bronze, and the standard a pound weight, which in the shape of a brick, with the sheep impressed, was, it is said, the coin of Servius Tullius. In course of time the square or rectangular shape was abandoned for the circular, and it is to be noted that the early Roman circular coins were cast, and not hammered into a die, as was the case with the Greek pieces. The first silver coin was the *Denarius* (10 ases) equivalent in value to the Greek drachma. The earlier gold coin was a *Scrupulum*; these had representations of the head of Mars on the obverse, and on the reverse the Roman Eagle with the thunderbolt. The latter coins of this series are very beautiful. The *Family* coins superseded the Republican, and

* *Vide* Demosthenes, "Against Aphobus," Orat. I.

were so called because the mastership of the mints was confined to certain families who acquired a right of placing their name on the pieces. The name was succeeded by a device of an ancestor's head, and by degrees this was changed to the head of a living person—Julius Cæsar being the first thus represented. The *Imperial* coinage bore the head of the Emperor or Empress, and the coins of Agrippina, Augustus and others are very beautiful. The Sestertius of Nero is for workmanship and artistic design unequalled in numismatics. The devices on the earlier coinages were, as we have said, the heads of deities or of those to whom divine honours were accorded. The first coin which bore a representation of a human head was one of Lysimachus, which bore a device of the head of Alexander the Great; he is represented with the ram's horns, which was an indication of his descent from Jupiter Ammon. But though exhibited in the divine character, the circumstance is interesting, as marking the transition from the pure worship of the gods to the compromising worship of the hero. Julius Cæsar (48 B.C.) had to obtain the permission of the Senate to impress his own portrait on the coins. The practice has been perpetuated, and the coins of nearly all countries are now adorned with a device of the sovereign's profile.

The Romans are said to have invented the science and business of Banking. The first mention of Banking in Rome that we find, refers to the year 352 B.C., when the Plebeians being in great distress, the State appointed certain persons to lend them portions of the public funds on security; hence sprung an authorised and recognised system of advances made by these Bankers, but their functions were limited merely to lending. There were other descriptions of Bankers which played an important part in the social economy of Rome. Of these there were three principal classes :—

(1.) The *Negociatores*, whose chief business consisted in lending money at high rates of interest to the inhabitants of the neighbouring provinces, and as the laws regulating Banking did not extend to the provinces, the *Negociatores* were enabled to ply an extensive trade at fancy prices, and not being restrained by any legal restrictions, they seem to have realized large profits. Their system degenerated into usury* and became such an evil that at length a law was promulgated to curb their practices—the *Lex Sempronia De Fœnore*.

(2.) The *Argentarii*. These were private Bankers, with whom individuals kept their private accounts, and who acted as disbursers of their clients' monies. From Cicero we learn that their chief business lay in attending to the payments due in Rome on account of the citizens dwelling in the country districts. They kept books of their customer's accounts. They sometimes acted as auctioneers. The *Argentarii* introduced, if they did not invent, perfect documents of the same nature as our cheques. These were called *præscriptiones* or *attributiones*, and were written orders by the owners of the money to the holders of it to pay certain amounts to specified persons.

(3.) The *Mensarii*. These were a class of Bankers called into existence by the State, and consisted of the Bankers of the Republic. They were created, Livy tells us, to counteract the usurious practices of the money-lenders and to abate the evils caused thereby to the citizens. This class appears in later years under the Empire to have merged into the *Argentarii* —at least the two terms are frequently applied to the same individual, for Suetonius speaks of one C. Octavius indiscriminately as *Argentarius* and *Mensarius*.

Besides these there was another class, the *Nummularii*— but

---

* The word *usury* is said to be derived from Latin usu-œris (for the use of money).

they can scarcely be regarded as Bankers. Their duties lay in assaying and weighing moneys, and they were recognized by the State and appointed to test the fineness of the metal and to estimate the current and the intrinsic values. Their nearest approach to Banking was in their business of changing the money thus estimated.

The important and prominent position occupied by the Roman Bankers can be judged by the fact that numerous laws were made regulating their practice, and by the frequent references to them in the Latin authors. There is no doubt that as a body they enjoyed a high reputation for honourable dealing in their profession, but nevertheless they were frequently a mark for uncomplimentary allusions in the comedies of the time. Usury, which originally conveyed no more than a payment for the use of money, came to have an opprobrious meaning, because the payment became extortionate, and the lenders extortioners. Nevertheless, outside the Roman Bankers we have described, private individuals were money-lenders at oppressive and ruinous rates. Pompey, Brutus, even Cato himself—perhaps in sustainment of "the dignity of man,"—lent money at 50 per cent. interest. And in one of his Satires, Horace speaks of one Furfidius, who, " wealthy in lands and in " money put out at interest," is afraid of having the character of a rake and spendthrift. Furfidius understood his business and saw the advantages of *discount*. "This fellow," says Horace, " deducts five per cent. from the principal at the time of " lending, and the more desperate in his circumstances any one " is, the more cruelly he pinches him. He hunts out the " names of young fellows just of age." And we are further told that Furfidius notwithstanding his wealth lived meanly, and was " no friend to himself." The rate he charged was five per cent. and if it means five per cent. per annum, which is doubtful, was remarkably moderate for those days. Laws against usury were enacted in Rome, as in England, and a legal rate of interest was fixed at 8¾ per cent. In the time of Cicero, the legal rate was fixed at 12 per cent., and in 528 A.D. the Emperor Justinian reduced it to 4 per cent. for loans to illustrious persons; 6 per cent. for loans for commercial purposes: and 8 per cent. for loans which did not come under either of these descriptions. One of the legal provisions in regard to Bankers is interesting and perhaps equitable. When a Roman Banker stopped payment, those citizens who had deposited money with him for safe custody alone ranked as preferential creditors, and were to be satisfied before those who lodged money at interest. The law forbade lending money to minors, *i.e.*, persons under 25 years of age.

By a constitution of Alexander Severus, A.D. 224, the absolute freedom of transfer of debt, by sale or otherwise, without the consent or knowledge of the debtor, was allowed and made legal. The debt was evidenced by an instrument, and by a simple process this was made transferable; hence we find in Rome the origin of our modern Bills of Exchange with their chief attribute — freedom of transfer — recognised by the Law.

We have reason to gather that foreign letters of credit were also understood by the Romans, as from Cicero again we learn, that when he was sending his son Marcus to Athens to study, he made inquiries as to obtaining in Rome a letter of credit on Athens, in preference to the alternative of Marcus taking money on his person. The inquiry would hardly have been made unless instruments of this nature were issued by the Bankers.*

---

* In the first century we find *permutare* and *cambire* used to signify " to ,' send a draft or bill for money."

After the division of the Empire in A.D. 364, the city of Rome was not the pleasantest or most profitable place for Banking. In the 5th century it was thrice taken, pillaged, and devasted, by Alaric, Genseric, and Odoacer. In the 6th, Totila the Goth seized it. In 553 the Senate was abolished, and in 600 the great and ancient "Eternal City" was at its very lowest ebb. During the long Middle Ages,—or as they are more appropriately called the "dark ages,"—commerce, like the arts and learning, was little attended to. Where Commerce was moribund there was little field for the development of Banking. But money-lending and money-changing were ever necessary, and the people who had a genius for money-trading —the Jews—established business in many parts of Europe about 800 A.D. It was the Jews of Lombardy, or Lombard Jews, who thus distinguished themselves. Some of these merchants were sent into England by Pope Gregory the IX., in 1229, to lend money to the convent communities and private persons who were unable to pay the tithes which in that year were rigorously collected throughout the Kingdom. These emigrants settled in that street in London which to this day is named after them (Lombard Street), and in which at present many Bankers have their offices. The transactions of the Lombard Jews—who are not to be confounded with the descendants of those Jews brought over by William the Conqueror—seem to have been conducted in the usual extortionate and usurious fashion, until at length their trade became so pernicious and mischievous, that in Queen Elizabeth's time they were expelled the Kingdom.

But though during the dark ages commerce was generally in a very feeble and exhausted condition, nevertheless, **Tuscany** stands out bright in its pre-eminence in learning, and also in mercantile trading; and **Florence** became the centre of the money transactions of the commercial word, and great success attended its commercial enterprises. Here Guilds were established in the 13th century, and so rapidly had the city progressed, that at one time it is said that eighty Bankers flourished and throve in Florence. About the year 1430, an association, formed of seventy-six Bankers, lent 4,865,000 gold Florins to the State. But these were still private Bankers, and though public Banks existed before this period, there was no State Bank there. Macaulay in writing of Florence in the early part of the 14th century, says:—"Four hundred thousand Florins "were annually coined. Eighty banks conducted the com- "mercial operations, not of Florence only, but of all Europe. "The transactions of these establishments were sometimes of a "magnitude which may surprise even the contemporaries of the "Barings and the Rothschilds. Two houses advanced to "Edward the III. of England upwards of three hundred thousand "marks, at a time when a mark contained more silver than fifty "shillings at the present day, and when the value of silver "was more than quadruple what it now is."

At this period **Litteræ Bancales**, or Drafts by Banks, had succeeded the **Litteræ Cambitoriæ**, or Bills of Exchange, of an earlier century. Italian writers—Genovesi, Galiani, and others—claim, and perhaps justly, for the Italians the honour of "having been the fathers, masters, and arbiters of Commerce, "so that in all Europe they are the Depositaries of Money "and are called Bankers."

II.

EARLY EUROPEAN BANKS.

THE earliest public Bank in modern Europe was the **Bank of Venice,** the formation and establishment of which is said to have taken place in 1157 or 1171. It originated as subsequent National Banks did, in a device of the State to extricate itself from its financial difficulties. Owing to foreign wars and conquests, the State was in an impecunious condition, and it sought relief from its straits in the creation of a Public Loan. It forced the citizens to lend their money, promising them interest at the rate of 4 per cent. This Relief Loan Fund, so far, can scarcely be considered a Bank, though to the Venetian State belongs the honour of having created the institution of a permanent National Debt on the funding system. The stock thus forced on the citizens was transferable, and a body of commissioners was appointed to manage the debt—to attend to the payment of the interest and to the transfer of the stock. The usual name by which this Loan and other subsequent similar ones were designated in Italy was **Monte,** plural **Monti.** The exact signification of the word is not, in its relation to a Bank, very apparent. Blackstone writes: "At "Florence, in 1344, Government owed £60,000, and being "unable to pay it, formed the principal into an aggregate sum, "called *metaphorically* a Mount or Bank." The original

Bank of Venice was called **Monte Vecchio**, and subsequent Loans established on the same principle was called **Monte Nuovo** and **Monte Nuovissimo**. The word Bank has an obvious connection with **Monte**, and in an Italian dictionary of 1659, the latter word is explained, "a Standing "Bank or Mount of Money." There were other **Monti** in Italy, as well as the State ones. There were the Banks of Charity, a species of pawnbroker's shop. Evelyn, in his Diary, under date 1645 (18 Feb.), writes: "Neere this (the Palace of "Cardinal Spada in Rome) is the Monte Pieta, instituted as "a Bank for the poore, who, if the Sum be not greate, may have "money upon pawns." And subsequently when in Padua, Evelyn observed a similar establishment there: "In the "Piazza is the Podesta and Capitano Grande's Palace, well "built; but, above all, the Monte Pieta, the front whereof is of "most excellent architecture. This is a foundation of which "there is one in most of the cities of Italy, where there is a con- "tinual banque of money to assist the poorer sort, on any pawn "and at reasonable interest, together with magazines for "deposit of goods till redeemed."

The Bank of Venice for centuries seems to have been little more than a body constituted to manage the public debt, for undoubtedly it did not engage in Banking business. It was an authorised mart for the exchange of foreign and clipped and worn coins, which, being assayed, were purchased and paid for in promissory notes payable to bearer. And as these notes were redeemable and not liable to depreciation, they were in high esteem, and bore a premium as compared with the current money. The Bank of Venice does not appear to have engaged in discounts, and it was not till 1587 that it received money on deposit—but, even then, the nature of the deposit was simply safe custody; the Bank, in fact, was only a bailee, a money changer, and the manager of the public debt, and cannot be considered to have been a true Bank. The Bank of Venice continued to exist until the fall of the Republic in 1797.

The Bank of Geneva was founded in 1345, but its functions were so restricted that it, neither, can be regarded as a Bank as we understand the expression.

The earliest public National Bank in the modern sense of the term, was the **Bank of Barcelona**, founded in the year 1401. For some fifty years previous to this date the cloth merchants of Barcelona, then a wealthy community, engaged in Banking, and in 1401 their business as Bankers was consolidated by the Spanish Magistrates into a public Bank under the auspices of the Government. Its liabilities to the public were secured by the city property, which was held in pledge on behalf of the Depositors. The Bank of Barcelona discounted Bills and allowed interest on Deposits, but it did not issue notes, nor does it appear to have been acquainted with cheques.

The Bank of Genoa, or as it was called the **Bank of St. George**, though its constitution was devised in 1345, was not established till 1407. Its operations for a couple of centuries cannot be characterized as Banking, for they were similar to those of the Bank of Venice, and like it, originated in the pecuniary exigencies of the State. The Republic borrowed from the citizens, consolidated the debt, and appointed eight "protectors," chosen annually by the stockholders, to manage it. However, in 1675, it appears to have extended its operations and engaged in genuine Banking business. The Bank was pillaged by the Austrians when the city was taken by them in 1746, and in 1750 it closed its doors finally.

The Bank of Amsterdam was founded in 1609 with the principal object of remedying the disadvantage and inexpedience arising from the circulation of the clipped foreign coins which circulated amongst the merchants. Its business was to purchase all worn and clipped gold and silver coins at their bullion value, and to give credit to the selling party for such value. On these transactions it charged a small commission, and the gold and silver purchased was re-coined. There was a State enactment, aimed at the evil of the defective coins, to the effect that all debts of 600 guilders (which was afterwards reduced to 300, equal to 25 guineas) should be paid in the money coined and issued by the Bank. At this period Amsterdam was a great commercial centre; the Exchange there was built in 1634. The Bank received moneys on Deposit, and declared that it had bullion in its coffers equivalent to the amount of deposits, as it avowedly lent no money and discounted no bills. But if these were its principles in the earlier days of the Bank, there was a departure later on, for when Amsterdam opened its gates to the French in 1795, it was ascertained that the Bank had lent a sum equivalent to one million sterling to the States of Friesland and Holland, and this discovery dissipated confidence, and wrought the ruin of the Bank of Amsterdam.* About twenty years later, in 1814, the **Bank of the Netherlands** was established to fill the void.

The **Bank of Hamburg** was established in 1619, on the same basis as the Bank of Amsterdam, and it is still in existence. The other Banking establishments on the continent, worthy to be classed with the National Banks, were the **Bank of Rotterdam**, founded in 1635; the **Bank of Stockholm**, which, according to the Hume and other authorities, was the first that invented Bank Notes in Europe, founded in 1688; the **Bank of Copenhagen**, in 1736; the **Bank**

* *Vide* Smith's "Wealth of Nations," book iv., chap. 3.

of Berlin, in 1765; the **Caisse D'Escompte** (France), in 1776; the **Bank of St. Petersburgh**, in 1786; and the **Bank of France,** which was instituted in 1803, by laws which were approved in 1808, and which, as Napoleon said, was established with the object of providing money at all times at 4 per cent. interest. Since the Joint Stock principle has become understood on the continent, many other Banks have been established under it, which have met with varying success.

III.

EARLY ENGLISH COINAGE.

Amongst the Ancient Britons, as amongst all primitive nations, metals were used as values,—the values being determined by weight; and we learn from a passage in Cæsar, that iron in the form of bars was used as money in England B.C. 55. Long previous to this period, however, there appears to have been a coinage in Britain, which is said to have originated about the year 200 B.C., in Kent, and to have spread thence, as far as Devonshire on the one hand and Oxford on the other. At the time of the Roman invasion the Britons had in use silver and brass coins, shaped oblong, square and round. Some of these coins are lettered, one series bearing the letters CVN, which is taken as being intended for Cunobelinus—the Cymbeline of Shakespere—who was King of Britain in the year 4 A.D. Some of the coins of this period seem to be copies of the *staters* of Philip of Macedon, having the chariot and horses on one side, and the head of Apollo on the other—evidently the coinage imposed by the Roman Conquerors. But rude and unintelligible as the majority of the early British coins are, we find, nevertheless, that the race was sufficiently advanced to have acquired the art of manufacturing spurious money. Forgery was a profession amongst the semi-civilized inhabitants, and base metal coins plated with silver, and even with gold, have been found. A coinage in tin was struck at a very early period, but immediately relinquished for obvious reasons, though it was re-introduced for a moment by Charles II. The Romans established a Mint at Camulodunum—now Colchester—and it seems that Constantine had a Mint in London. With the departure of the Romans the coinage relapsed into its former barbarous condition. The earliest coins we have of the post Roman period are the *skeatta* of silver and the *styca* of copper. These appear to have belonged to Northumbria, and are of the rudest description. The silver pennies superseded the *skeatta*, and these seem to have been the sole coin in circulation till the reign of Edward III. The coinage, inartistic and debased as it was, was nevertheless under regal authority. Athelstan enacted regulations for the Government of the Mint and the coinage in 928. In the Anglo-Saxon and early Anglo-Norman Mints the coins were devised and made by the "moneyers," who were officers of the Mint, and who were supervised by an authority called the "reeve." Upon the introduction of Christianity rude attempts at a cross are impressed on the coins. The grotesquely designed pennies of King Alfred had a monogram of London, where they were minted, and on the reverse an absurd-looking head supposed to have been his portrait. The portrait was soon abandoned, apparently, for on subsequent pieces the cross re-appears now within a circle. The Cross with three pills at each angle continued to be the design for many centuries, and the coinage made no advance toward artistic beauty till the reign of Edward III. After the conquest, the Royal Mint in London was placed under the jurisdiction of the Court of Exchequer, and the officers and master were sworn into their offices before the Barons of that Court. Henry I. established a Mint at Winchester, in 1125. But at this period, besides the Royal Mint, there were several other coin manufactories. The Barons and Bishops coined money in Stephen's time, and the privilege of issuing coins was sometimes accorded to the higher monasteries. In King's John's reign there was an episcopal Mint in Chichester. In Henry II.'s reign the moneyers were exempted from taxes, and various concessions were made to them by subsequent monarchs. Coin was made *sterling* in 1216, and before this time, as Stow informs us, rents were mostly paid in kind, and money was only to be found in the coffers of the Barons; and he further says that the Royal Mint was kept at this time by Italians, as the English were ignorant of the art of coining.

The first English gold coins on reliable record were struck by Henry III. in 1257, and the first entry of gold being brought to the Mint for coinage is under the date 1343 (Edward III.). To Edward the credit is due of having reformed the coinage and advanced it artistically to a degree of excellence even beyond that of contemporary States. He struck in addition to pennies, silver halfpennies, farthings, groats, and half groats. On his groats first appeared the legend, "Dei Gratia," and "Rex "Franciæ," and the motto, "Posui Deum adjutorem meum," which latter continued on the coinages till the reign of Richard III. Under this Edward's reign gold Florins, six shilling pieces, nobles, and half and quarter nobles were introduced. The noble was value for six and eight pence, and it was this coin that fixed the lawyer's fee, which is still unchanged. The noble had on the obverse a beautifully designed representation of the king in a ship, bearing a shield, upon which the arms of England and France are quartered, and having his sword in his right hand, and on the reverse a cross within an eight-arched circle, and a lion with a crown in each angle. Edward IV. added much to the coinage, both to its utility and its ornate character. In Henry VIII.'s reign the coinage suffered, and became debased

in value and execution. On his coins the title "Hiberniæ
"Rex" first appears; his predecessors had styled themselves
"Dominus Hiberniæ" only. The coinage was reformed by
Edward VI., who coined crowns and half-crowns (1547-53),
and by Elizabeth, who also was a reformer, and who caused
all the base coin which was in circulation to be called in and
genuine money issued; but the standard of artistic excellence
is not maintained in these reigns. In Elizabeth's reign the mill
and screw were introduced, as an improvement on the hammer
and punch of former reigns, and her coins are therefore more
regularly executed. Under the Stuarts, clipping was a general
practice, and debased spurious money was largely circulated,
all of which was called in by William III., when the expenses of
a new coinage (£1,200,000) were raised by a house duty.
The coins of the Stuarts had designs of great variety. James I.,
on his shillings and minor silver coins, is represented by an
armed bust, crowned. On his larger pieces he is on horseback;
and in his reign the harp of Ireland is first quartered as the
arms of that kingdom, with the motto, "Quos Deus conjunxit
"nemo separet." In his reign also the first copper royal coinage
since the Saxon *styca* was struck. Copper farthings (with a
harp on the reverse) were coined for England and Ireland in
common. Charles I. coined silver twenty-shilling pieces, a
magnificent coin, with the king on horseback represented upon
it. In this reign guineas were also first coined, their original
value being twenty shillings. They were so called because
made of gold brought from Guinea in Africa. The unroyal
coins of Cromwell with the legends "The Commonwealth of
"England," and "God with us," were succeeded by those bearing
his laurelled bust and title of Protector, and on the reverse his
own paternal coat of arms, with other designs. In Charles
II.'s time the device of Britannia, taken from the Roman

British coins, appeared on the copper halfpennies, the face and figure of the female having been designed from those of Barbara Villiers, his mistress, afterwards Duchess of Cleveland. The same representation is on our modern copper coins. There was great scarcity of coins in this reign, and Evelyn tells us that the practice of clipping—a capital offence, for which many then were hanged—was carried on to such a degree that the coins were not worth one half the amount they purported to represent. In William and Mary's coins the profiles are one over the other, whereas in Philip and Mary's the faces were opposite to each other. In George III.'s reign copper pennies were first coined, and the improvements made in the coinage in his time and since have been of a very doubtful character. The legend "one shilling" is as poor and paltry a design on a coin as can be conceived.

English and Irish money were assimilated in 1826. Sovereigns were first coined by the Mint in 1489; shillings in 1504; crowns and half-crowns in 1553; one guinea, two guinea, and five guinea pieces in 1664; quarter guinea, in 1716; gold seven shilling pieces in 1797; silver florins in 1849; fourpenny pieces in 1836; and threepennies 1861. The first large copper coinage was made in 1640 to supersede the private leaden tokens in circulation. The amount of current coin of the realm was, in 1711, valued at £12,000,000, and in 1853 at £60,000,000. From the year 1840 to 1878 inclusive, the respective amounts of gold, silver and copper coined at the English Royal Mint were:—Gold £181,453,645; silver, £15,216,770; and copper, £1,630,886; making a total of £198,301,301, or an annual average of £5,084,648.

IV.

EARLY LONDON BANKERS.

For the early history of Banking in London, we are largely indebted to the valuable researches of Mr. Hilton Price, whose most interesting work on the subject, the "Handbook of "London Bankers," has been our authority for many of the following particulars. Mr. Price finds the precursor of the goldsmiths, who developed into Bankers, in one Otto, a Goldsmith, who is quoted in Doomsday Book as holding lands in Essex and Suffolk, and whose lineal descendants continued in the trade for over a century. In the reign of Henry I., Leofstan was at the head of the profession, and a namesake, and presumably a descendant, was a Goldsmith and Mayor of London for twenty-four years, from 1189 to 1213, from which it may be premised that the trade of Goldsmith was an honourable and enriching pursuit. But these and their successors were not Bankers in any sense of the word. The bankers of the period were Jews, descendants of those brought over by William the Norman. These were not money-changers only; they introduced Bills of Exchange and lent out, at the customary usury, large sums to the nobility on the security of landed estates. They accumulated immense wealth by their conscientious adherence to the law of Moses, to "take usury from the stranger." Their wealth, real and reputed, made them conspicuous objects of persecution. Every Sovereign ill-treated, imprisoned and robbed them. They were massacred wholesale on the coronation-day of Richard I., at the instigation of the priests; their eyes were torn out and their teeth drawn, and they were cruelly butchered by King John—all in order to extract their treasures from them.

But they were supreme extortioners. Stow tells us of a Jew who had lent a Christian twenty shillings, and because he enforced the payment of a higher interest than 2s. a week thereupon—a modest 400 per cent.—he and seven hundred of his race were slain in London. A Jew was disqualified from enjoying a freehold, and every Jew who was a money-lender at interest was compelled to wear a plate on his breast announcing that he was a usurer; and failing compliance with this regulation he was to quit the Kingdom. The Jews settled in Oxford and extorted 45 per cent. from the students in the colleges, till their trade was repressed by the King (Henry III.). In 1278, two hundred and sixty-seven Jews were hanged and quartered, having been accused of clipping the coin, and the persecution culminated in the year 1290, when Edward I. robbed them of all their hoardings, and banished them, to the number of 16,511 persons, out of the Kingdom. The Lombards, who had been sent over by Pope Gregory IX. some fifty years previously, then became the only Bankers in England. They combined the three lucrative trades of Banker, Pawnbroker,* and Goldsmith, and they settled in Lombard Street. But they do not seem to have been regarded with much favour, and in the reign of Elizabeth their practices had

---

* Their sign was the Three Golden Balls, which is still used by modern pawnbrokers. Our word "lumber" is derived from their name. The room where they kept the goods pledged or pawned with them was known as the "Lombard Room"—corrupted into lumber-room.

become so detestable and pernicious that they also were banished the Kingdom.

The trade of Goldsmith gradually increased in importance and respectability, so much so that Henry VIII. condescended to borrow £300 from Robert Amades—a remarkably constitutional course for Henry VIII. to pursue under the circumstances. In Elizabeth's reign there were 107 enrolled Goldsmiths, of whom 76 resided in "the Chepe," and 31 in "Lum- "berde street," but these seem to have been no more than dealers in bullion and money changers, traders whom we would now term jewellers—and not to have any claim to be considered Bankers. They used to deposit their superfluous cash and bullion in the Tower for safety, until the saintly Charles I., in a moment of need, seized what was lying there, to the amount of £200,000, and having thus robbed them, commanded them by his Royal authority to consider him their debtor. The creditors were, however, ultimately paid, but they trusted the King no longer, and kept their cash in their own houses.

Under Cromwell, Banking considerably developed. In fact, Banking in England, as we regard the term, may be said to have commenced under the Protectorate. Then the systems of deposits of money with the Goldsmiths arose, and for those deposits, receipts, or "cash notes," which were also called "Goldsmith's notes," were issued. These were payable on demand, bore interest, and were transferable. A London Goldsmith-Banker, Mr. Samuel Lamb, recommended Cromwell, in 1656, to establish a national public Bank, and repeated his recommendation in 1658, but his advice was not acted on.

Noblemen, country gentlemen, and merchants, learned to deposit their money with these Goldsmiths, and it was received either payable at call or after a certain notice given. There was no fixed rate of interest allowed, the interest being regulated by the length of the period for which it would remain deposited, and the rate and period were a matter of agreement between banker and customer. The practice arose of the depositor drawing portion of his money by a written order on demand, and the making of such orders constituted the account a "running account," or, as we now term it, a current account, and the orders were the forerunners of our cheques. Then it became a recognised business of the Goldsmiths to lend out on security at interest—usually at a high rate—the sums so deposited; and though the security was sometimes of a nature which made the Goldsmith no more than a Pawnbroker, nevertheless, the pawnbroking instances are the exception.*

Perhaps it was the unsettled state of the country and the fact that the securities were rather unsatisfactory (as the tenure of land was unsteady during these periods of civil commotion), or perhaps it was owing to Royal pressure to hold the funds available for Royal use, but it seems that the profitable private discounting by the Goldsmith-Bankers was curtailed. For we find in Charles the Second's reign that they were in the habit of making advances to the Exchequer, at such a low rate as 5, or perhaps 6, per cent. Charles lived in a chronic state of impecuniosity, and in 1671, the pressure for money for the Royal pocket was peremptory. He hesitated to apply to the faithful Commons, fearing that a further demand might be as a last straw and break their patience and forbearance. So he counselled with his ministers as to the best means of obtaining one million and a half sterling, without the humiliation of again applying to Parliament, promising the Lord Treasurership—a

---

* For a very interesting account of the doings of money-lenders in London at this period, see an article on "Usurers of the Seventeenth Century," in *Disraeli's* "Curiosities of Literature."

post of much honour and emolument—to the successful inventor of a feasible scheme. At this time the Goldsmiths had money deposited in the Exchequer to the amount of £1,328,526, on which they received some 5 or 6 per cent. interest, and the device which was to supply the King's needs was, plainly, to rob the Exchequer of this amount. The scheme was the invention of Lord Ashley, but *alter tulit honorem.* He unguardedly confided his patent plan to Sir Thomas Clifford, who had been made Comptroller of the Household on the King's Restoration. Clifford is described by Evelyn as "a bold young gentleman of a small fortune in Devon, "but advanced by Lord Arlington, to the great astonishment of "all the Court." He unfolded it to the King, who approved of it readily. "'Odds fish," he said, " I will be as good as my "word to thee." And accordingly the Exchequer was closed, and payments out of it were suspended by the Royal authority on the 2nd January, 1672. Nearly all the Bankers were beggared, their customers were ruined, and Sir Thomas Clifford obtained a peerage—Lord Clifford of Chudleigh—and his Lord High Treasurership. The following are the names of the Bankers thus plundered and the amounts they lost :

BANKER-GOLDSMITHS PLUNDERED BY CHARLES II.

Sir Robert Vyner	£416,724	13 1½
Edmund Backwell ...	295,994	16 6
Gilbert Whitehall ...	248,866	3 5
Joseph Horneby ...	22,548	5 6
George Snell	10,894	14 5
Bernard Turner	16,275	9 8
Jeremiah Snow	59,780	18 8
John Colville	85,832	17 2
Robert Welstead	11,307	12 1

Thomas Rowe	17,615	17	8
John Portman	76,760	18	2
John Collier	1,784	6	4
Others	64,139	7	3½

The total amount of this plunder was £1,328,526.

The King said he intended to re-open the Exchequer in a year, but it was not re-opened, and no payment of principal or interest was made to the Bankers. However, in 1677, a Royal Covenant was made by letters patent to pay interest at the rate of 6 per cent. to them, which covenant was fulfilled up to 1683, when it ceased.

An Act was passed in 1699, reducing the aggregate claim of the Bankers to £664,263, i.e., half the debt, and charging the hereditary revenue of excise with interest at the rate of 3 per cent. after 25th December, 1705. This Act was the result of a suit against the Crown, wherein a verdict was given in favour of the Bankers and against the Crown, but which verdict was reversed by the Lord Chancellor Somers.

Sir Robert Vyner (or Viner) who heads the foregoing list, has found a place in history. He was the son of a Goldsmith, Sir Thomas Vyner, who was Lord Mayor of London in 1654, was knighted by Cromwell and created a Baronet by King Charles. He had his shop in Lombard Street, on the site of the present Post Office. To Sir Thomas Viner, Robert Viner, and Daniel Bellingham, Esquires, Goldsmiths, King Charles in 1662 granted a patent for 21 years, to coin silver money for Ireland, from a halfpenny to a fourpenny. This Daniel Bellingham (who was afterwards created a Baronet, and was the ancestor of the Castle Bellingham family), was the first Chief Magistrate of Dublin who was honoured with the title of Lord Mayor. Sir Robert, the son of Sir Thomas Vyner, was at the head of his profession; he made the crown for Charles II.

at a cost of £21,000. Like his father, he was Lord Mayor, and the following well-known story related by Grammont, of an incident of the banquet given by him to Charles, at the Guildhall, has immortalized him. "Sir Robert was a very loyal man, "and if you will allow the expression, very fond of his Sove- "reign ; but what with the joy he felt at heart for the honour "done him by his Prince, and the warmth he was in with con- "tinual toasting healths to the Royal Family, his lordship grew "a little too fond of his Majesty, and entered into a familiarity, "not altogether graceful in so public a place. The King under- "stood very well how to extricate himself in all such difficulties, "and, with a hint to the company to avoid ceremony, stole off "and made towards his coach, which stood ready for him in "Guildhall yard. But the Mayor liked his company so well, "and was grown so intimate, that he pursued him hastily, and "catching him fast by the hand, cried out, with a vehement "oath and accent, 'Sire, you shall stay and take t'other bottle !'

"The airy monarch looked kindly at him over his shoulder, "and with a smile and a graceful air, repeated this line of the "old song :

"'He that's drunk is as great as a King,'

"and immediately returned back and complied with his host's "invitation."

Pepys kept his account at Vyner's, and from the Diary we learn that Vyner allowed interest at the rate of 7 per cent., for Pepys left " clear in his hands to call for when I pleased," two thousand pounds, and he received at the end of three months interest amounting to £35. Pepys visited him at his mansion at Swakeley, "a very pleasant place," and there saw the black boy " that had died of a consumption, and being dead, he (Sir

"Robert) caused him to be dried in an oven, and lies there "entire in a box." Pepys there saw Lady Vyner, who had brought her husband "near £100,000, and no man now lives "in England in greater plenty, and he commands both King "and Council, with his credit he gives them."—This was in 1665, many years before the plundering. Vyner was also an acquaintance of Evelyn's.

Edward Backwell, or Bakewell, was an Alderman of the city, and had carried on his business of banker and goldsmith for some years at the Sign of the Unicorn in Lombard Street. Mr. Hilton Price identifies the locality as the present No. 69 in the street, and informs us, from an inspection of the Alderman's books that the rate charged varied between $2\frac{1}{2}$ and 10 per cent., but that it was usually 6 per cent. With Backwell Royalty banked. The King, the Queen's mother, the Duke of York, the Duke of Monmouth, the Countess of Castlemaine and many of the nobility, kept their accounts with him. In 1665, the rates of interest allowed by him were : at call, $3\frac{1}{2}$ per cent. ; at 10 days' notice, 4 per cent. ; at 14 days' notice, 5 per cent. ; at 20 days' notice, 6 per cent. In the following year he raised his rates by 1 per cent. He is described by Granger as "a banker of great ability, industry, integrity, and very exten- "sive credit. With such qualifications he, in a trading nation, "would, in the natural event of things, have made a fortune, "except in the days of Charles II., when the laws were overborne "by perfidy, violence, and rapacity." Backwell was a Jeweller and Silversmith as well as Banker. He manufactured Prince Rupert's plate, which "with fashion and engraving" cost £960 3s. 9d., and he made silver candlesticks for Pepys. Pepys knew him well,—liked his conversation, and sometimes had a glass of "Lambeth ale" with him. One of the old gossip's allusions to him is worth repeating : "This evening, coming

"home, we overtook Alderman Backwell's coach and his lady,
"and followed them to their house and there made them the first
"visit, where they received us with extraordinary civility and
"owning the obligation. But I do, contrary to my expectation,
"find her something a proud and vain-glorious woman in telling
"the number of her servants and family and expenses. He is
"also so. But he was ever of that strain. But here he showed
"me the model of his houses that he is going to build in Cornhill and Lombard Street; but he hath purchased so much there
"that it looks like a little town, and must have cost him a great
"deal of money." Such was a private banker a few centuries ago. Backwell retired to Holland after the Plundering, and there died in 1679.

Of **Gilbert Whitehall** we know little or nothing.

Joseph Horneby kept his place of business at the Sign of the Star, in Lombard Street, and notwithstanding his heavy loss, continued his establishment.

George Snell's house was at the Sign of the Fox, in Lombard Street, and **Bernard Turner's**, at the Sign of the Fleece, in the same street. The latter continued business with one Samuel Tookie in partnership.

Jeremiah Snow was at the Golden Anchor in the Strand at the time of the Royal robbery, but previously, during the Commonwealth, he had lived in Lombard Street. The closing of the Exchequer was not his first misfortune, apparently. In the *London Gazette* of 28th February, 1666, there is the following curious advertisement:—" Whereas, Jeremiah Snow, late of
"Lumbard Street, Goldsmith, now living in Broad Street, did
"owe divers persons, Anno 1652, eight thousand three hundred
"pounds in full, and gave him discharges absolute, (which was
"occasioned by the failing of two French merchants, who were,
"at the time, indebted to him three thousand four hundred

"pounds, but never paid him a fifth part, as by the Testimonials "remaining with the Publick notary it may appear), since which "time it hath pleased God to bless his endeavours with some "small Estate; he, therefore, in gratitude and justice, invites "them to receive the full remainder of their principal money, "excepting such as by his Oath he shall affirm to have paid in "part or in whole. And he declares this Publication is not for "vain-glory, (retribution in this kind being indispensable) nor to "get more credit, but because his friends have adjudged it con- "veniently necessary that his vindication might be as Publick, as "then was the Scandal." He surely deserved a better fate than that with which Charles visited him. Some half-century later, Snow's Bank—then "neere Temple Bar"—attained to a considerable reputation for the wonderful sagacity of Thomas Snow in connection with the South Sea Bubble. A panegyrical epistle to him by Dean Swift, "occasioned by his buying and selling "the third South Sea subscriptions, taken in by the Directors at "1000 per cent.," is certainly very creditable to his solvency :

> "Disdain not, Snow, my humble verse to hear,
> "Stick thy black pen awhile behind thine ear.
>
> * * * * *
>
> "When credit sank and commerce gasping lay,
> "Thou stood'st ; no bill was sent unpaid away ;
> "When not a guinea chinked on Martin's boards
> "And Atwill's self was drained of all his hoards,
> "Thou stood'st—an Indian king in size and hue,
> "Thy unexhausted shop was our Peru."

It is worthy of observation that this high spirit of probity and integrity did not continue to his successors. The bank founded by the upright Jeremiah Snow, became in the progress of a century, the Bank of **Strahan, Paul and Bates**, the notorious collapse of which, in 1856, and the prosecution of Sir

John Dean Paul and the other partners, have not faded from the memory of the present generation.

John Colville, or John Lyndsay, as we have seen the name in some returns—(owing to the fact that Colville's widow married John Lyndsay)—was in Lombard Street also. He was also a Silversmith, for Pepys got "a dozen silver salts" from him, and it is further recorded in the Diary, that his wife "is indeed one of the prettiest, modest black women that I ever saw;"—and Pepys saw many. It was Colville's note for £600 that paid Pepys' sister's portion. He also was "building a very fine "house in Lombard Street" after the Fire.

Of **Robert Welstead,** or Wealstead, we find no particulars.

Thomas Rowe was at the "George," in Lombard Street.

Of **Portman** and **Collier,** we have no information.

Remembering how the foregoing houses were plundered, we are not surprised that none of them or their successors are to be found amongst the London private Bankers of to-day. But some of the existing Bankers were founded anterior to the Royal robbery. The present Banking House of **Child and Co.,** Fleet Street, had its origin in the Goldsmith's establishment of John Wheeler in "Chepe," whose name is in the books of the Goldsmiths' Company, under the year 1559. His son John moved to Fleet Street, and when he died in 1660 the business was continued by William Wheeler and his son William at the Sign of the "Marygolde." Thence it passed into the hands of their apprentices, Blanchard and Child. Child became Sir Francis Child—relinquished the Goldsmith's business, became a true Banker and "the Father of the Profession," and his descendants own the Bank at present. The offices were for generations beside and over Temple Bar, until its removal in

1877. The earlier device of the marigold on the cheque-forms of Messrs. Child, was succeeded by a view of Temple Bar, and now Temple Bar like the marigold is amongst the things of the past. The following celebrated and historical persons kept their Banking accounts with Child and Co. : Oliver Cromwell ; Nell Gwynne ; Stillingfleet ; John Churchill the great Duke of Marlborough, and his Duchess, Sarah ; John Dryden ; King William III. and Queen Mary ; Harley, Earl of Oxford ; the Duke of Tyrconnell ; Archbishop Tenison. The house also possesses, amongst numerous other autographs of extreme interest, that of Dr. Titus Oates—his endorsement on a cheque of the Duke of Bolton.

Again, the existing Bank of Messrs. **Goslings and Sharpe** boasts a respectable antiquity. As early as the year 1650 Henry Pinckney was a Goldsmith in Fleet Street, at the Sign of the Three Squirrels. He is described as "Major" Pinckney in a conveyance of 1667, when his property was being marked out in that year, after his house had been burned down in the great fire of 1666. Pinckney's business was subsequently, in 1693, carried on by a Mr. Chambers, and about the year 1745 it passed into the hands of Messrs. Gosling, who still conduct it, and on whose cheques is still retained the device of the Three Squirrels. Pinckney or Pinkney was an acquaintance of Pepys, for on the 1st December, 1660, Pepys called upon him and " he took us to the taverne and gave us a pint of wine."

The present Bank of Messrs. **Hoare** is unique in one respect—the business is to-day carried on by the lineal male descendants of James Hoare, or Hore, who in the year 1677 kept " running cashes " at the " Golden Bottle " in Cheapside. This Hoare was an eminent person ; he was Comptroller of the Mint in 1661, Clerk of the Coins in 1665, and subsequently Warden of the Mint. About 1690 he removed from Cheapside to Fleet Street, where, ever since, the Bank has been conducted. The early sign of the house is still exhibited over the entrance door, and is retained on the cheques; and in one place we read that it is a leathern bottle and not a golden one, and that the meaning implied by a leathern bottle is "that it is not easily broken."

The Bank of Messrs. **Martin and Co.** was originally that of Charles Duncombe and Richard Kent, at the sign of the Grasshopper (a device of which still adorns their cheques) in Lombard Street. Kent had been established before Charles plundered the Exchequer, and Duncombe was an apprentice of Backwell's, and when the latter was ruined entered into partnership with Kent, and carried a good many of Backwell's customers to the new firm. The house evidently had a most successful career. From Evelyn's Diary we learn that in 1696 Duncombe, who a short time before had been but 'a mean goldsmith,' had recently " made a purchase at neere £90,000," of the Duke of Buckingham's estate of Helmsley, in Yorkshire.* On Jan. 25th, 1697-8, Duncombe, then an M.P., was charged with making false endorsements on Exchequer Bills, and was committed to the Tower, where he was detained a close prisoner. He confessed his guilt and was expelled the House. A Bill was brought in in the Commons for a seizure of his estate, and the "punishment of C. Duncombe, Esq.," and was passed by 138 against 103 votes. The Lords, however, refused the Bill, and ordered his discharge from the Tower. On the 31st March the Commons recommitted him, but nothing further seems to have been done towards punishing him. He was knighted in 1700. The present Earl of Feversham and Viscount

* " And Helmsley, once proud Buckingham's delight,
  " Slides to a Scrivener or a City Knight."—POPE.

Helmsley is his descendant, and the estate is now called Duncombe Park. When Duncombe relinquished the banking business it was carried on by Richard Smyth, from whom it passed to Messrs. Stone and Martin, and eventually to Messrs. Martin and Co. It is claimed for this Bank that it actually originated with Sir Richard Gresham, the "King's Exchanger" in the reign of Henry VIII., whose son was the celebrated Sir Thomas Gresham, of Elizabeth's reign, and who undoubtedly carried on his business of Goldsmith at the Grasshopper, in Lombard Street, where Messrs. Martin are now located.

Messrs. **Barnetts, Hoares, and Co.**, are the successors of Mr. Stokes or Stocks, who was Pepys' "own little Goldsmith," and who moved from Paternoster Row to the Black Horse in Lombard Street, where Humphrey Stocks was established in 1677. The business descended to John Bland and Son, who were the owners in 1740, and they were the immediate predecessors of Messrs. Barnetts, Hoares, and Co.

Messrs. **Coutts**—who are now at the head of the private Bankers—are the successors of George Middleton, who was a Goldsmith at the Three Crowns, in St. Martin's Lane, in 1690, and whose business was subsequently moved to Durham Yard, in the Strand, on the site of which the present Banking House is built. The English Royal Family keep their accounts at Coutts', and during the French Monarchy, the French Kings also patronised this establishment.

The foregoing are the private Bankers at present existing in London, who can trace a descent from the firms whom we find as Goldsmiths "keeping running Cashes" in the year 1677. A list of these is given in the "Little London Directory," republished by Mr. J. C. Hotten, and is worth here reproducing :

John Addis and Co., at the Sun, in Lumbard Street.

John Bolitho and Mr. Wilson, at the Golden Lane, Lumbard Street.

John Ballard, at the Unicorn, Lumbard Street.

Job Bolton, at the Bolt and Tun,* Lumbard Street.

Richard† Blanchard and Child, at the Marygold, Fleet Street.

Thos. Cook and Nichs. Carey, at the Griffin, Exchange Alley.

Mr. Cuthbert . . . . Cheapside.

Mr. Coggs, at the King's Head, Strand.

Mr. Churchill . . . . Strand.

Chas. Duncombe and Richd. Kent, at the Grasshopper, Lumbard Street.

John Ewing and Ben. Norrington, at the Angel and Crown, Lumbard Street.

Mr. East . . . . Strand.

Thomas Fowles, at the Black Lion, Fleet Street.

Joseph and Nathl. Hornboy, at the Star, Lumbard Street.

John Hind and Thos. Carwood, over against the Exchange, Cornhill.

Benjn. Hinton, at the Flower de Luce, Lumbard Street.

James Heriot, at the Naked Boy, Fleet Street.

James Hore, at the Golden Bottle, Fleet Street.

James Johnson, at the Three Flower de Luces, Cheapside.

Thos. Kiborne and Capill, at the King's Head, Lumbard Street.

Mr. Kenton, at the King's Arms, Fleet Street.

Mr. Ketch, at the Black Horse, Strand.

Henry Lamb, at the Grapes, Lumbard Street.

James Lapley, at the Three Cocks, Cheapside.

John Mawson and Co., at the Golden Hind, Fleet Street.

Henry Nelthorpe, at the Rose, Lumbard Street.

* Possibly a pun on the name.   † Should be Robert.

Thos. Price, at the Goat, Lumbard Street.

Peter Percefull and Steph. Evens, at the Black Boy, Lumbard Street.

Thomas Pardo, at the Golden Anchor, Lumbard Street.

Thomas Rowe and Thomas Greene, at the George, Lumbard Street.

Humph. Stocks, at the Black Horse, Lumbard Street.

John Sweetaple, at the Black Moore's Head, Lumbard Street.

John Snell, at the Fox, Lumbard Street.

Michl. Shrimpshaw, at the Golden Lion, Fleet Street.

Richd. Stayley . . . . Covent Garden.

John Temple and John Scale, at the Three Tuns, Lumbard Street.

John Thursby, at the Ball, Lumbard Street.

Bar. Turner and Saml. Tookie, at the Fleece, Lumbard Street.

Major John Wallis, at the Angell, Lumbard Street.

Peter Wade, at the Mermaid, Lumbard Street.

Peter White and Churchill, at the Plough, Lumbard Street.

Thomas White, at the Blew Anchor, Lumbard Street.

Thomas Williams, at the Crown, Lumbard Street.

Robt. Ward and John Townley, at the Ram, Lumbard Street.

An insight into the manner in which Bills of Exchange were negotiated and Banking conducted in the earlier years of the eighteenth century will be afforded by the following extracts from Swift's "Journal to Stella." Under date, Chelsea, 7th June, 1711, he writes: "What an old bill (one for £200) is that "you sent of Raymond's! A bill upon one Murry of Chester, "which depends entirely not only upon Raymond's honesty "but his discretion; and in money matters he is the last man "I would depend on. Why should Sir Alexander Cairnes in

"London pay me a bill drawn by God knows who upon Murry
"in Chester? I was at Cairnes's and they can do no such
"thing. I went among some friends who are merchants, and
"I find the bill must be sent to Murry, accepted by him and
"then returned back, and then Cairnes may accept or refuse it
"as he pleases. Accordingly I gave the bill to Sir Thomas
"Frankland, who has sent it to Chester, and ordered the post-
"master there to get it accepted and then send it back, and in
"a day or two I shall have an answer. Raymond should have
"written to Murry at the same time, to desire Sir Alexander
"Cairnes to have answered such a bill if it come. But Cairnes's
"clerks (himself was not at home) said that 'they had received
"'no notice of it, and could do nothing,' and advised me to
"send it to Murry." On the 30th June, he writes thus: "I
"believe my £200 will be paid; but that Sir Alexander
"Cairnes is a scrupulous puppy. I left the bill with Mr. Strat-
"ford, who is to have the money." And on the 9th July he
writes: "I was to-day in the city and dined with Mr. Stratford,
"who tells me Sir Alexander Cairnes makes difficulties about
"paying my bill. To-morrow I shall have a positive answer.
"That Cairnes is a shuffling scoundrel; and several merchants
"have told me so. What can one expect from a Scot and a
"fanatick?" Such was a Bill of Exchange experience of the
great grim Dean. This Cairnes was "of Monaghan, Baronet."
There is no mention of him in Mr. Hilton-Price's book, though
Sheridan describes him as "an eminent banker."

The following houses, which are the principal private Banking firms at present doing business in London, were subsequently established :—

Glyn, Mills, and Co.—This house, which does the largest
business of any London private Bank, was established about
the year 1750, as Vere, Glyn and Hallifax, and a Glyn was

always a chief partner in it. The present Lord Wolverton is the representative of the family and a senior partner in the firm. **Barclay, Bevan and Co.**, commenced business very early in the 18th century, probably about 1710, at the sign of the Black Spread Eagle in Lombard Street, in the names of Feame and Gould, subsequently Feame and Barclay. **Drummond's** Bank was founded about 1712 by Andrew, a son of Sir John Drummond. When George III. quarrelled with Mr. Coutts because he advanced £100,000 to Sir Francis Burdett for the expenses of the celebrated Westminster Election, he removed his account to Drummond's; but the Prince Regent returned to Coutts' (where the Royal Family have since banked) because Drummond declined further advances to his Royal Highness. All the partners are Drummonds. **Fuller, Banbury, and Co.** date from about 1735, when the Bank was established as Atkins, Honeywood and Fuller. **Herries, Farquhar, and Co.** was founded in 1770 by Robert Herries, who seceded from Coutts' Firm, and to him the honour belongs of having invented "circular notes" for Continental travelling purposes. Sir Walter Farquhar, Bart., is the present head of the Bank. **Praeds' London Bank** dates from 1803, the partners having previously been bankers at Truro for a considerable period. Mr. Praed, the poet, was a member of this Firm. **Prescott, Grote, and Co.** was established in 1766 under that title. Mr. George Grote, the historian, was one of the family whose name is in the Firm. **Ransom, Bouverie, and Co.** was originally founded in 1786 by Mr. Ransom and others. It absorbed Bouverie's Bank in 1856. Lord Byron kept his account at Ransom's, his friend Mr. Kinnaird being a part owner. Lord Kinnaird is head of the house at present. **Robarts, Lubbock, and Co.** was founded in 1772 by Sir William Lennon and others, and the title of the firm has experienced many mutations.

Sir John Lubbock, Bart., M.P., whose name is identified with banking, and who is as eminent in the scientific as in the banking world, is a chief partner. **Sir Samuel Scott, Bart., and Co.** dates from 1825. **Smith, Payne, and Smiths** was, under the name Smith and Payne, carrying on business in 1759. Mr. Smith had originally been established at Nottingham, where his grandfather founded, and his descendants still conduct, a Banking House. **Williams, Deacon, and Co.,** was originally Sir Charles Raymond, Bart., Williams and others, and was established about 1770. **Cocks, Biddulph, and Co.** dates from 1750. The London Private Bankers continued to issue their own notes till near the end of the last century.

Besides these, there are several other private banking firms in London, but we have made mention only of those more notable ones, whose names are familiar to every bank official in this country. The numerous houses, eminent and prosperous in their day, which have been absorbed by, or merged in, other establishments—which have ceased from choice, or stopped from misfortune—we have not referred to, as it is beyond the scope of this sketch. Those curious on these points should consult Mr. Hilton Price's admirable and trustworthy volume, where they may read the histories of the Banks of Hankey; Jones, Loyd, and Co.; Strahan, Paul, and Bates; Willis, Percival, and Co.; Price and Co; Olding's and Co. (where Samuel Rogers the poet, the friend of Byron and the society-father of Lord Beaconsfield, was a partner); and many others dead and forgotten, or still flourishing with various degrees of prosperity and various shares of business. The history of the London private banking firms stands out in strong contrast with those of the Edinburgh and Dublin ones. Several now transacting business in London, have been established over a century—some over two centuries; whereas in Dublin, the oldest of the three private banks now existing (Ball and Co.) can show no greater antiquity than about 60 years; and in Edinburgh a private banker is a thing of the past.

V.

THE BANK OF ENGLAND.

IN 1694 the Bank of England was established, having been projected in 1691 by a Scotch merchant, William Paterson, to relieve King William III. from the difficulties experienced in raising supplies to prosecute the war against France. The same year (1694) Paterson also promulgated his plan for the colonization of Darien, for which end a company was formed in 1695, and expeditions set sail. But this project was attended with disastrous results; the colony had to surrender to the Spaniards, and Paterson narrowly escaped a death by famine and disease. His National Bank project was more successful. He, in conjunction with one Michael Godfrey, influenced forty London merchants to subscribe half a million sterling towards the sum of £1,200,000, which was to be lent to the Government at 8 per cent., with a further allowance of £4,000 a year for management, in consideration of the subscribers being incorporated into a bank with certain monopoly privileges. The scheme was violently opposed in Parliament, and also by the private bankers, but the Bill received the Royal assent on the 25th April, 1694, and the Bank obtained its Charter of Incorporation on the 27th July following. On the 1st July, Evelyn writes: "The first great Banke for a fund of money "being now established by act of Parliament, was filled "and completed to the sum of £120,000, and put under the "Government of the most able and wealthy citizens of London. "All who adventured any sum had 4 per cent. so long as it lay "in the Bank, and had power either to take it out at pleasure "or to transfer it." The Charter was first granted for eleven years, but it has since been renewed from time to time down to 1844, when Peel's Bank Charter Act renewed it for the usual eleven years, and longer, "if the debt due from the "public to the Bank, £11,015,100, with interest, be not paid "after due notice." The Bank commenced its business on 1st January, 1695, at the Grocers' Hall in the Poultry*—Sir John Houblon being the first Governor and Michael Godfrey the first Deputy-Governor. Houblon was "a French merchant, whose "father had fled out of Flanders on the persecution of the Duke "of Alva, and who had his house furnished *au Prince*, and gave "splendid entertainments." At the time of its founding it issued notes for £20 and upwards,† and discounted bills at rates varying from 4½ to 6 per cent. In 1696 there was a run on the Bank which caused its temporary suspension, when its notes

---

* Dickens' *Dictionary of London* states that "the business of the Bank "was originally carried on in the Mercer's Hall; thence it was removed to "the Grocers' Hall; and thence again to the buildings at the back of the "present Court towards Threadneedle Street, the existing not very satis-"factory pile being the work of Sir John Soane half a century later."

† In the "Bankers' Magazine" for March, 1845, "R. W. D." writes as follows :—"A gentleman near Aylesbury, it is said, has in his posses-"sion a Bank of England note for 6d. (sixpence) issued in the year 1700, "of which the following is an exact copy :—

No. 105.
I promise to pay T. Caddel or bearer,
on demand, the summe of sixpence.
London, 8th day of May, 1700,
—6d. For the Governor and Company
of the Bank of England.
John Wage."

were at 20 per cent. discount. The capital was then increased by about a million, to £2,201,171 10s. In 1710 its capital was further increased to £5,559,995 10s. In 1734 it moved from the Poultry to Threadneedle Street, the present building, which stands in four parishes, and is reared on the site of Sir John Houblon's house and many other buildings, including the Church of St. Christopher-le-Stocks, the burial ground* of which is now "the Garden" of the Bank, and is known to every visitor to London. The first erection comprised what constitutes the present centre, with the courtyard, hall, and Bullion Court. In 1770 the eastern wing was added; and in 1804 the western wing, with the Lothbury front was completed. In 1738, the Bank invented and issued Bank Post Bills; in 1759 it issued £10 notes; in 1793 £5 notes; in 1797 £1 and £2 notes; but it relinquished the issue of all notes under £5 in 1844. In 1826 and 1827, acting under Government advice, it opened its few country branches, and in 1856, its Burlington Gardens Branch. In 1718 its notes in circulation amounted to £1,829,930; in 1800, to £15,450,000.

The Charter originally stipulated a payment by the Government on the amount lent it at the rate of 8 per cent., but at each renewal the Government used the opportunity to reduce the rate, or the Bank took advantage of the Government, and to secure its Charter offered advances at a lower rate, and sometimes free of interest. In this way the debt, which was £1,200,000, increased: in 1708 it stood at £3,375,000; in 1781 at £11,686,000; in 1816 at £14,686,000. Upon the renewal of the Charter in 1833, the Act (3 & 4 William IV., c. 98) provided that the Government should repay one-fourth part of the debt due to the Bank, and it now stands at £11,015,000.

* In this burial ground was buried, in the last century, a clerk of the Bank named Jenkins, who was six feet and a half in length, and was interred here to save the corpse from the Resurrectionists.

The Bank had certain privileges conferred upon it at the time of its formation, some of which have since been rescinded and some of which are still enjoyed. In 1708 an Act was passed forbidding the formation in England or Wales of a Bank having more than six partners, for the issue of notes payable on demand. This was partially repealed in 1826, the restriction then being made to apply only to Banks within a sixty-five mile radius of London.

The Bank of England is prohibited from engaging in any commercial undertaking—it must adhere rigidly to its legitimate business of "buying or selling coin, bullion, and bills of Exchange." It keeps current accounts, but allows no over-drafts. It receives money on deposit, but allows no interest. By the first Charter it was permitted to issue notes to the extent of its then capital, £1,200,000, and by the Bank Act of 1844, the Issue Department—which is separate and distinct from the Banking Department—could issue to the amount of £14,000,000 against certain securities, of which the Government debt of £11,015,000 is the chief; and no notes can be issued over and above this £14,000,000,* except against coin and bullion held by the Bank. The Banking Department was separated from the Issue Department in 1844, the object being to prevent a note issue beyond a certain amount, unless against gold coin held, so that a mixed currency of gold and notes should expand and contract in unison, and thus mitigate financial convulsions. This idea was based on the assumption that the Bank could issue its notes, and get them into circulation to any amount, that excessive issue meant increased currency and increased prices, and ultimately a foreign drain of gold—a theory not supported by experience.

The Bank of England has sometimes been in difficulties. It failed in 1696, and in its earlier years it was subjected to

* Exclusive of a small addition subsequently referred to.

many runs—some organized by the jealous private bankers; some the result of political causes. The Rebellion of 1745 caused a serious run, during which the Bank notes were redeemed in silver. In 1797 the panic caused by the expectation of a French invasion was so great that an Order in Council was issued to protect the Bank. By this order the Bank was prohibited from paying its notes in gold till Parliament had spoken on the subject, and Parliament continued the protection till six months after the signature of a definite treaty of peace between the nations. In 1801, owing to over-issue, the notes of the Bank were at a discount of 10 per cent. In 1810 they sunk to a discount of 15 per cent., and in 1824 to 25 per cent., from the same cause and sundry disturbing anticipations. In 1825, during the great panic which brought down 770 Banks throughout the Kingdom, the Bank found extrication from the difficulties caused thereby in the issue of some £1 notes, which were found in an old chest, the existence of which had been forgotten, but which was happily discovered at an appropriate time. In 1847, during the panic which arose from the railway mania, the restriction on the issue was suspended by Lord John Russell, but the favour was not used.

In 1857, during the panic caused by the American failures, Lord Palmerston sanctioned an addition to the authorised issue, and £200,000 over the limit were issued. In the panic of 1866 the Bank Act was also suspended.

If any country Bank of issue should cease to issue notes, the Bank of England may apply, and will be authorised on such application by an Order in Council, to increase its issue by two-thirds of the authorised issue thus discontinued, but the profits of the increased issue do not belong to the Bank but to the Government. In this way the Bank's issue was, in 1857, increased by £475,000, and now it can issue, against securities allocated for the purpose, notes to the amount of £14,475,000;

but for any amount in excess of this, gold and silver must be held in accordance with the Act of 1844. Bank of England notes are a legal tender in England, except if tendered by the Bank itself. The Issue department in the Bank is distinct from the Banking Department, and all the notes issued by the Issue Department must necessarily be either in the Banking Department or in the hands of the public. The amount of those in the Banking Department is known as the "Reserve," and the amount of those in the hands of the public is known as the "Active Circulation." The "Reserve" is the basis upon which the variations of the Bank rate are regulated; if it be low the rate is increased, and if large the rate is lowered. It increases as the amount of circulation from the Issue Department increases, and diminishes in sympathy with diminished or restricted out-put.

For the £14,000,000 which the Bank issues by authority, and which represents the sum lent to the Government, it receives interest at the rate of 3 per cent. But this is not clear profit, as it has to pay Government £180,000 a year as a set-off for its privileges and exemption from stamp duty; and the cost of production and management of the circulation is estimated at about £115,000 a year. Thus the profit on the issue is about £125,000 a year only. An additional source of profit is the purchase of gold bullion, upon which it clears 1½d. per ounce. As the Bank allows no interest on Deposit Receipts or on Current Accounts, and permits no over-draft, it has also means of profit which other Banks do not possess. It did not open any branches till 1826; at present it has a dozen offices. There are twenty-four directors who must each hold £2,000 of the stock of the Company; a Deputy-Governor, who must hold £3,000; and a Governor, who must hold £4,000. An anomalous and remarkable custom prevails whereby Professional Bankers are excluded from the Board,

The History and Progress of Banking.   65

which is solely composed of eminent merchants; a custom which, as Mr. Dunning Macleod observes, is indefensible and unsupportable in theory and is fraught with errors in practice. Twelve Directors and the Governor or Deputy-Governor are necessary to form a court, and they meet each Thursday. The Bank of England differs from other Banking establishments in having the management of the Public Debt, upon which it pays the dividends: in holding the Government Deposits and making advances to the Government: in aiding in the collection of the Revenue, and in being the Banker of all the London Banks. For the management of the Public Debt it receives about £250,000 a year, of which about half covers the actual charges in connection therewith. The following, which is the account for the week ending 13th July, 1881, will show the position of this great concern:

Issue Department.

Debit.		Credit.	
Notes Issued... ... ...£41,239,015		Government Debt ...£11,015,100	
		Other Securities... ... 4,734,900	
		Gold Coin and Bullion 25,489,015	
£41,239,015		£41,239,015	

Banking Department.

Debit.		Credit.	
Proprietors' Capital ...£14,553,000		Government Securities £16,271,339	
Rest 3,326,858		Other Securities... ... 20,195,229	
Public Deposits (including Exchequer, Savings Banks, Commissioners of National Debt and Dividend Acts) 4,754,329		Notes 13,978,645	
		Gold and Silver Coin 1,164,728	
Other Deposits 28,716,904			
Seven days and other Bills 258,850			
£51,609,941		£51,609,941	

The dividend paid by the Bank of England, in 1694, was 8 per cent.; it rose as high as 9, and fell as low as 4½ (1753), during the 18th century. In 1807, 10 per cent. was paid and maintained till 1822. The present dividend is at the rate of 9½ per cent. per annum.

There is one curious circumstance in the History of the Bank of England of which mention has been made—its having stopped payment in 1696. This was owing chiefly to the failure of the **National Land Bank**, which was projected by a Dr. Chamberlain, and established by Act of Parliament in that year (1696), with the object of advancing money on the security of unencumbered freehold estates. This project, though supported by Lord Sunderland, Harley, and the Tory Ministers, and patronised by the King, who subscribed £5,000 to it, never made any progress. Its capital was not subscribed for, but its rivalry of the Bank of England was of such import, that when it failed the Bank of England stopped payment and the notes fell to a heavy discount. A contemporary fly-sheet announces, "the trial and condemnation of the Land Bank at "Exeter Change for murdering the Bank of England at "Grocer's Hall:" and another gives an epitaph: "Here lies "the body of the Bank of England, who was born in the year "1694 and died 5th May, 1696, in the third year of its age." A complete and most interesting "History of the Bank of "England" has been written by Mr. John Francis, and a perusal of it will amply repay the reader.

VI.

ENGLISH PRIVATE AND JOINT STOCK BANKS.

BEFORE the passing of the Act of 1826, English Banking was confined to the Bank of England, which had the monopoly of issuing notes within a radius of 65 miles; and to the private Banks scattered extensively over the country. The oldest country Bank is stated in some works to have been Wood's Bank in Gloucester, which was founded in 1716, but the present Banking House of Samuel Smith and Co., of Nottingham, claims to have been established so far back as 1688. The origin and history of this veteran establishment is pleasantly told in Mr. F. Martin's book—"Stories of Banks and Bankers"—and therein we learn that it was a grandson of the founder who entered into partnership with Payne, of London, in 1759, and established the eminent firm of Smith, Payne & Co. The History of the English Country Private Banks of the last century that have failed or disappeared, has yet to be written; but there are at present several establishments which were formed over a century ago, now carrying on business and enjoying valuable connections. **Alexanders and Co.**, of Ipswich and elsewhere, dates from 1744;[*] **Beckett and Co.**, of Leeds, from 1750; **Miles, Cave, Baillie and Co.**, of

---

[*] It was at the Woodbridge branch of Alexander's Bank, that Bernard Barton, the poet, was a clerk from 1806 till near his death.

Bristol, from 1750 also; **Pease's**, of Hull, from 1754; **Garfit and Co.**, of Boston, from 1755; **Wright and Co.**, of Nottingham, from 1759. The majority of the English private Banks at present existing were founded late in the eighteenth, and early in the present century. Few have been established during the past fifty years; for the rapid spread of Joint Stock Banks, founded in accordance with the Act of 1826, discouraged, if it did not render impracticable, the formation of new private Banks, which could not, unless in exceptional cases, succeed in creating a business, in seducing it from the older private Banks, or in obtaining it in preference to the Joint Stock Banks.

The old private Banks could not have more than six partners, but the restriction does not seem to have been an obstacle to the formation of such establishments. In 1792, it is said there were over 350 private Banks in England, of which more than half failed in the panic of 1792-3, consequent on the French War; but subsequently they increased with amazing rapidity. In 1809 there were no fewer than 782; in 1814, their number was 940; but the great panic which shook the country in the winter of 1825 made great havoc amongst them. At that time 770 Banks of all kinds stopped payment, and the following year (1826) the Joint Stock Act was passed. A majority of the private Bankers issued their own Bank notes; and the Act of 1844 regulated the future issues of these Banks as it did of the public Joint Stock Banks. At present (1881) the number of private Banks in England and Wales is 241, of which 103 issue notes. The total amount of their authorised issue is £3,548,166, and of their actual issue, about £1,700,000. The Bank of England monopoly privilege, whereby no bank of more than six partners could issue notes within 65 miles of London, was discussed publicly in 1833, and it was decided that, as the restriction only applied to Banks of Issue, Banks on the Joint Stock principle, not being Issuing Banks, could carry on business in and near London; and thereupon the London and Westminster (1834), the London Joint Stock (1836), the Union of London, and London and County (1839), and other Banks, were established in the Metropolis. In an Appendix is a statement of the present position of the English Joint Stock Banks.*

* See Appendix I.

VII.

BANKING IN SCOTLAND.

In Scotland the system of private Banking never attained the same proportions that it reached in England and Ireland. This is due chiefly, if not solely, to the earlier formation of Chartered and Joint Stock Banks, and the plentiful establishment of branches throughout the country. In this respect Scotland has had a very sensible advantage over the sister countries, and especially over Ireland, where there was no Bank, except the private ones, before 1783, when the Bank of Ireland was founded, and, as will be seen, it did not deign to open a branch till the year 1824. In Scotland it was far different. The first notice of Banking in that country which appears in the Statute Book is in the Act passed in 1695, under which the **Bank of Scotland** was chartered. To this establishment the *exclusive* privilege of Banking "within the Kingdom of "Scotland" was granted for a period of twenty-one years from the 17th July, 1695. The following year it commenced operations and opened branches. Its original capital was £1,200,000 *Scots*, in 1,200 shares of £1,000 *Scots* each, which was equivalent in sterling money to £100,000, in shares of £83 6s. 8d. each. Unlike the Bank of England and Bank of Ireland, the Bank of Scotland was, by its Charter, prohibited from lending money to the Crown. It commenced its issue of £1 notes in

1704. In 1774 the capital was increased to £200,000 sterling, and at present the subscribed capital is £1,500,000 sterling, of which £1,000,000 is paid up. It will be observed that the paid-up capital of all the Scotch Banks, is, in proportion to the subscribed capital, greater than that of the English and Irish Banks. The Bank of Scotland continued to be the only Bank in Scotland until 1727, in which year a Charter of Incorporation was granted to the **Royal Bank of Scotland**. It was formed with a capital equal to £151,000 sterling, but now it stands at £2,000,000, of which all is paid-up. The **British Linen Company** was incorporated in 1746 for the purpose of manufacturing and trading in linen, but the project, as such, was almost immediately abandoned, and the Company entered upon Banking business solely. Its capital was originally £100,000 sterling, but it has been increased to £1,000,000. The foregoing are the three Chartered Banks of Scotland, and in these the liability of the shareholders is in effect limited to the amount of their shares. In 1765 an Act of Parliament was passed whereby it was rendered compulsory on the issuing Banks to make their notes payable on demand; hitherto they seemed to have retained to themselves the option of paying their notes six months after presentation, allowing legal interest from the date of demand to the date of payment.

Notwithstanding the spread of Banking facilities as afforded by these institutions of unquestionable solvency, Private Banking firms were established and enjoyed a fair share of prosperity. Those of them which were still in existence half a century ago were:—

Sir Wm. Forbes, Bart., and Co., of Edinburgh, established in 1802.
Carrick and Co.   „ Glasgow   „   1749.
Hunters and Co.   „ Ayr   „   1773.

Ramsay, Bonar, and Co.	of Edinburgh	established in	1738.
Kinnear and Sons*	,,	do.	,,	1748.
Donald Smith and Co.*	,,	do.	,,	1773.
Robert Allen and Co.	,,	do.	,,	1773.
Alexander Allan and Co.	,,	do.	,,	1776.

Of these the most eminent was Forbes's Bank. It merged in the Glasgow Union Bank, which subsequently became the Union Bank of Scotland; Carrick's and Hunter's Banks were also absorbed by the Union Bank; Ramsay's was wound up; Kinnear's and Allen's failed.

The Private Bank of John McAdam and Co. was founded in Ayr in 1763; this and the firm of Alexander Johnston, Hugh Lawson and Co., of Dumfries, were purchased, in 1771, by Douglas, Heron, and Co., a private bank which was established in 1770, and which collapsed after a career of three years. About 1765 were started the Merchant Banking Company of Glasgow, and the house of Andrew, George, and Andrew Thompson. The Bank of Aberdeen, founded in 1767, and absorbed by the Union Bank of Scotland in 1854, is an instance of remarkable success. Its paid-up capital at its formation was £30,000, in 200 shares of £150 each. The capital was largely augmented from the surplus profits, and in 1836 the shares were worth over £3,000 each.

There were sundry other establishments dignified by the title of Banking "Companies," *quasi* Joint Stock concerns, the business of some of which, having commenced during the last century, continued for many years. These, however, were generally in effect Private Banks. They had few partners; their capital was unknown to the public; and their constitution

---

* These two concerns afterwards amalgamated under the title of Kinnears Smith, and Co., and subsequently failed.

and the methods and extent of their businesses were only imparted to the members of the partnership. They have mostly failed or been absorbed by the later-established Joint Stock Banks. Of these, the Dundee Bank (1763);* the Fife Bank (1802)†; the Leith Bank (1792); the Renfrewshire Bank (1802); the Montrose Bank (1814); the Perth Bank (1766); the Shetland Bank (1802); and the Stirling Bank (1777) failed; and of the Joint Stock establishments the most notorious failures of recent years have been those of the Western Bank of Scotland and the City of Glasgow Bank. The **Western Bank**, which was established in 1832, had a capital of £1,500,000, and an authorised circulation of £337,938, about 100 branches, and 1,300 shareholders, stopped payment under circumstances of grave reprehension in 1857. In the Western Bank the following establishments had been merged :—

The Dundee Union Bank.
The Greenock Banking Company.
The Ayrshire Banking Company.

The **City of Glasgow Bank** was established in 1839, and failed in 1878. The cause of stoppage in all these instances was culpable recklessness of management. The **Edinburgh and Glasgow Bank**, being in difficulties, was taken over by the Clydesdale Bank in 1858. Its authorised issue (£136,657) went, by arrangement, to increase the issue of the Clydesdale Bank. It consisted of the following companies :—

The Edinburgh and Leith Bank.
The Southern Bank of Scotland (Dumfries).
The Glasgow Joint Stock Bank.

* Paid its creditors in full.
† Originally George Dempster and Co., with a capital of £1,260; the first bank established in Dundee, was amalgamated with the Royal Bank of Scotland in 1864.

The **Royal British Bank**, though not strictly a Scotch Bank, was promoted by Scotch gentlemen with the object of transplanting to English soil the peculiar system of Scottish Banking. It was established in 1849, and stopped payment in 1856, under such management that entailed (as in the case of the City of Glasgow Bank failure also) the prosecution and imprisonment of the directors.

The following Joint Stock and Private Banking Companies are merged in the existing Union Bank of Scotland :—

> The Glasgow Union Bank.
> The Paisley Union Bank.
> Glasgow Banking Company.
> Carrick and Co. (The Ship Bank) Glasgow.
> Sir William Forbes, Bart., and Co.
> The Thistle Bank, Glasgow.
> Hunters and Co., Ayr.
> The Aberdeen Banking Company.

In the Commercial Bank of Scotland is merged,
> The Arbroath Banking Company.

In the National Bank of Scotland is merged,
> The Commercial Bank of Aberdeen.

The British Linen Company has absorbed,
> The Paisley Bank.

Banking, as practised in Scotland, differs in some marked respects from that of England and Ireland. The Banks are all chartered or joint stock companies; they all issue notes, they all have numerous branches. Banking is better understood by the rural population of Scotland than in the sister countries. The smallest town in Scotland has one, and frequently more than one, bank, and the system of "cash credits" which obtains there is in accordance with the habits of the people, and is a great impulse to industry and an incentive to thrift. A "**cash credit**" is simply an advance by way of a debit balance in current account, which advance is secured to the bank by a bond entered into by a couple of solvent parties who are guarantors for the borrower. It was an invention of the Royal Bank, and was designed to get its superfluous capital into circulation by inducing parties to borrow and embark in business. "In the very contracted sphere of Scottish com-"merce at that time," writes Mr. Dunning Macleod, "there "were not sufficient commercial bills to exhaust the credit of "the Banks. They had, as it were, a superfluity of credit on "hand, and the Royal Bank devised a means of getting it into "circulation." This means was the "cash credit." It is no more than an open credit, to be availed of as the party requires, and to be reduced at his convenience. The advance enables the person obtaining it to start or to develop a trade or business— be he shopkeeper or farmer. Thus the industrious poor are supplied with capital and enabled to commence life under favourable conditions, and the profits realised, or surplus moneys received, are lodged in the bank towards the reduction of the debit balance. It is obviously the policy of the borrower to conduct his business and himself to the satisfaction of his sureties ; and it is his interest to cultivate habits of industry and frugality in order to clear off his debt and save the interest paid thereon. It is unanimously acknowledged that the practice has been of immense advantage to the country materially and morally. Capital is more extensively employed for the benefit of the poorer classes, and labour, thrift, and foresight are encouraged. The enterprise of the nation is exemplified by the fact that the chief offices or headquarters of the Banks are not confined to the metropolis, but various local institutions have their directors and chief management in their own districts. The laws affecting the circulation and note issues are similar in effect to those which apply to Ireland, and, like them, are the result of Sir Robert Peel's legislation. The Scotch and Irish Banks of issue have an advantage over the English, in that the latter cannot, under any circumstances, exceed their authorised issue, while the Banks in Scotland and Ireland can issue to an unlimited extent, on the condition that the amount in excess of the authorised issue is covered by coin held; and of this the amount of silver cannot exceed one-fourth the amount of gold.

The following table shows the existing Scotch Banks; their date of establishment; their head offices; their capital subscribed and paid-up; number of branches; their authorised circulation; and their average circulation on 22nd November, 1879 :—

NAME.	Date	No. of Branches.	Head Office.	Capital. Subscribed.	Capital. Paid-up.	Circulation. Authorized.	Circulation. Average.
				£	£	£	£
Bank of Scotland	1695	105	Edinboro'	1,875,000	1,250,000	343,418	890,130
Royal Bank of Scotland	1727	121	Do.	2,000,000	2,000,000	216,451	831,035
British Linen Company	1746	99	Do.	1,000,000	1,000,000	438,024	696,506
Commercial Bank	1810	105	Do.	1,000,000	1,000,000	374,880	846,182
Aberdeen Town and County	1825	54	Aberdeen	720,000	252,000	70,133	237,674
National Bank of Scotland	1825	96	Edinboro'	1,000,000	1,000,000	297,024	697,763
Union Bank of Scotland	1830	129	Glasgow	1,000,000	1,000,000	454,346	818,217
North of Scotland Banking Co.	1836	59	Aberdeen	1,968,000	394,500	154,319	371,514
Caledonian Banking Company	1838	19	Inverness	600,000	150,000	53,434	49,237
Clydesdale Banking Company	1838	95	Glasgow	1,000,000	1,000,000	274,321	555,462

The total paid-up capital of the Scotch Banks is £9,046,500, while of the Irish Banks the total is £6,984,230. The total number of branch Banks in Scotland has within the past twenty years increased about 50 per cent. At present there are 882 to a population in round numbers of 3,500,000, whereas in Ireland the total number, including sub-offices, is less than 500 to a population of 5,500,000.

VIII.

EARLY IRISH AND SCOTCH COINAGES.

GOLD was known from immemorial times in Ireland, not as an import, but as a native product. In Keating's *History of Ireland* we are informed that the first golden mine in Ireland was discovered near the "Liffee," in the reign of Tighermhas, who is said to have begun to reign in the Kingdom in the year 1188 B.C.—from which statement it appears rational to conclude that the County Wicklow gold mines ought to have been exhausted, if they were not, when mining ceased there some 50 years ago.*

When Aldfrid, a Saxon prince, afterwards King of Northumbria, came as a student to the Irish schools, he made a tour of the kingdom, about 684 A.D., and wrote in the Irish language, it is said, a poem, in his "Itinerary," in which he says :

"Gold and silver I found, and money."

And one Donat, who flourished about 850, sung of Ireland :—
" *Insula dives opum, gemmarum, vestis et auri.*"

* These gold mines were unfortunate. In Mr. Richey's "Lectures on Irish History" we read that one of the misfortunes of the country in Henry VIII.'s reign was "the importing of German Protestants to work "the mines of Wicklow, who turned out to be 'idle vagabonds, not worth "their keep."

> "—— exhaustless is her store,
> Of veiny silver and of golden ore."

Gold, of advanced and chaste workmanship and design, was undoubtedly in use for personal adornment and religious vessels at a very early period in Ireland; and it was a standard of value and an exchange medium considerably over 1,000 years ago. It was shapen into rings, and circulated in this form, as it did in many countries at a primitive period; and it is curious to discover that spurious money was then manufactured. In the Royal Irish Academy are examples of this—base metal carefully coated with gold.

The same veracious historian who chronicles the discovery of the "Liffee" gold mine, informs us that St. Patrick erected mints at Ardmagh and Cashel and "coined money for the service of the State," about the year 450 A.D. If this were so, the art of coinage fell into disuse, for in subsequent years we find gold for ransoms, religious offerings, &c., mentioned as being weighed by ounces and not specified as coins; and the first reliable record of a coinage in Dublin that we possess is under the year 1210, when King John, who was then in Dublin, ordered a coinage of pence and farthings. Pope Adrian's Bull to Henry II. in 1155, authorising him to invade Ireland, contained a condition that the King should compel every Irish family to pay a *carolus* to the Holy See, but this stipulation was not fulfilled at the invasion in 1172, for the simple reasons that the Irish families had not got caroluses, and if they had, it would have been beyond Henry's power to levy the tax. Silver marks, value for 13s. 4d., appear to have been coined also about this time, and in 1251 a new coinage was *stamped* in Dublin, bearing on it the King's Head in a triangle with the inscription "HENRICUS REX III.," and the name of the Mint-master, "RICHARD ON DIVE."

In 1279, Edward I. commanded the coinage to be made in accordance with fixed standards, and in his reign there were four mints in Dublin. Base coin was also manufactured largely and circulated widely, and in 1300 a King's proclamation was issued, whereby the "base coins called 'pollards and crocards'" were cried down. But though there were the Royal mints, there were also, as in England, other coiners; but whereas in England these others coined under authority, in Ireland there was apparently no restriction exercised, or, if it were, it was disregarded. The trade of these coiners was "a great hurte and " destruction" to the country, and in 1447 an Act was passed against clipped money, unlawful money, and O'Reyley's money. Who this "O'Reyley," or "Reyley," was, or where he minted his money, we are not aware; but from this and subsequent enactments, it appears that the "King's money" did not enjoy as large a circulation as clipped money and O'Reyley's coinage.

In 1459 brass money was coined at a mint in the Castle, and in 1462, groats, twopennies, pennies, half-pennies, and farthings were issued from the Dublin mint. The public estimate of these coins may be inferred from the fact that the English money was at a premium at this time. Henry VIII. first placed the harp, as the national badge, on Irish coins. In 1540 the Dublin mint coined silver testoons (testers, or sixpennies), twopennies, and pennies, and in 1548 a new mint was established, "which soon failed for want of bullion." In 1552, a year of great famine, the mint testoon was ordered to pass for two shillings—four times its value. In 1662, King Charles II. granted, as we have seen, a patent for coining money for Ireland to the Viners and Daniel Bellingham, and this is the first time money for Ireland was coined in England. The Irish mints, previous to this period, were mere temporary institutions, and the trade of the country was facilitated by frequent issues of "tokens" by the traders. These were either brass or copper, and were a kind of transferable promissory note. They bore the maker's name and the value, and were supposed to be redeemable by him on demand. The issue of tokens was, however, prohibited in 1661 by Charles, and an improvement was effected by the coinage which was minted under the patent granted to Viner and Bellingham.

When James II. arrived in Ireland he improved his financial position by a proclamation that all English Guineas — the coin he brought with him—should be current for £1 4s. in Ireland, and he granted a patent for coining to Sir John Knox. But when his circumstances grew more shattered he annulled the grant, confiscated Knox's engines and stock of metal, and set up a Mint in Capel Street* and coined the most worthless and debased imperial coinage ever issued to a people. Old bells, old cannon—even pots and pans and kitchen utensils—were molten down, and struck into half-crowns, shillings, and sixpennies. The people were compelled to surrender their gold and their plate, and to take in exchange this wretched dross, the value of which may be estimated from the circumstance that the half-crowns were ordered to circulate as pennies by William III. when he had established his power in Ireland.† The value of the old metals melted down is stated at £6,500, while the nominal value of the coinage is alleged to have been £1,496,799.

* At No. 28, nearly opposite the Scots' Church. In this house, subsequently, Dr. Thos. Sheridan, father of Richard Brinsley, kept his school.

† It has been alleged that the word "humbug" is a corruption of the Irish words *uim bog*, pronounced "oombug," signifying soft copper, or pewter, or brass, or worthless money, such as was made by James II. at the Dublin Mint, and twenty shillings of which was worth about only one penny sterling. At first applied to worthless coin, the word in time became the general title of anything false and counterfeit.

The grant, or purchase, of the patent for coining £180,000 in half-pence and farthings for Ireland, which was obtained by William Wood, of Wolverhampton, from the Duchess of Kendal, is remarkable, because of the violent and successful opposition to the coinage which was conducted by Dean Swift, and which made him the most powerful and popular man at the time in Ireland. The proposed coinage was stated by the Dean to be "of such base metal and false weight as to be six parts in seven below the real value." An essay by Sir Isaac Newton, however, in 1724 reported that it exceeded the conditions of the patent in weight and fineness. But the conditions of the patent provided for a very depreciated coin. Some of Swift's denunciations under the signature of "The Drapier" are of extraordinary violence. For example, in one of those manifestoes he writes :—" For " my own part, who am but a man of obscure condition, I do " solemnly declare in the presence of Almighty God, that I will " suffer the most ignominious and torturing death rather than " submit to receive this accursed coin." The outcry against it was so great, and the opposition so overwhelming, that Wood's half-pence never circulated as current coin in Ireland. After this period, the Irish coins were always struck in England,—one of the "wrongs of Ireland" that Swift bitterly inveighs against. " We are denied," he wrote, " the liberty of coining gold, silver, " or even copper. In the Isle of Man they coin their own " silver ; every petty prince, vassal to the Emperor (of Germany) " can coin what money he pleases. In this we are an exception " to all other States or Monarchies that were ever known in the " world."

Tampering with the coinage was a serious crime in the last century in Ireland, and was punished by death in a barbarous and shocking manner, so late as 1750. In *Esdall's News Letter*, under date 14th July, 1715, we read the following item of horrible intelligence :

"Last Wednesday, Edward Costelowe and Mary, his wife, "were executed at Stephen's Green (Dublin), for filing and di-"minishing guineas. *The man was hung, drawn, and quartered, "and the woman was burnt to ashes.*"

There was a difference in value of the coins of the respective countries, £1 Irish being equivalent to 18s. 5½d. English. In 1826, however, the values were assimilated, and at present the same coinage is common to the two countries in every respect.

It does not appear that there was in Scotland any native coinage before the 11th century, when Somerled, Prince of the Isles, issued a rude money. The early silver pennies are like the early English ones, bearing the name of the "moneyer" and the place where they were minted. The native art and workmanship were much behind the contemporary English— the attempts at portraits are much ruder, and the deteriorated coinage—the billons, or base pennies—which were issued by authority, are poor specimens of a national coinage, even in those ages. Placks, and half-placks, or groats, likewise of billon, were minted by James III., who also issued some rather well-designed and well-executed gold coins, called "unicorns," from an image of that animal upon them. "Riders," so-called from a representation of the King on horseback, were coined by James IV., and the "bonnet-piece" of James V. is a very beautiful coin. The coins of Queen Mary present several different portraits of her—some with a crown, some without ; and some, coined after Francis's death, represent her in a frilled dress and a widow's cap. Pistoles and half-pistoles, made of gold brought from Darien, and equal respectively to about a guinea and half-guinea, were struck in the reign of William III. These, bearing the inappropriate emblem of a rising sun, were the last pieces of gold coined in Scotland. An evidence of the worth of the currency of Scotland is to be found in the fact that upon the junction of the Crowns of England and Scotland in 1605, the relative value of the Scottish and English coins was as 12 to 1 ! The coinages of the two countries were assimilated in 1707.

IX.

BANKING IN IRELAND.—EARLY DUBLIN BANKERS.

IN Ireland, as in England, the Joint Stock Banks were preceded by the Private Bankers, and the latter by Goldsmiths, who super-added to their legitimate trade the pursuits of money-changing and money-lending. But apparently before usury was carried on by the Goldsmiths, there was a system of money-lending existent in Ireland, the curious characteristic of which was that there was an intermediary, or touter, who plied a recognised trade, and whose business consisted in introducing the needy borrower to the usurer, and in drawing up and witnessing the bonds given in connection with the loan. As early as 1634 the Irish Parliament passed an Act to restrain usury, and one of its provisions is that no " driver of bargains for contracts "—*i.e.*, no person who induced one man to borrow from another—was to charge more than five shillings for *procuring a loan* of £100 for one year, or more than twelve pence for making the bond in reference to the loan. This Act restricted the rate of legal interest to 10 per cent. It was reduced to 8 per cent. in 1704, to 7 per cent. in 1721, and to 6 per cent in 1737.

Private Bankers were established in Dublin in the latter part of the 17th century. Previous to this time Goldsmiths carried on a deposit business, and issued " notes"—as they were called

—in acknowledgment of such deposits. But it seems that these notes were not transferable, and were merely acknowledgments for deposits, which deposits were to be returned to the depositor only, on application, and were to be returned in the state and form in which they were lodged. The Goldsmiths were no more than safe custodians, and they possessed no power to utilise or convert the deposits with which they were entrusted. In process of time, these notes were passed from hand to hand, and were treated as negotiable, till some question was raised as to their transferability, and in 1709 an Act of Parliament enacted that notes issued by any " Banker,* Goldsmith, Merchant, or Trader," whether made payable to bearer or order, should be assignable and transferable by delivery or endorsement, and an endorsee could sustain an action on them. Bankers' notes thus became instruments recognized by the Irish Laws, and many subsequent enactments were passed in regard to them. Thus, in 1721, it was enacted that Goldsmiths' or Bankers' notes not paid on demand should carry legal interest from the day of demand; and further, that a Banker's real estate should be liable at his death for his notes current.

The more regular Bankers naturally superseded the Goldsmiths. In 1721, a preamble to an Act states that " the trade " of this Kingdom was partly carried on by the means of cash " notes given by Bankers, and that the trade or calling of a " Banker was followed by the keeping of a public shop, house, " or office, for the receipt of the money of such persons as " were willing to deposit the same in their custody." Forgery of Bankers' notes was made a felony in 1729, punishable by burning in the hand and transportation of the convicted party.

The most noted of those early Bankers was one **John**

* This is the first mention of the word Banker in an Irish Act of Parliament.

Demar or **Damer**. He had been a captain of a troop of horse under Cromwell in the Civil War, and at the Restoration of Charles II., he sold his estates in Somerset and Dorset, and settled in Ireland. He plied his trade of usury for many years at a noted tavern in Dublin, called "The London," where "he "touched the pence while others touched the pot," and he died on the 6th July, 1720, at the age of ninety-one. At his death Dean Swift wrote a punning elegy upon him, wherein are described his threadbare cloak and his miserable appearance in public. He was altogether such a dilapidated sight that he seemed as if he were asking alms, reminding us of the Furfidius of whom Horace wrote. The following, which constitute the epitaph, are the concluding lines of the Dean's elegy on him:

> "The sexton shall green sods on thee bestow;
> Alas! the sexton is thy *banker* now!
> A dismal banker must that banker be,
> Who gives no *bills*, but of mortality!"

He amassed great wealth, and, being childless and unmarried, he left most of it to his nephew, John Damer,—from whom the present Earls of Portarlington are descended,—and some in charity;—Damer's Almshouse is, we believe, still in existence in Dublin.

Another of the same class as Damer, who flourished at this time, was **James Southwell**, who left a large sum for charitable purposes connected with the parish of St. Werburgh's, where he had been born in 1641. There was a temporary run upon the Dublin Bankers in 1720, possibly occasioned by Damer's death, and in the panic some succumbed.

The so-called Bankers of this period were, generally speaking, not men of wealth or property, but the exigencies of exchange and trade helped to circulate their notes, and thus put them in credit; and as there was no restriction on the amount they were allowed to issue, their notes became almost the only circulating medium, and silver and gold became quite scarce in the country. There were no qualifications or licence, or authorization required in any Banker. Any person so disposed could set up in the business, and the condition of the country was such that he was sure to get his cash-notes into circulation, and having issued beyond his powers of redemption, they were frequently not redeemed in full, or not redeemed at all. In Swift's *Short View of the State of Ireland*, in 1727, he shows what those Bankers were, and gives a very unmistakable opinion of them and their trade : " The lowness of interest, in all " other countries a sign of wealth, is in us a proof of misery, " there being no trade to employ any borrower .... Hence " the daily increase of Bankers, who may be a necessary evil in " a trading country, but so ruinous in ours ; who, for their private " advantage, have sent away all our silver and one-third of our " gold ; so that, within three years past, the running cash of the " nation, which was about five hundred thousand pounds, is " now less than two, and must daily diminish, unless we have " liberty to coin as well as that important kingdom the Isle of " Man, and the meanest principality in the German Empire. " I have sometimes thought that this paradox of the kingdom's " growing rich is chiefly owing to those worthy gentlemen the " BANKERS, who—except some custom-house officers, birds of " passage, oppressive thrifty squires, and a few others who shall " be nameless—are the only thriving people among us. And I " have often wished that a law were enacted to hang up half a " dozen bankers every year, and thereby interpose, at least, some " short delay to the further ruin of Ireland." After events fully justify the Dean's bloodthirsty desires.

These unrestricted note-issues, by men without capital, became such a scandal and serious injury to the trade and commerce of the country, that an endeavour to arrest the business carried on by the Bankers was made in 1720. The Bank of England had been established in London, and maintained an honourable position, and a public establishment in Ireland was deemed advisable. But it was projected on a very different basis. The Earl of Abercorn, Viscount Boyne, Sir Ralph Gore, and others, petitioned the Crown in that year (1720) for a charter for the institution of a Joint Stock Bank of Issue, the capital of which (£500,000) was to be invested in land, and the rental of these lands was to form a fund, which fund was to be issued against in notes. The main design was to establish a reliable and solvent currency to supersede the variable, and sometimes worthless issues of the private Bankers. The project was favourably entertained, and leave given in Parliament to introduce the Bill. But it was met by a counter petition from Lord Forbes* and others, for a charter to establish a Bank with a capital of £1,000,000. This would almost certainly have been granted in preference to Lord Abercorn's project, but it was stated that one of the provisions of the Bill would be to obtain for the Bank a monopoly of Banking in the country; and to ensure the passing of this part of the measure a bribe of £50,000 was said to have been offered to the Members to influence their votes in favour of it. Unfortunately the Bill was rejected, not on its merits, but through jobbery and scheming, and the business of the Bankers was not interfered with.

Some of the early Bankers were very respectable, and apparently did a very large business, but the early history of Irish Banking is a record of failures, windings-up, and runs. And of all the multitudinous Private Banks established about this period, but one—that of **LaTouche and Co.**—survived to

* Son of the Earl of Granard.

the latter half of the nineteenth century, an honourable exception to its ephemeral contemporaries.

In 1731 the Bank of **Meade and Curtis** failed. Another Bank, which had been established previous to 1700 as **Burton and Falkener's** Bank, in Castle Street, Dublin, and which at the time of its failure, in 1733, was Burton and Harrison's, failed ignominiously, and the landed estates of the partners were sold in satisfaction of the claims of the creditors, and after the realisation, the liabilities were yet £65,000 in excess of the assets. This Bank had a great reputation—"as safe as Ben Burton" was a proverb. Burton was Lord Mayor in 1734, and four times M.P. for the City, and Falkener had been Sheriff in 1720. The Marquess Conyngham is descended from Burton.

Two years after the failure of Burton's Bank, that is to say in 1735, there were five Private Banking Firms in Dublin— James Swift and Company, of Eustace Street; Hugh Henry, Esq., of Upper Ormond Quay; Nuttall and M'Guire, of Lower Ormond Quay; LaTouche and Kane, of Castle Street; and Joseph Fade and Co., of Thomas Street. Of these, the firm of **LaTouche and Kane** was the most eminent. The Bank had been established in 1725, and in this year (1735) it was removed to the edifice, still existing, where the business was carried on till 1871, when the Bank merged in the Munster Bank. This house was built by David LaTouche, jun., son of the founder of the firm. Nathaniel Kane, the partner, was Lord Mayor in 1734, and had been accused by Dr. Lucas, M.P., of appropriating some of the City funds, but successfully vindicated himself. LaTouche was returned as Member of Parliament for the City, but was unseated on petition. At the termination of Kane's partnership, the firm became David LaTouche and Sons, which was its style and title till its absorption.

7

LaTouche's was one of the three Banks pronounced by a committee of the House of Commons, which sat in 1760 to inquire into the state of credit in the country, to have much more than enough funds to suffice for all claims upon them. In 1778 we find it advancing £20,000 to the Lord Lieutenant, the Marquess of Buckingham, for State emergencies, and declining to make a further advance as the security offered was unsatisfactory. LaTouche's Bank never issued a paper currency, but adhered to the legitimate and simple business of receiving money on deposit and current account, and making advances. Five members of the family had seats in Parliament in 1800, and of them, only one voted for the Union.

The Union, which terminated the Irish Houses of Lords and Commons, and transferred the Irish Peers and the Parliamentary representatives across the Channel, reduced Dublin from a metropolis to a mere provincial city. The Irish Lords and Members of Parliament became chronic absentees, spending their time and their money in London, and their absenteeism of course wrought detrimentally on LaTouche's Bank, where chiefly they did their banking business. However, previous to the Union, no single Private Bank, in our opinion, transacted the same kind and extent of business that LaTouche's did. It is no exaggeration to say that the entire Irish Peerage and Landed Gentry kept their accounts with substantial balances there.* Names which have become historical and famous are

---

* The following list, which is taken from the Current-account Legers of 1765-1790, and which does not include any of the opulent Commoners who were customers of LaTouche's, will give an idea of the magnitude and respectability of the business done :—

Duke of Leinster.	Marquess of Cornwallis.
,, Rutland.	,, Lansdowne.
Marquess of Buckingham.	,, Westmeath.
,, Headford.	,, Hertford.

to be found in their books. Lord Edward Fitzgerald, Lord Castlereagh, Flood, Grattan, Curran; Lord Clare, the Chan-

Earl of Clanricarde.	Lord Dungannon.
,, Carhampton.	,, Bective.
,, Drogheda.	,, Carbery.
,, Kerry.	,, Callan.
,, Athlone.	,, Glentworth.
,, Antrim.	,, Hawarden.
,, Camden.	,, Clifden.
,, Desart.	,, Clonbrock.
,, Granard.	,, Macartney.
,, Inchiquin.	,, Cremorne.
,, Kenmare.	,, Mulgrave.
,, Leitrim.	,, Blayney.
,, Longford.	,, Doneraile.
,, Lanesborough.	,, Farnham.
,, Meath.	,, Grandison.
,, Nugent.	,, Gormanston.
,, Wicklow.	,, Glandore.
,, Belmore.	,, Lifford.
,, Belvidere.	,, Loftus.
,, Cork.	,, Lismore.
,, Egremont.	,, Massareene.
,, Upper Ossory.	,, Maxwell.
,, Aldborough.	,, Muskerry.
,, Altamont.	,, Mountmorres.
,, Bellamont.	,, Portsmouth.
,, Brandon.	,, Percy.
,, Carysfort.	,, Ranelagh.
,, Courtown.	,, Southwell.
,, Castlestewart.	,, Sherborne.
,, Clanbrassil.	,, Sunderlin.
,, Carrick.	,, Templeton.
,, Donoughmore.	,, Dillon.
Lord Eyre.	,, Crosbie.
,, Knapton.	,, Chas. Fitzgerald.
,, St. George.	,, Henry Fitzgerald.
,, Louth.	,, Robert Fitzgerald.
,, Kilmaine.	etc., etc.
,, Cloncurry.	etc., etc.

cellor; Foster, the last Speaker of the Irish House of Commons; Lord Norbury, when he was plain John Toler; Barry Yelverton; Sir Boyle Roche; the Countess of Mornington, the Duke of Wellington's mother, were account-holders in LaTouche's in its years of greatest prosperity. An anecdote records a peculiar form of cheque drawn on the bank by Whaley, a noted character in Ireland in the last century, and usually known as Buck Whaley, or Jerusalem Whaley. It is said he wrote:

> "Dear Mister LaTouche,
> Pray open your pouch,
> And give my heart's darling (*i.e.* his wife or daughter),
> One thousand pounds sterling."

—a form of cheque more creditable to his heart than his head.

LaTouche's was agent for the London firms of Coutts; Ransom; Pybus, Call and Co.; and Puget; and for the Provincial Irish Bankers, Newenham, Pike, and Hewitt—all of Cork; Newport, of Waterford, etc. In fact, for the space of a century, it was the chief bank of the country.

Swift's Bank, originally in Eustace Street, Dublin, moved in 1741 to Castle Street, to "two houses opposite the Castle gate." It ceased to exist in 1746, and was succeeded by the Bank of **Thomas Gleadowe and Co.** William Gleadowe, the head of the firm about 1770, married a Miss Newcomen, and assumed that name in addition to his own. His Bank moved to 19, Mary's Abbey, in 1777, but returned to Castle Street in 1781, to the edifice now occupied by the Hibernian Bank. In the same year he was created a baronet, and in 1800, as a reward for his vote in Parliament in favour of the Union, he received £20,000, and his wife was raised to the peerage as Baroness Newcomen, and in 1803 she was advanced to the further dignity of a Viscountess. In 1799 the partners in the

Bank were registered as Sir William Gleadowe-Newcomen, baronet, Arthur Dawson, and Thomas Gleadowe-Newcomen.

Joseph Fode and Co., of Thomas Street, took into partnership, in 1738, Isaac or Isacher Willcox and John Willcox, and subsequently John Dawson, and failed on 3rd March, 1755, principally through the dishonesty of Richard Brewer, the cashier. The principal partner in **Nuttall and McGuire's** Bank, (Nuttall), was Lord Mayor in 1732. Of **Hugh Henry** we know nothing beyond that he was the ancestor of an existing Kildare family of wealth and position.

A Bank was established, in 1739, on Ormond-quay, by **William Lennox.** He took George French into partnership in 1751, and the Bank ceased in 1755, when both the partners absconded. The creditors were both numerous and respectable, from which we gather that the firm enjoyed a good business.

The Bank of **Malone and Clements**—which, in respect to the brevity of its existence, is unique in the history of banking—was established on the 3rd July, 1758. Its partners were the Right Hon. Anthony Malone, the Right Hon. Nathaniel Clements, and John Gore. It granted receipts payable seven days after demand, with interest at the rate of 10 pence per week for each £100—a little over 2 per cent. per annum—the interest to commence three days after the date of issue. But neither great names, nor terms meant to be alluring, could endow it with solvency or permanency. It died in the first November of its life, aged 4 months. Clements, undeterred, seems to have started on his own account, for a Bank kept by a person of that name failed in 1760. Malone was a celebrated man.* He was Prime Serjeant, and was leading counsel for

---

* Malone, who was son of Richard Malone, of Baronston, a well-known lawyer and orator, was M.P. for Westmeath. He was appointed Prime Sergeant in 1740, dismissed in 1754, and was appointed Chancellor of the

the Earl of Anglesey, in 1743, in the celebrated Annesley Peerage case—a case which has furnished two novelists—Sir Walter Scott and Charles Reade—with the groundwork for two romances.

In 1748, in addition to the houses already mentioned, we find in the Dublin Directory:—

Richard and Thomas Dawson, of Jervis Street. **Henry Mitchell and J. Macarell*** of Ormond Quay, both of which failed in 1760, not, we read, from want of means, but from want of money in the country, wherewith to pay the demands on them. This year (1760) drew down all the Dublin Private Banks, with the exception of LaTouche's and Gleadowe's; these alone surmounted the crisis and survived the panic, and these were the only firms which did *not* issue notes.

And in 1751—**Theobald Dillon and Sons**: afterwards Thomas Dillon, Richard Farrell (or Ferrall) and Co., of Inns Quay. This firm failed in 1754.

And in 1760—**Thomas Finlay and Co.**, of Jervis Quay.

The public feeling which culminated in the panic of 1760 was not of sudden or intemperate growth. The power to issue notes by the Private Bankers had been grossly and preposterously abused, and the disasters consequent on the reckless creation of liabilities that could never be paid came inevitably. In 1753, a Committee of the House of Commons which inquired into the condition of Banking, reported that the paper in circulation was largely in excess of the assets of the issuing

---

Exchequer in 1757. He was uncle to Edmund Malone, the well known Shakesperian commentator. Clements (son of the Right Hon. Theophilus Clements, M.P. for the Borough of Cavan, and Teller of the Exchequer in Ireland) was also one of the Tellers of the Exchequer, and was Deputy Vice-Treasurer of Ireland. He was father of the first and ancestor of the present Earl of Leitrim.

* Lord Mayor, 1739.

Bankers; and the following evidence in respect to the state of Banking in Ireland in this year (1753) was given by Mr. William Colvill, a Director of the Bank of Ireland, before a Parliamentary Committee which sat in 1804:—

"I remember perfectly well that in 1753 the circulation of paper in Dublin from the Private Bankers was so general and extensive that in receiving £1,000 there was not £10 in gold at that time. I remember that exchange was near three per cent. above par; the consequence of which was that the Bankers of Dublin, of whom there were as many as there are at present (1804) if not more, were in competition with one another to send their specie over to London and to get Bank bills at four per cent. above par, bringing a clear profit to that extent. The consequence of this showed itself in the succeeding year; all the Banks failed except Messrs. LaTouche's and Sir William Newcomen's (under the name at that time of Gleadowe and Co.); and these two Banks paid off their entire paper.* There followed a total annihilation of Bank-paper in Ireland at that time, and I remember it was said with triumph that Ulster, the great seat of our linen manufactory, was safe, because she had no such think as Bank-paper in that province. The consequences were that exchange fell two or three per cent. under par, and the whole circulation of Ireland was turned from paper into gold; but the result was that multitudes of people were ruined. The convulsion was exceedingly severe,—many tenants threw up their lands, and there was no person connected with the three southern provinces of Ireland, that did not suffer either immediately or remotely."

In addition, the commercial morality of the Bankers was at a low ebb. In those days there were few channels for the investment of moneys, and lending it on Discounts was an unsatisfactory trade in a poor and unsettled country. Therefore, we find that the Bankers were addicted to investing all surplus cash they held—that is, all their deposits and all received on account of their note issues which was not lent nor used for every day purposes—in land. They purchased estates—and landed estates were not always an immediately realisable asset; it was an almost useless asset as far as meeting a run was con-

* These were *not* issuing Bankers.

cerned. This practice of sinking their funds in realty was recognized as an evil that should be counteracted; and to this end the Banker's Act (33 Geo. III., c. 14), which was the principal enactment for the regulation of Bankers in Ireland, was passed in 1759. The object of the statute was to endeavour to protect the public against the frauds of Bankers, who used to thus acquire, and then alienate, estates, to the detriment of their creditors; and to fix the manner of winding up insolvent or bankrupt Bankers. By it all deeds of conveyance executed by Bankers are declared void unless registered within one month after execution, or within three months if executed out of Ireland—except leases not exceeding three lives or 31 years, made at the full improved rent without fine. All grants of real estate or leasehold interest made by Bankers to their children or grandchildren, although made for a good consideration, are void against creditors, and although such creditors were not creditors at the time of the making of such grants; the receipt of a Banker given after he has stopped payment is no discharge; and the conveyances of Bankers who have absconded are void, and their estates and effects are subject to their debts, without regard to priority (except in case of debts incurred before they became Bankers, or of those duly registered); and the persons of such absconding defaulters are only protected in case they are Peers or Members of Parliament. Within three months after stopping payment a Banker may invest his estates in trustees to be approved by the majority of the creditors or by the Lord Chancellor. No person entrusted with the public money was allowed to become a Banker. No Banker was allowed to issue notes bearing interest; but if the issued notes were not paid on demand, the holder could claim interest until the date of payment. All demands upon Bankers must be made within three years after they have stopped payment or ceased to transact business, and if the creditor fails in making his demand within the said three years, he shall be barred from suing in law or equity; and the Banker, in the event of his being sued by any creditor after the expiration of the said three years, can plead payment and discharge of liability, and give this Act in evidence.

But notwithstanding the attempts of the legislature, failures were not prevented. In 1764 we find the Bank of **Sir George Colebrooke, Bart., and Co.,** was doing business in Mary's Abbey. This was a branch of a London Bank of the same name, which, established about 1720 as James Colebrooke and Co., behind the Royal Exchange, was Sir George Colebrooke, Burns, and others, about this period. The Dublin house suspended payment in 1770, and the panic engendered thereby grew to such dimensions that the Lord-Lieutenant and a number of the nobility, gentry, and merchants issued a manifesto wherein the solvency of some of the other Bankers was vouched, and a declaration made of their willingness to receive the notes of these houses in lieu of cash payments. The Banks whose credit was thus guaranteed, and which alone outlived this panic, were—LaTouche's, Gleadowe's, Finlay's, and Dawson's.

In 1797 there were altogether but nine Private Bankers in Ireland, of which three were in Dublin—LaTouche's, Gleadowe's, and Finlay's. Over-issuing had wrought panics; and panics, and the Rebellion, and the scarcity of coin in the country, had swept the majority of the Private Banking Firms into the limbo of bankruptcy. But unhappily, after the Rebellion, new establishments called Banks sprung up throughout the country. In Dublin **John Claudius Beresford and Co.** were, in 1798, established at Beresford Place. This Bank is notable for the circumstance that the populace, to wreak their vengeance on the unpopular Beresford, collected all his notes and *burned them in order to ruin him.* **Sir Thomas Lighton, Bart., Thomas Needham, and Robert Shaw**, was also established in the same year in Foster Place. This firm became Sir Robert Shaw, Bart., and Co., and was ultimately merged in the Royal Bank. In 1804 **William Williams and Robert Finn**, which had been established in Kilkenny in 1800, moved to Dublin and had its offices in Dame Street. This establishment failed in 1820 for £300,000; and Sir John Newport, in evidence before the Lords in 1826, positively swore it was never worth a shilling, and had commenced on no capital whatsoever. **Lord Ffrench's Bank**, and **Alexander's Bank**—two other Dublin concerns which enjoyed a great business and a great circulation—also failed in 1820, Alexander's owing half a million. The panic of 1820 made havoc of the Private Bankers throughout Ireland, and a few years later saw Joint Stock Banks established, and the progress of Joint Stock Banking was fortunately a prevention of the birth of new private firms.

In 1826, LaTouche's, Finlay's, Shaw's, and the newly-established Ball and Co., of Henry Street, were the Private Dublin Banks. Finlay's, which flourished for many years in the office which is now the counting-house of Messrs. Todd and Burns, went under in the panic of 1835-6. Shaw's, as has been said, was purchased in 1836 by the Royal Bank, and LaTouche's by the Munster Bank in 1870. **Ball and Co.** is now the premier private Bank in Dublin. **Boyle and Co.**, who are Stockbrokers and Notaries as well as Bankers, and **Guinness, Mahon, and Co.**, who are also land agents, were established about 1832; and these three firms are now the sole surviving representatives of Private Banking in Ireland.

Private Banking firms were numerous throughout the country

during the latter portion of the last and early in the present century. Many of them were extremely respectable—many no better than peddlers in money; some of them were disreputable—nearly all were extremely insolvent. A history of the Rise and Fall of Irish Country Banks at this period would be a continuous record of note-issues, panics, failures, and bankruptcies. It is a matter for amazement that the people can have been so credulous as to place any trust in these banks, their failures were so frequent, their note issues so often proven to be worthless. In 1799 there were seven Banks in Wexford; four in New Ross; four in Galway—all issuing their notes in careless profusion. Panics were, of course, of frequent occurrence. In 1804, 1810, and 1814, numbers of those bankers failed; and in 1820 the crowning panic occurred which effectually stopped this reckless and dishonest establishment of firms of note-issuers.

In 1784 a Bank was established in Belfast, the operative principle of which was to have a very restricted paper currency, and to make its payments almost exclusively in gold. It was suspended in 1798. In 1793 a Banking Company, called the **Belfast Discount Company**, was founded in the Northern Capital, the partners being Messrs. Thompson, Bradshaw, and M'Ilwaine, trading under the title of Robert Shaw and Company. The firm changed to the style of Gilbert M'Ilwaine and Company in 1800. Besides these there were three other Banks in Belfast—the **Commercial Bank, the Northern,** and **the Belfast.** The joint circulation of these three Companies was estimated at £225,000, when, owing to the scarcity of gold in the country, they failed in 1797. Among the more respectable Provincial Bankers were **Simon Newport and Co.,** of Waterford, which was established about 1775, and existed till 1820.

In Cork, in 1775, **Travers, Sheares, and Travers**, was flourishing, and is now remembered because the Sheares of the firm was father of John and Henry Sheares, who were executed during 1798. In 1799 **Sir James Cotter, Bart., and Co.** and **Sir Thomas Roberts, Bart., and Co.**, were the chief Cork firms. **Maunsell's** in Limerick (which failed in 1820), and **Redmond's** in Wexford, were also respectable concerns. In 1800 three more Banks were registered in Cork, **Newenham's, Roche's,** and **Pike's**; and in Fermoy, **John Anderson's.** In 1801 **Delacour's** in Mallow was registered; it was the last private provincial Bank; it failed in 1835. In 1803 **Scully's** in Tipperary was established. In Tuam, the Hon. **Sir Thomas Ffrench's Bank** flourished, and subsequently opened an office in Dublin.

But besides these there were scores of others, the careers of which were briefer, the positions of less importance, and the memories even more unfortunate. Banking was a pursuit open to all, and not confined to persons of social distinction, personal worth, or financial strength. Humble folks, seeing that a Banker required no capital when he started, and that when he collapsed he was generally wealthier than when he began, adopted the business, and—in addition to the registered Banks, which were mainly kept by respectable members of society—most of the little shopkeepers and publicans—more especially in the South—could, and did, issue their I. O. U.'s, call them, with a cunning ignorance of the paradox, "silver money," and call themselves Bankers, and their little shop a Bank. The records of the "Banking" of some of these impostors would be ludicrous, were it not a thinly veiled system of robbery and swindling. They issued "notes" for sums as low as 3d., and, with too much success, deluded the ignorant country folk. But the chiefest evil to the country was wrought by the regularly constituted registered Banks. One fact will convey much of the condition of the paper issues of Ireland's Bankers in 1803. The total stamp duties paid for the notes and post bills issued that year by 41 firms of Private Bankers were as follows:

Three-halfpence.	Threepence.	Fourpence.
1,110,217.	256,801.	90,265.

The three-halfpenny duty was on all notes under three guineas; if we average the amount at two guineas, the duty represents an issue of £2,220,434
Those under £10 required a threepenny duty.
   An average of £5 per note would be ... 1,284,005
Those under £50 required a fourpenny duty.
   An average of £20 would represent ... 1,805,300

Or a total note and bill issue by private firms in 41 places of business of £5,309,739
The present (June, 1881) issue of all the Irish joint stock banks with about 400 places of issue is £6,354,494

A contrast of the two statements is, perhaps the most effective commentary on Irish Private Banking eighty years ago, and is sufficient to cause a regret that Swift's panacea for the country—"hanging a dozen bankers every year"—was not applied when the century was young.

X.

IRISH JOINT STOCK BANKS.

THE BANK OF IRELAND was established by the 21 and 22 George III., cap. 16, an Act passed in 1782, on principles somewhat similar to those upon which the Bank of England was founded. The capital was to be £600,000, which was to be lent to Government at 4 per cent. The Bank was not to charge more than 5 per cent. for money lent, nor was it to undertake or engage in any business other than Banking as defined in its Charter. The Charter was granted on 15th May, 1783, and by it the Bank obtained a monopoly of Joint-Stock Banking, as it restricted the constitution of all other Banks of issue to six partners each. The individual Stockholders, though not burdened with unlimited liability, are nevertheless, under the Act, answerable to the extent of their means to the creditors, in case of the downfall of the establishment, *in proportion to their subscriptions*. The Subscribers were to constitute a Corporation, of which there should be a Governor, whose qualification was a holding of £4,000 Stock ; a Deputy Governor, with a holding of £3,000 ; and fifteen Directors, with an individual holding of £2,000.

The Bank commenced business in Mary's Abbey, Dublin, on 25th June, 1783. The first Governor was David LaTouche, junior, and amongst the Directors were Messrs. John and Peter

LaTouche, Colvill, D'Olier, Jaffray, Hoffman, &c. In 1791 the capital was increased to £1,000,000, the additional £400,000 being also lent to Government. In 1797 it was further increased to £1,500,000, and in the same year the Bank was allowed to suspend payment of its notes, the circulation at the time being £622,000. In 1799 it obtained the monopoly to issue notes of amounts from 20s. to £5. In 1800 the Union was accomplished and the Houses of Parliament were left derelict till 1802, when the buildings were sold to the Bank for £40,000 Irish currency. In 1808 the capital was increased to £2,500,000, and by the same Act (48 Geo. III., cap. 103) the management of the public debt was given to the Bank, and it was to pay the dividends thereon without expense to the Government. In 1821 the capital was further increased to £3,000,000,* its present figure, and the set-off for the advantage of the augmentation to the capital was the abandonment of the monopoly whereby more than six persons were precluded from forming themselves into a Banking Company.

But the ostensible abandonment of this monopoly was accompanied by certain provisions in respect to the partners of any new Banking Company that might be established, of such a character that the concession it appeared to make operated as a confirmation, rather than a reversal, of its monopoly privileges; and when the legal effect of the proceeding was understood, the Bank was vigorously denounced for having "broken faith with Parliament and the Public."

The Bank had not at this period any Country Branches. For over forty years it enjoyed its monopoly entirely for its own advantage, and not in the interests of the country, and when it did open Branches, its design was not to benefit the people but to try to discourage a rival. We have never seen

* Irish currency—equivalent to £2,769,230 sterling.

any defence of the Bank's position during the first forty years of its career. It saw the country ruined with the corrupt and valueless issues of the Private Bankers, but it never made any move to protect the people in the provinces from the depredations of these firms. The losses to the people of Ireland from about 1770 to 1820, through the paper money of the Private Banks, has been estimated at £20,000,000, and the Bank of Ireland, during the greater part of this period, had the monopoly of that description of Banking which offered some security to the public. But it did not open any Branches, and resented so strongly the opening of country offices by another Bank, that it put in motion all its powers of oppression and suppression to prevent an interference with its privileges. It was the Provincial Bank that fought the Bank of Ireland on the occasion, and therefore, to the Provincial Bank we are in a measure indebted for the present position and extent of Banking in Ireland.

The circulation of the Bank, which in 1797 amounted to £621,919, rapidly increased, owing to the failures of the Private Bankers and the withdrawal of their notes from circulation. In 1808 it reached £2,827,000; in 1813, £4,212,600; in 1821, £5,182,600; in 1825, £6,309,300. The establishment of Joint Stock Banks of Issue throughout the country diminished its circulation considerably. In 1848 it had dwindled down to £3,100,000, and at present (June 1881), with an authorised issue under the Act of 1844 of £3,738,428, the actual amount of notes in circulation is about £2,910,000 only. From 1784 to 1799 the dividend paid oscillated between 5 and 6 per cent. In 1800 it was 7 per cent. From 1809 to 1814, 7½ per cent. In 1829, on its capital of £3,000,000, it paid 10 per cent., and from 1829 to 1835 it distributed 9 per cent. In 1864 the Bank broke through its old rule, and consented to allow interest on money deposited with it—thus assimilating its procedure to the Joint Stock Banks, its rivals. In 1872 the dividend rose to 13½ per cent.; of late years it has been at the rate of 12 per cent., and in 1879 it was 11 per cent. Over and above the dividends, bonuses to the amount of £800,000 have been distributed amongst the proprietors. The Bank publishes no Statement of Accounts.

The Provincial Bank.—By the 6 George IV., c. 42, the enactment which prevented the formation of Banks with more than six partners to carry on business within fifty miles of Dublin was repealed. Previous to this, however, in 1824, the Provincial Bank was established. It was mainly an English Company, the Directors being chiefly residents in London. Its subscribed capital was £2,000,000, in shares of £100. In May, 1826, it had opened the following branches, all beyond the fifty mile radius from Dublin—Cork, Limerick, Clonmel, Londonderry, Sligo, Wexford, Belfast, Waterford, and Galway. It issued notes; and in these early days of antagonism the Bank of Ireland required gold from the Provincial Bank in payment of its Bank notes, but refused to redeem its own notes in gold to the Provincial Bank. Whereupon the Provincial Bank, on 17th August, 1825, in Clonmel, protested a Bank of Ireland note for £100, with the ulterior object of a civil action. These proceedings seem to us now to be childish and petulant on both sides, but undoubtedly the course of oppression pursued by the Bank of Ireland towards the Provincial Bank warranted and necessitated the action of the latter. The Provincial Bank notes were payable in Dublin at LaTouche's Bank, and the Bank of Ireland construed this agency for note paying as a violation of its privileges, and on 5th December, 1823, it brought a vexatious action against the Provincial Bank therefor and obtained a verdict with sixpence damages.

Through the action of the Provincial Bank, the Act which abolished notes under £5 in England was not extended to Ireland.

In its earlier years the Provincial Bank paid a dividend of 4 per cent. In 1831 it was increased to 5 per cent.; in 1833 to 6 per cent.; in 1834 to 7 per cent.; in 1835 to 8. In 1836 it had thirty-three branches in operation, and the paid-up capital, which had hitherto been £500,000, was increased to £540,000 (its present amount) by the creation of 4,000 new shares of £10 each, which were fully paid up. From 1859 to 1874 a dividend of 20 per cent. was paid; in 1875 one of 18 per cent.; in 1876 15 per cent.; and in 1881 13 per cent. per annum has been distributed. The Provincial Bank does not publish its accounts.

The Hibernian Bank was projected in 1824, under the title "Hibernian Joint Stock Loan and Annuity Company," by prominent Catholic Dublin gentlemen, and its object was to provide a Catholic Bank for Catholic customers, and thereby to maintain on their behalf the exclusiveness into which the laws and narrow prejudices of the day drove them. The capital was £1,000,000, in £100 shares, of which £25 is paid up, but was subsequently increased to £2,000,000—its present figure. It has never issued notes. It did not originally grant interest on money deposited, and it charged discount at the rate of 5 per cent. per annum. It issued no post Bills, nor did it allow interest on cash balances. It paid a dividend of 4 per cent. from its establishment to 1839, when it increased it to 5 per cent., which was paid down to 1848. Twelve per cent. was paid from 1872 to 1876; 11 in 1878; 9 in 1879. The Bank narrowly escaped being wound up in 1827, but surmounted its difficulties and enjoyed a very good business in its sole office (Dublin) for many subsequent years. It had the entire of the

Catholic business of the city, and had no rivals there, except the Bank of Ireland and the private Bankers, till the establishment of the National Bank in Dublin in 1843; for the Royal Bank, which was established in 1836, did not interfere much with its exclusive business. The Hibernian purchased the Dublin and some other offices of the Union Bank of Ireland in 1867. This establishment has become limited under the provisions of the Act of 1879.

The National Bank.—The National Bank was formed in 1834, under the title of "The National Bank of Ireland," by Daniel O'Connell and others, with the object of being a Bank for the People, and an engine to assist the movement for Repeal of the Union. With the exceptions of O'Connell, his son Maurice, and Mr. C. Fitzsimon, the Directors were Englishmen. The notable conditions of the establishment were that a Branch should be formed in each suitable town in Ireland, and that the profits of each Branch should be divided amongst the local shareholders: and until the year 1850 the Carrick-on-Suir and Clonmel Branches were separate establishments in almost every particular. There were to be local Directors to each office. The capital was to be £1,000,000 in shares of £50 each. The first Branch opened was at Carrick-on-Suir on 28th January, 1835. The Dublin office was opened in 1843, and the Bank commenced to issue notes in Dublin in 1845.

In 1848 it absorbed the business of the London and Dublin Bank, a Bank established in 1842 by a Mr. Medley. In 1856 it commenced to transact Banking business in London (the office there having hitherto been a mere place of meeting for the Directors, and a Head Office for receiving and checking the accounts of the Branches), and it further opened seven Metropolitan Branches. The title was then changed to "The

"National Bank," and the paid-up capital increased to £1,500,000. In the earlier years of its career the return to the shareholders was about 5 per cent. The dividends paid from 1859 to 1867 were at the rate of 13⅓ per cent. From causes unnecessary to recapitulate, under a new management they fell to 7 per cent. in 1869, and increased to 8 per cent. in 1871, to 9 in 1872, to 10 in 1873, to 11 in 1874, to 12 in 1876. In 1879 11 per cent. was paid. The National Bank has also become limited under the Banking Act of 1879.

The Royal Bank (Limited).—The deed of settlement of the Royal Bank is dated 1st September, 1836, and on the 26th September the newly-established concern took over the Private Bank of Sir Robert Shaw, Bart., and Co., which had carried on business in Foster Place since 1799. The Royal Bank was a Bank of Deposit and Discount only. It has no note issue, and originally had no branches, though at present it has four City offices, and one Suburban branch. The capital was and is £1,500,000 in 30,000 shares of £50 each, upon which £10 per share has been paid up. The Bank rapidly developed a good and prosperous business. In its third year of existence it had over £1,500,000 in discounts, and paid a Dividend at the rate of 5 per cent. per annum on £208,850, the amount of the capital paid up at the time. In 1848 the paid-up capital stood at £209,175; the Reserve Fund at £45,475; the year's net profit was £19,877, of which £10,458 was appropriated to a dividend of 5 per cent. per annum. The dividends of late years have been as follows :—12 per cent. in 1870; 13 in 1872; 15 in 1873; 14 in 1875; 15 in 1876; 14 in 1879. The Royal Bank has registered under the Banking Act of 1879, and become a Limited Bank with a Reserved Liability.

The Munster Bank (Limited) was originally projected as The National Investment Company (Limited), in Cork, but was established as a Bank in 1864 with its Head Office in Cork, and its Directors were exclusively Cork gentlemen. Its Branches were at first confined to the Southern Province, but subsequently were spread over Leinster. It took over the business of the European Bank* in Dublin in 1865, and it purchased some of the country branches of the Union Bank of Ireland in 1867. In 1870 it obtained by purchase the business of La Touche's Bank. The capital was £1,000,000, in 100,000 shares of £10 each, upon which £3 10s. has been paid up, but in 1880 it was increased by £500,000 by the issue of 50,000 New Shares. In December, 1865, it paid a Dividend of 6 per cent.; in 1870, 8 per cent.; in 1871, 10 per cent.; in 1872, 12 per cent., which rate it continued till 1879, when it relapsed to 10 per cent. The Bank has no note issue. It has also registered under the Act of 1879—the Reserved Liability being £750,000.

The Northern Bank is the oldest Irish Joint Stock Bank. It was originally a Private Bank under the same name, and was incorporated as a Joint Stock concern in 1825. Its early years seem to have been very prosperous, as a bonus of £5 per share was added to the capital in 1839; a bonus of £2 per share was distributed amongst the shareholders in 1853; one of £1 per share in 1861; one of £2 in 1864, 1865, and 1866; one of £1 4s. 6d. in 1867, and smaller ones in subsequent years. The dividend has been as high as $18\frac{1}{2}$ per cent. in 1871, and latterly it has been at the rate of 15 per cent.

The Belfast Bank, like the Northern, was formed on a private Bank of the same name. It was founded in 1827, and

* A Bank called the English and Irish Bank, which had purchased the business of Gray and Son, private Bankers in College Green, was merged in the European Bank.

incorporated in 1865. Its paid-up capital is but £250,000 in old and new shares, and a uniform dividend of 20 per cent. has been paid on the old shares for some years. The Belfast Bank issues no public Balance Sheet.

The Ulster Bank was established in Belfast in 1836, and a branch was opened in Dublin in 1862. The dividend and bonus paid to shareholders in 1864 was 16 per cent.; in 1865, 18; in 1866, 1867, 1868, 1869, and 1870, 20 per cent.; in 1871, 18 per cent.; in 1872 and 1873, 22 per cent.; and since then 20 per cent. has been divided.

The following is a table of the Irish Joint Stock Banks; their number of branches; capital—subscribed and paid-up; note circulations as authorised by the Act of 1844; and the average circulation during the four weeks ending 17th January, 1880.

NAME.	Date	No. of Branches and Sub-Branches	Capital.		Circulation.	
			Subscribed	Paid-up	Authorised	Average
Bank of Ireland	1783	59	2,769,230	2,769,230	3,738,428	2,703,975
*Hibernian	1824	52	2,000,000	500,000	—	—
Provincial	1824	47	2,040,000	540,000	927,677	727,887
Northern	1824	69	961,538	300,000	243,440	443,525
Belfast	1827	57	1,000,000	250,000	281,611	407,719
National	1835	116	2,500,000	1,500,000	852,269	1,138,054
Ulster	1836	48	1,200,000	300,000	311,079	610,390
*Royal	1836	5	1,500,000	300,000	—	—
*Munster	1864	44	1,500,000	525,000	—	—

The foregoing are the Joint Stock Banks at present established in Ireland. There have, however, been others founded, which have disappeared. Some have merged in other banks; some of them have hardly left a memory, they had such a transient existence; while some can never be forgotten, their collapses were so destructive and disgraceful. Want of support ruined some; folly and ignorance, more; fraud, others.

* These are not Banks of Issue.

The London and Dublin Bank was founded in 1842 by a Mr. Medley, who was connected with the Provincial Bank. It had a nominal capital of about £1,000,000. It had branches in Athy, Carrickmacross, Dundalk, Kells, Mullingar, Parsonstown, and Wicklow; and in 1848 it merged in the National Bank of Ireland. The **Union Bank of Ireland**, after an unsuccessful career of a few years, was purchased in 1867—the Southern Branches by the Munster Bank, the Dublin and some of the Leinster branches by the Hibernian.

The following establishments failed :—

The Agricultural Bank.—This concern was projected in 1834 by Mr. Thomas Mooney, a baker in Dublin, Mr. John Chambers, and Mr. James Dwyer. The paid up capital was £1,000,000, in 1,000,000 shares of £1 each. Before the end of 1835 it had twenty-two Branches in operation. The general manager was Mr. Wm. Mitchell, who was subsequently connected with the ill-fated Western Bank of Scotland. The Reports were of a gaudy description and superlatively optimist character. Mismanagement, incompetence, and fraud ruined the concern, and it stopped payment in 1836, hopelessly insolvent.

The Southern Bank of Ireland was established in Cork upon the failure of the Agricultural Bank. It commenced operations in July, 1837, and stopped payment two months after. It was a Bank of Issue.

The Provident Bank was a creation of Mr. Thomas Mooney, the same gentleman who projected the Agricultural Bank, and a Mr. W. H. Holbrooke. It was established in 1837, and stopped payment soon after.

The Tipperary Bank.—The Tipperary Bank, better known as Sadlier's Bank, was established upon the foundation of Scully's private Bank, in the year 1839, by Mr. John Sadlier, a young man then aged twenty-seven. His family was respectable and wealthy, and was related by marriage to the Scullys. John Sadlier was a solicitor, and practised as such in Dublin, and afterwards in London as a Parliamentary Agent.

The Tipperary Joint Stock Bank was an immediate success. Under the auspices of the family connection it obtained a great amount of the deposits of the rich farming classes of the county Tipperary, but the discounting was principally in sums of great magnitude to landowners who could mortgage their property. Mr. John Sadlier, his brother James, and Mr. Wilson Kennedy were the three Directors. What the capital was we have not ascertained, but in 1848 a dividend at the rate of 6 per cent. was declared, and £2,513 added to the doubtful debt fund.

Mr. John Sadlier was M.P. for Carlow, and subsequently for Sligo, and James was M.P. for Tipperary. John, in the financial world of London, played a prominent part, and occupied a conspicuous position. He became Chairman of the Royal Swedish Railway Company, Director of the East Kent Railway and of several other enterprises, and Chairman of the London and County Bank. He was appointed a Junior Lord of the Treasury, and was the cynosure of the "Irish Brigade" in Parliament. The business done by the bank was large, respectable, and remunerative; but the amount it held from the public was at the disposal of, and disposed by, John Sadlier in his London projects and enterprises, and the available resources were yearly diminishing, until in 1856 they ran dry.

In February, 1856, the Tipperary Bank Drafts were dishonoured by Messrs. Glyn & Co., the London agents, and a few days after, on the 17th February, John Sadlier's body was found on Hampstead Heath, dead from poison self-administered. The Bank had smashed; and it was discovered that Sadlier

had been engaged for years in a career of robbery, forgery, and fraud. The defalcations under these frauds were estimated at £1,250,000, and the deficiency in the assets of the Bank was considerable. It has never been satisfactorily ascertained what became of these vast sums, for John Sadlier lived frugally and unostentatiously. The dividends paid to the creditors (the last of which was paid in 1879) have already reached 7s. 11d. in the £1. The Bank had many Branches, and the excitement occasioned a panic which was the greatest that ever occurred in Ireland. An article of the London *Times* published shortly after his death referred to him and his transactions in the following terms:—" John Sadlier was a national calamity.
" It is not often that an individual rises to a position of such
" infamous notoriety; but the truth is, now that the whole story
" of his frauds is beginning to assume shape and form, that the
" prosperity of a province has received a severe shock from his
" proceedings. He has forged title-deeds of estates, he has forged
" private acceptances and securities, and by his connection with
" the Tipperary Bank he has contrived to swindle the population
" of the South of Ireland to an amount which is already stated at
" £400,000, and which will probably reach the full proportion of
" the half million."

XI.

CONCLUSION.

The existing well-developed system of Banking is the natural amplification and expansion of those primitive practices which were the necessary creation of commerce and money-dealing. A strong and secure place where valuable property could be deposited with safety, where risk and apprehension of plunder and loss were minimised, and where the person depositing remunerated the custodian for the care-taking, has been succeeded by an establishment where the depositor is paid for having his money taken care of, and from which ideas of risk and apprehension are almost eliminated. The Goldsmith and Money-Changing businesses have been relinquished and left to traders and brokers. A Bank is something higher than a mere strong room and a barter house, and usury is replaced by a Bank of England rate. Banking has become a science.

The word "Bank" is popularly supposed to be derived from the Italian *Banco*, a bench*. The root of the word, however, appears in Anglo-Saxon and in all the Latin languages, and the Italian word is said to be derived from the German, and the German from the Low Latin. The original meaning of the word *banc* in the Anglo-Saxon and Dutch languages was *a hillock, a heap*. It was transferred to mean any elevated or

* See *ante* pp. 28, 29.

eminent place for sitting, and was applied to express a *bank* of oars, and a *bench* of rowers. It thus came to be applied generally to the seats of the moneychangers in the later Roman market-places, as those persons occupied more elevated seats than the common traders. The word was next applied specifically to the tables at which they sat and to their occupation, as Mensarii was the designation of the Bankers in classic Rome, from *mensa, a table*. The word **Bankrupt** is usually deduced from the French *banqueroute*, which is derived from the Italian *banco* and *rotto*—a broken Bank. But the old French idiom conveying the expression of bankruptcy is *qui font banque route*—translated literally in the first English Bankruptcy Law (34 Hen. VIII., c. 4) as "such persons as do make bankrupt." This French word *route* is, however, rendered by *vestigium*, a track or mark; and as *cart route* is the mark which the cart wheel has left, so *banque route* is the mark which the *banque* or bench has left. The explanation offered for this derivation is in the circumstance that when in Rome the Banker failed or absconded, he took his bench with him, or else that it was removed by the authorities and nothing left but the *route* or sign and mark where it had been. Others say that the absconding or failing Banker had his table broken (*ruptus*) by the exasperated populace. At all events it seems allowed on all sides that *banque* or *banc* or *banco*, meant a bench or table,* and that our modern word Bank is derived therefrom.

 The functions of a Bank at the present day are not only manifold and of paramount importance, but are of vast benefit to the community individually and to the country at large. A Banker is the intermediary of capital. He borrows money from those who have it—to their advantage—and lends it to those who legitimately require it—to their advantage. By

* "Overthrew the tables of the money-changers."—MATT. xxi. 12.

his means the numberless sums, large and small, which would be unproductive and unused in the possession of individuals are amassed together, and the Banker employs the amount in lending it at interest, thereby increasing the capital of manufacturers, traders, and farmers, who utilise it for the purposes of advancing commerce and developing trade. Thus these moneys, which without his intervention would be unused, are gathered together and made to increase the productive capital of the Kingdom. The country, if it is not positively so much richer, is negatively so—for it is saved from being so much poorer. He lends out the money deposited with him, at a greater rate than he allows to those from whom he receives it, and the margin constitutes his main profit. It is thus apparent that the common phrase of statisticians—" so many millions in Banks "—is not correct, for the millions are not in the Banks but lent out over the country. Therefore the amount that Banks apparently hold on Deposit Receipt is an unreliable index, or no index at all, of "the wealth of the country." Indirectly, however, it is a criterion, for, presumably, if the country was not solvent and prosperous the Banks would not lend out the millions they have on deposit. These sums must be either lent or not lent. If lent in the country, the country is *prima facie* prospering, for the classes requiring temporary use of capital are solvent; if not lent, *prima facie* those classes are not solvent, and thus it is possible that the amount of deposits in Bank may be greater when the wealth of the country is less. To cite a possible case, and not an extreme one: A. has possessed a certain business, which a few years ago, as a going business, was valued at £30,000—his then profits being the basis of the estimate. This year, after a few depressed and unsuccessful seasons of trading, he discontinues his business—sells the interest of it for £5,000, or say £10,000, which amount he places with his Bankers on Deposit Receipt. Statistically, then, the "wealth of the country" has increased £10,000. In reality, it has decreased considerably. Again, a more usual case: A., a wealthy person, overdraws his account and lends to B., who places the amount on deposit. Again the "wealth of the country" from a statistician's view-point has increased, though in reality there is no increase. Thus such statistics cannot be deemed to be conclusive on the subject of the national wealth.

Besides the amount he has received on Deposit Receipt and Current Accounts, the Banker has the capital of his Bank to trade on. Though the money he holds from the public is repayable always at the call or disposal of the depositor, nevertheless, except in special cases (such as during a panic) which are specially provided for, there is but a limited portion daily called for; and for this portion which he has to surrender each day it is necessary that he should maintain a floating balance of cash and available resources on hands.

Banks of Issue possess a source of revenue which is denied to non-issuing establishments. As will be explained in the subsequent pages, some Banks are legally enabled to issue and keep in circulation a greater value in Bank Notes than that of the coin they hold. If they were compelled to hold gold or bullion equivalent to the value of their notes in circulation a note-issue might be a loss; but when the actual circulation is largely in excess of the gold and silver coin held, it is manifest that this excess is a source of profit; the interest upon this super issue, less the cost of manufacture and maintenance, is net profit to the Bank. The benefits also to the State and the country conferred by paper issues of solvent Banks are not inconsiderable—by reason of the saving of wear and tear, of the attrition and waste of the coinage. The amount of Bank Notes at present in circulation in the United Kingdom is about fifty millions sterling.

A further function of a Bank, and one which is also a source of profit, is to afford a rapid and secure transfer of money from one part of the Kingdom or the world to the other, by means of Letter of Credit, Circular Note or Credit-advice. This portion of a Bank's business is usually profitable, rather because of the commission paid on such transactions than that they add to a Bank's productive capital. There are minor functions of a Bank noted subsequently. A consideration of the scientific aspect of Banking is not suited to these pages.

A banker, accordingly, is burdened with a grave and serious responsibility, and clothed with a great trust. To his ability, skill, discretion, and honesty is consigned the duty of advancing the prosperity of the country, by assisting legitimate industry, encouraging diligence, and aiding the worthy. In the use he makes of the money entrusted to him he proves whether he is fulfilling his duty and benefiting society. Gilbart, in speaking of a Banker's position and authority, says: "He "holds out inducements to uprightness, which are not dis- "regarded by even the most abandoned. There is many a "man who would be deterred from dishonesty by the frown "of a Banker, though he might care but little for the admoni- "tions of a Bishop." Whether the frown of a Banker is as omnipotent now as in the days when Mr. Gilbart wrote thus, is a question that need not now be discussed. But there is no doubt that a Banker's powers for good or evil are superlative, and not easily overrated. The advantages bestowed by Banks are now extended to almost every town in the Kingdom, and are appreciated by the public, who regard them in a proper light and manifest their appreciation by extending to them the fullest confidence. It is a long step from Egibi and Son to the

National Provincial Bank and from Pasion to Coutts and Co., but it is a pleasant and assuring circumstance that in all ages and countries Bankers have as a rule enjoyed a good reputation and borne themselves so as to deserve and maintain the confidence of the public.

It is true that, from time to time, public confidence in our Banking system has been shaken. Such scandalous failures as those of the Western Bank of Scotland, of the Tipperary Bank, and, in later years, of the City of Glasgow Bank—events that occurred not because of outward panic but because of internal mismanagement and fraud,—were calculated to permanently weaken public reliance on, and trust in, a Banking system under which such occurrences were possible. The effects, however, of such collapses have been of ultimate benefit to Banking, and, notably, the City of Glasgow Bank failure occasioned the passing of a protective Act of Parliament, which, whatever its defects in detail may be, must be regarded as one of large and wide benefit to Shareholders in Banks. It is a frequent complaint that Bank Shareholders are too apathetic in regard to their own position and interests, and exercise too little supervision over the management; but it must be admitted that if interference of this nature were allowable, it would probably degenerate into inquisitiveness and obstruction, and serve no really good end—and, moreover, the Directors of our Banks are, as a rule, chosen from those classes to whom suspicion cannot readily attach. In the selection of proper Directors greater protection lies than in holding the Board under control and supervision.

The numerous great men—great in Literature, in Politics, in Science, in Wealth—that have been connected with Banking since the time of Egibi of Babylon; the many failures and accidents since the days when Icetas, the father of Diogenes the

Cynic, fled, a swindling Banker, from the town of Sinope; the great, though gradual, progress the Banking of the present shows when compared with the days when Seneca had a sum equal to two millions sterling lent out at usury, and wrote, the while, in praise of poverty,—or with the more modern times in our own country, when in the town of Bury St. Edmunds, seven centuries ago, Benedict, the Jew usurer,* a representative Banker of the time, having lent forty marks—some seven and twenty pounds—to the Abbey, prefers at the end of four years or so a claim for "Twelve hundred pounds besides interest"—a circumstance that causes Mr. Carlyle to almost hope this Benedict was one of those who hanged themselves in beleagured York City soon afterwards—these are subjects too large to fully discuss in this volume, but they will claim the attention and interest of all students of Banking, its History and Literature.

* Carlyle's *Past and Present*.

PART II.

THE LAW AND PRACTICE OF BANKING.

THE

LAW AND PRACTICE OF BANKING.

I.

THE RELATIONS BETWEEN THE BANKER AND HIS CUSTOMER.

A BANKER is a medium between those who have money and those who require it; he receives money for temporary keeping from the one class to advance it temporarily to the other.

The relations are simply those of debtor and creditor. The Banker does not occupy the position of a **trustee**. If he did, the remedy, for instance, against him in case of his wrongfully dishonouring A.'s cheque to B. would be a suit in Equity by B., whereas the remedy is a Common Law suit by A. The drawer only of a cheque can proceed against a Banker for wrongful dishonour, because there is no privity or contract, actual or implied, between any parties to a cheque, except the drawer and drawee; the debtor is liable only to his creditor, and the Banker cannot be the debtor to the bearer or holder of a cheque, being other than the drawer. Neither does the Banker occupy the position of a **bailee**. If he did, he would be bound to re-deliver to the drawer of a cheque, A., the identical moneys which A. had lodged. Nor is the Banker the

agent of his customer; for if he were, he would be bound to apply the actual money lodged with him only in the manner the person so lodging might direct. The relations, therefore, are, at law, simply those of debtor and creditor, or borrower and lender.

Under some circumstances the Banker pays the depositor for the use of his money, and in almost all cases he charges those who borrow from him a certain rate of interest for the amounts so lent. There is, however, the general distinction between those who deposit with the Banker—*i.e.*, those who lend to him,—and those who borrow from him. The Banker is practically obliged to repay, or account to, the depositor on demand or notice, whereas the borrower does not repay the Banker till the term of the contract between them has been fulfilled. Thus the Banker holds himself liable to an immediate call on him to return the funds of others which he holds, while he cannot obtain on demand the sums he has lent for a stated term. Primarily, the extent and nature of a Banker's business are regulated by his capital and the extent and nature of the sums he receives from the community; secondarily, the extent and method of his business are regulated by the circumstance that the sums so received are not generally repayable at any certain and stated time, but may be demanded on any day. The ordinary experience of the Banker is, however, that the aggregate amount held from the public varies with circumstances within his knowledge. In rural districts, they diminish in the Spring and increase in the Autumn season; but, as a rule, they seldom decline below a certain line. He thus calculates on retaining a gross permanent amount, estimated by previous experience and a foreknowledge of the consequences of any exceptional occurrences.

There are two descriptions of lodgment with a Banker: one, where the amount shall bear interest and be repayable on call, or at a short notice, upon returning the Banker the receipt he has given for such lodgment; the other, where the amount shall not bear interest, and shall be repayable on demand from time to time, on written orders from the lodger. The former description is known as on *Deposit Receipt*, the latter as on *Current Account*. It has been observed that the relations of the Banker to his customer are not fiduciary; neither is he a legal agent to the customer, nor does the customer occupy the position of a principal. "Money paid into a Bank ceases altogether to be "the money of the person paying it in; it is the money of the "Banker, who is bound to return an equivalent by paying a "similar sum to that deposited with him, when he is asked for "it. To all intents, it is the money of the Banker to do as he "may please with it; though it is true that, in a popular sense, "it is spoken of as 'my money at my Banker's' and 'my "'balance at my Banker's'; and though no one can doubt that "in ordinary language the term 'ready money' includes the "speaker's balance at his banker's."*

A Banker is arbiter of his own business, and can decline to open an account for, or to receive lodgments from, any individual. But if an account be opened, the Banker thereby impliedly undertakes to transact the party's Banking business (but not necessarily to discount bills or make advances), and to obey the orders of his customer which are within the scope of a Banker's business as understood in the country and neighbourhood. Failing obedience in these respects on the Banker's part, he is liable to his customer, should the customer be in any way damnified, or put to loss, by reason of the neglect or disobedience, notwithstanding that he (the Banker) derives no

* Grant.

profit or benefit from the business. Negligence in transacting the customer's business entails liability, as disobedience does. "A Banker may fairly be considered," says Grant, "to be in a "situation or position in which skill is implied, and therefore "an omission to use due skill, even on an occasion of a gra- "tuitous employment, is taken as gross negligence."

II.

DEPOSIT RECEIPTS.

UNLESS a Banker expressly stipulates to allow interest on money lodged with him he is under no obligation to do so, nor can he be compelled to do so. Such express stipulation, subject to certain conditions, exists in the case of Deposit Receipts, the usual form for which is as follows :

Deposit Receipt.

     The Anglo-Indian Bank.

      London, _____ 1881.

  Received from _____

of _____   *the sum of* _____

_____ *to be accounted for at our Office here.*

     For the Anglo-Indian Bank.

_____ *Acct.*   _____ *Manager.*

On the back of each such Receipt there is a printed memorandum of the conditions on which Deposits are received by the Bank, generally to this effect : "Sums deposited for one month "or longer, bear interest at the rate allowed by the directors on "such deposits. Notices of the rate allowed, and of any

"variation thereof, are posted from time to time in the public
"offices of the Bank, and no other notice of such variation
"will be given to any depositor. When payment of either
"Principal or Interest is required, the Deposit Receipt must
"be produced, and endorsed by the depositor, and delivered
"up to the Bank. Ten days' notice previous to withdrawal is
"required to be given by the depositor."

The **Rate of Interest** varies in accordance with the variations in the Bank of England rate, and the interest accrues on the deposit at the varied rates. The ten days' **notice of withdrawal** is not always and under ordinary circumstances required by a Bank. It can be claimed, however, and has been in times of panic, should there be a "run" on the Bank; but even in this extreme case it is not always demanded, as the tendency of a regulation to defer payments at such a time would be to increase the panic. The rule dates from the ante-steam and ante-telegraph days, when the transit of coin to meet such emergencies was a matter of a delay of some days.

A Deposit Receipt can be issued in **two or several names**, in which case the endorsement of each is required on repayment. But if the receipt is surrendered by one of the parties, bearing his endorsement only, for the purpose of adding to the amount and obtaining a fresh receipt in the same joint names, the discharge of one will, with the evidence of such an additional deposit, protect the Banker. It can be issued in **joint names** payable to either or any of them, and as a rule a joint deposit is made accountable to "the survivor." This course is supposed to obviate, in the case of the death of one of the parties, the necessity to take out Letters of Administration, a certificate of death being deemed sufficient. But as a matter of law such a precaution is unnecessary, as the parties whose names are joined in a Deposit Receipt are not tenants in common, but joint tenants, and, consequently, on the death of one his property in the amount accrues to, and is absorbed by, the survivor. If a Deposit Receipt is lodged by another party in the name of an **infant**—that is, a minor—it cannot be repaid or withdrawn until the infant attains majority. A Banker is not competent to bind himself by a Deposit Receipt issued to an infant. A Deposit Receipt is a contract between the Banker and depositor; and not alone is an infant incapable of entering into a legal contract, but should he be a party to a contract, he cannot now make it valid by ratification when he is of age, as all infant contracts are absolutely void by the Infant Relief Act, 37 & 38 Vic., c. 62. A Deposit issued in the name of a **spinster** who subsequently marries, requires her husband's endorsement supplementing her own before repayment can be made. A deposit can be received from a **married woman**, but unless she alleges at the time of depositing that it is her separate estate, and for her own separate use and enjoyment, and that it is so stated on the receipt; or that the receipt is issued under the husband's knowledge and consent; it is necessary that the receipt should bear the husband's endorsement on repayment. The amount of a Deposit Receipt in a married woman's name which is her separate estate, vests at her death, not in her husband, but in her executor or administrator. If a married woman represent herself as a spinster or widow when lodging money on Deposit, and her husband subsequently apprises the Bank that the money so deposited is his property, the Banker should refuse to pay either party, and let a Court of Law decide whether the money was the wife's separate estate, or whether in depositing it she was merely her husband's agent, in which case it would be his property.

A Deposit Receipt, though by the American law it is held

capable of transfer, is not, in this country, intended to be a transferable document; and where it is not presented for payment by the depositor, but by a second party, payment is not made until the Banker is satisfied that the discharge is *bona fide* that of the depositor, and that it has been his intention to transfer the amount. As the Banker is in all cases accountable to the depositor, he must satisfy himself as to the identity and *bona fides* of the person to whom he repays the amount. In the case of payment to a wrongful holder the Banker is liable to the depositor, unless he can prove that the latter has been guilty of fraud or of such negligence that the responsibility for the mispayment attaches thereto.

The non-transferability of a Deposit Receipt is, however, in some quarters, still a debatable question. Mr. Dunning Macleod, in his *Theory and Practice of Banking*, thus expresses himself:—

"Formerly these Deposit Receipts were what was termed non-negotiable. They were made payable to the Customer himself only, and consequently, if the Customer transferred his Deposit Receipt to any one else, the transferee could not sue the Banker, at Law, in his own name, though he might in the name of the Transferor; but he might sue him in Equity. But since the Supreme Court of Judicature Act, which enacts that the rules of Equity shall prevail over those of Common Law, a Deposit Receipt is as transferable as a Bank-note or cheque."*

Mr. Macleod does not give any authority for this sudden conclusion, nor has the Judicature Act, as far as we can learn, caused the Banks to make any distinction in the treatment of their Deposit Receipts, and at no time have they been regarded as transferable as a Bank-note or cheque. In a case (Moore (administratrix of) *v.* The Ulster Bank), the Irish Courts distinctly affirmed that a Deposit Receipt was not a transferable instrument. In this case, A., shortly before his death, *endorsed*

---

* Third Edition, vol. ii. p. 469.

a Deposit Receipt which was in his name, and *delivered it* to B., stating that the amount was for his (A.'s) niece C. B. endorsed the document, and after A.'s death, presented it to the Bank, who paid him (B.) the amount. The Bank had not had notice of A.'s death. In an action by the administratrix of A. against the Bank, it was held that the Deposit Receipt was not a negotiable instrument passing by endorsement.* A Deposit Receipt is not "made payable" to the Depositor. It is a simple contract between the customer and the Banker, wherein the latter undertakes to account to the Depositor for his Deposit, and the Banker is strictly within his right in refusing to saddle himself with the responsibility of vouching the *bona fides* of any transfer of the Receipt—for paying a transferee amounts to vouching for such *bona fides*.

In a will, Deposit Receipts should be specifically mentioned. It has been held that they were not included in a bequest in the following words: "all bonds, promissory notes, and other "securities for money in my hands at the time of my decease, "and all moneys due thereon." A Deposit Receipt, it will be observed, cannot strictly come under any of these terms, and therefore, in this case, the amounts on Deposit passed under a residuary clause.

It has happened that a Deposit Receipt has been issued in such a way and under such circumstances and conditions as to cause a double liability of the Bank, as will be seen from the following case of Cochrane *v.* O'Brien:—"John O'Brien, "father of Daniel O'Brien and Catherine Callaghan, lodged "£150 in Bank, upon a Deposit Receipt, in his own name. "Upon Daniel's producing the receipt some time afterwards,

---

* It was further held that there had been no equitable assignment in this case; that even if the transaction constituted B. an agent of A., the authority was revoked by A.'s death; and that the transaction did not amount to a *donatio mortis causa*.

"and demanding the interest, he was refused, the Bank paying
"only to the depositor in person; John, upon this, used, for
"some time, to come along with Daniel, and receive the
"interest, taking the fresh receipt in his (John's) name, on each
"occasion; afterwards he obtained permission that Daniel
"should receive payments upon producing the receipt endorsed
"by John. Then Daniel, by his directions, paid an additional
"sum of £5 into the Bank, and obtained a new Deposit
"Receipt for the whole amount then in the hands of the Bank,
"being £155, but in the name of Catherine O'Brien (after-
"wards Callaghan), Daniel telling the Manager that his father
"intended £155 to be the portion of his daughter Catherine,
"*but desired to retain control over it during his life, and that
"*he wished the Deposit Receipt should be drawn in her name.*
"In a few days afterwards John O'Brien died, Daniel took out
"administration *testamento annexo*, and, as administrator,
"claimed the £155. Shortly after, Catherine married, and
"she and her husband demanded payment of this money.
"Both Daniel and Catherine, with her husband, commenced
"actions against the Bankers, who filed a bill of interpleader
"against both; but the bill was dismissed, this not being the
"case of a double demand for one duty, but a case in which
"there may be two liabilities : and a mere pretext of conflict-
"ing claims will not support a bill of interpleader; and the
"court is bound to see that there is a question to be tried.
"Here the transaction created a debt from the Bank to
"Catherine, in consequence of the mode of dealing adopted
"by the Bankers; they were not at liberty to resist her demand,
"or to treat the case as one of interpleader, because John's
"representative, who made the last deposit and took the new
"receipt, chose to rescind the whole transaction. It is quite
"consistent with this view that John's representative might

"still be able to recover against the Bankers; but it was their "own fault if they created a new liability in themselves without "obtaining a sufficient discharge from the original title to the "money in their hands. The Bank in this case applied for "the bill of interpleader; but it was pointed out by the Court "that in so doing they asked it to destroy their own mode of "dealing, for if the cancellation of the old receipt and the "issuing of the new receipt did not create a liability to the "person named in the new receipt, the Bankers' system of "Deposit Receipts was defective."*

It frequently happens, especially in country districts, that a **Depositor becomes security** for a person who is obtaining accommodation from the Bank. In such a case the Banker usually obtains from the guaranteeing depositor his deposit receipt duly discharged; he then has a lien upon it, and is entitled to hold an equivalent to the amount guaranteed. If the Banker has not possession of the receipt, there is nothing to prevent the depositor obtaining payment of the amount of his deposit while the Bill he has secured is running and before it has matured. A Banker's action, however, in this as in many such cases, is to be governed by the character, etc., of the guaranteeing-depositor.

A Banker's Deposit Receipt is exempt from stamp duty; but as it is necessary that the Banker should obtain from the depositor, on repayment, a receipt for the amount repaid, and as there is no corresponding exemption on behalf of the depositor, the receipts issued by the Banks generally bear an impressed receipt stamp. This impost legally falls on the depositor, and on this account the practice obtains in some Banking establishments of deducting the price of the stamp from the amount of interest payable—a practice not in favour

* Grant.

with the public, who are not aware of the reason of the deduction, or of the right of the Bank to enforce it.

Lost Deposit Receipt.—In the event of the loss of a Deposit Receipt, the amount is repaid to the Depositor upon a satisfactory indemnity.

III.

CURRENT ACCOUNT.—CHEQUES.

A CURRENT ACCOUNT differs from a Deposit in that, as the term conveys, it does not consist of a fixed balance, but varies from day to day, being increased by lodgments and diminished by cheques. The customer lodges with the Banker sums consisting of money, cheques, drafts, bills, and other negotiable documents, and the Banker makes repayment upon written orders from the customer. These written orders are called Cheques. The fact of the Banker receiving lodgments on Current Account for his customer creates a contract and engagement on the Banker's part to honour the customer's Cheques to the extent of those lodgments.

A Cheque on a Banker is, according to its legal definition, an Inland Bill of Exchange payable on demand. It is an order in writing by the person who has deposited the moneys, or in whose name they have been deposited, for the payment on demand, without interest, of a specified sum, to a person named therein, or to his order, or to the bearer. The person making such order is the Drawer; the person to whom the order is made payable is the Payee; the Banker on whom it is drawn is the Drawee. The usual form of an unfilled Cheque is as follows:—

```
-------------------------------------------------
|   No.                                         |
|                    London,_____188        |
|              THE ANGLO-INDIAN BANK.           |
|   Pay_____ or bearer     |
|   the sum of_____ _____sterling.|
|   £_____                         |
-------------------------------------------------
```

But it is not requisite that any precise form should be employed.* It is not even absolutely necessary that the Drawer's signature must be subscribed at the foot of an order to pay. One couched, for instance, in the following terms, in the customer's handwriting, is equally a valid Cheque, if fulfilling all the legal requirements as to dating, stamping, etc. : — "*Mr. Henry Wilkinson requires the Anglo-Indian Bank to pay bearer fifty pounds.*" It seems, however, that the terms of the order must be such that payment of the amount is not asked as a favour but required as a right, that is, that it must be so framed that payment is not at the option of the Drawee, but that it is compulsory on him.

The Essential Constituents of a Cheque are (1) that the Drawee's name be set forth on it; (2) that it be dated; (3) that it be stamped; (4) that the amount to be paid be expressed; (5) that it be payable to the bearer, or to some person or persons, or his or their order; (6) that it be payable on demand unconditionally; (7) that it be signed by the Drawer, or by an authorised person for him.

(I.) **The Drawee's Name.**—The name of the company,

---

* For convenience in after reference it is to be recommended that a place be indicated on cheque forms, to contain the folio and number which will mark its posting in the Banker's ledger.

firm, individual, or establishment upon whom the Cheque is drawn, together with the locality where the Cheque is to be presented, are necessary. A Cheque addressed to the "National Provincial Bank" is not sufficient—the office or branch of the Bank must be stated. But presentation at the Bank's Head Office, of a Cheque thus vaguely addressed, is a sufficient presentation.

(II.) **The Date.**—A Cheque may be dated on any day of the week, Sunday not excepted. If a cheque is **undated** it is an imperfect instrument, and therefore inoperative; and the Drawee can decline to honour it on that ground. Further it is possible that an undated cheque may have been issued such a length of time before its presentation as would raise a presumption of *mala fides* if the date of issue was known to the Banker; and he is entitled to such an adverse presumption in case the Cheque is undated. It is said to be **"post dated"** if it bears a date subsequent to the day upon which payment is demanded. A post-dated cheque is not an illegal document, nor does any penalty attach to the maker of it. "It is," says Grant, "a legal, valid, and unimpeachable instrument." If a Banker, however, cash such a Cheque before the day of its date, and that the Cheque has been lost or stolen, or fraudulently obtained, the Banker will be liable to the rightful owner. It is doubtful if liability in any shape would attach to a Banker who paid such a Cheque to a *bona fide* holder, or direct to the Payee, because it is an inherent quality of a Cheque that it is payable on demand, and unconditionally. It is the opinion of some persons that a Cheque, being post-dated, is transformed into a Bill, and requires an *ad valorem* stamp duty; but this is an erroneous idea.

(III.) **The Stamp.**—Formerly the stamp duties on cheques were of a varied, complex and confusing character, but now a stamp duty of one penny is imposed on each Cheque, irrespective of its amount. This duty is denoted either by an impressed stamp (which of late years has been reduced from a large unsightly roughness to a neat shape and size), or by an adhesive postage and inland-revenue stamp, affixed and cancelled by the Drawer, or, failing him, by the Drawee. If the affixing and cancellation of the stamp is the act of the Drawee, it operates to make the instrument valid and to protect himself, but not to relieve the Drawer or negotiator. The consequences of negotiating an unstamped cheque, are liability to a penalty of £10, and inability to sue upon the instrument, unless upon payment of the duty and a penalty. The Stamp Act of 1870 fixed the stamp duty on Cheques payable on demand at one penny; but by it any Draft or Order drawn by one Banker upon another in payment of any differences, for the purpose of settling or balancing or clearing any account between such Bankers, is exempt from the duty. A subsequent Act extends the exemption to Drafts or Orders drawn by the Paymaster-General. Cheques drawn by Benefit Building Societies and the like are not exempt.

(IV.) **The Amount.**—The sum payable must be set forth in words or figures, or both. It must be denoted in English money. A Cheque may be written for any sum. There is now no restriction of the amount for which it may be drawn. The supposition that Cheques for a less sum than £1 are illegal, is erroneous, as the Act making such a Cheque void and illegal has long since been repealed. If a Cheque has the amount in figures or in writing only, it is yet a valid instrument. If the amount as expressed in words differs from that as expressed in figures, the amount in words is the sum the Bank can pay, irrespective of the circumstance that the figures may be the lesser amount; but it is open to the Bank to decline payment until the Drawer has indicated which of the two amounts is the correct one, as a Cheque with differing amounts is a contradictory order. It is not essential to a Cheque's validity that the amount should be fully designated as pounds, shillings, and pence. Thus an order to pay "ten, eleven, seven," has been held to mean ten pounds, eleven shillings, and seven pence; and where an amount so stated is supplemented by confirmatory figures, no hesitation to pay on the Banker's part is necessary.

Altered Amount—Forgery.—The law on the subject of a forged or altered Cheque is that the loss occasioned by the payment of such an instrument falls on the Banker, and not on the Drawer whose signature has been forged or whose Cheque has been altered. A Banker is bound to know his customer's signature and his handwriting; and therefore, he is bound to know what is not his customer's handwriting. If a Cheque is a forgery *in toto*, it is manifest it is not the customer's order, and that therefore his account cannot be charged with it. If a Cheque is altered fraudulently, and that the alteration is the result of the Drawer's gross negligence, the loss would probably fall on the Drawer; but the question of the negligence is one for the jury. In a case where a Cheque was filled for fifty pounds, but in such a manner as to admit of the words "three hundred" and the figure "3" being inserted in the body and margin respectively, it was held that the loss should fall on the Drawer, as it was his own negligence induced the fraud. But Bankers should not rely too strongly on this case, as the judgment may have depended on the fact that the body of the Cheque was in the handwriting, not of the Drawer, but of his wife. Had it been apparently in the Drawer's penmanship, it might have been ruled that it was the Banker's duty to know his customer's handwriting, and that he should have discovered that the added words were not written by him. But, of course, if such fraudulently added words or figures were manifestly in a handwriting different from the other words and figures, the Banker would *prima facie* be guilty of negligence, and would therefore be undoubtedly liable. The rule of law is, that in a case of this kind, where a loss must fall on either of two innocent parties, it falls on him whose conduct opened the door and created the opportunity for the fraud, and in case the Drawer cannot be made liable for this, the loss falls on the Banker. In case of a forged endorsement of the Payee's name, the Banker is protected where he has paid the holder without knowledge of the forgery, but the protection does not extend to any other person who takes the cheque upon the faith of such forged endorsement (16 & 17 Vic., c. 59, s. 19).

Any **alteration** whatsoever in any material portion of a Cheque requires the confirmation of the Drawer in order to constitute the Cheque valid and negotiable; in fact it may be laid down as a general rule that no alteration can be made in a Cheque, except by the Drawer, or by his authority, save in so far as regards altering the tenor of the Cheque from *bearer* to *order*, as is subsequently stated. The words "pounds," "shillings," "pence," are not material words, and an alteration, for instance, from a misspelling to a correct spelling of them, or *vice versa*, is not a material alteration. But such alterations in the number of pounds, shillings, or pence, or in the name of the Payee, or in the date, are material alterations and require the confirmation of the Drawer. An alteration from "bearer" to "order," though a material alteration, does not require the Drawer's initials in confirmation, because its effect is to restrict the negotiability of the Cheque, and being a restriction, the presumption is that it is authentic; and, besides, it operates also as a protection to the Drawer. Moreover, it is a received opinion that a Payee of a Cheque drawn to "bearer," can, for his own protection and security, change it, and make it drawn to "order." But where a cheque drawn to "order" is altered to "bearer," such alteration requires the Drawer's confirmation, for it operates to enlarge the negotiability of the Cheque, and the presumption is against such an act. Therefore, where a restriction is removed by an alteration, the alteration must be authenticated by the maker of the instrument.

(VI.) **The Payee.**—"**Bearer.**"—A Cheque is called an open Cheque, when it is not crossed. The nature and effect of "crossing" is treated subsequently; at present we deal with uncrossed instruments. A Cheque must be payable to some one. An order filled thus, "Pay twenty pounds" and signed, is not a Cheque, as the Payee is not specified. The Payee may be denominated as the "bearer," or the Cheque may be payable to initials "or bearer," or a number "or bearer," and may be payable to a specified party "or bearer." In all such cases the amount is payable by the Drawee to the presenter of the Cheque, it being an open Cheque and not crossed. The presenter is the bearer and it is not incumbent on him to endorse the Cheque. By its nature, as we have seen, a Cheque is payable on demand and unconditionally, and being payable to bearer and not crossed or its negotiability otherwise restricted, the holder is entitled to immediate payment, if the Banker has funds of the Drawer in his possession. The Payee of a Cheque payable *to bearer* can make it payable *to order* by altering the word "bearer" to "order." But a Cheque payable on the face of it, "to bearer," cannot have its negotiability restricted and be made *by endorsement*, payable to a further party's *order*.

"**Order.**"—Cheques payable to "order" were introduced into the Statute Law by 16 & 17 Vic., c. 59, s. 19. When a cheque is made payable to an individual, *or order*, it is necessary that it should be endorsed, or purport to be endorsed, by him, before it becomes negotiable. The Payee is empowered to endorse it making it payable to the order of a third party, the third to a fourth, and so on; and it must bear, or purport to bear, the endorsement of each subsequent Payee, the same as if he had been the original Payee. If a Cheque payable to "order" is duly endorsed, or purports to be endorsed, by the Payee, in blank—that is, if he does not limit the negotiability of it by making it payable to another party—it then becomes a cheque payable to bearer, and, as such, is negotiable without further endorsement. A cheque drawn, "*Pay me* or my order," if presented to the Drawee by the Drawer, and he is known to be the Drawer, can be paid without his endorsement. If he refuses to endorse he cannot be compelled to do so, but a memorandum to the effect that the amount has been paid to him, in the terms of the drawing, is advisable. Making the payment to the drawer in person fulfils his command to "Pay me."

"**Specially Payable.**"—A Cheque is said to be specially payable when it is an order, the payment of the amount specified in which is restricted to the Payee alone: this is effected by writing it payable to a party without either of the alternative words "bearer" or "order." In this case the Banker on whom it is drawn is empowered to pay it to the Payee only. Consequently its negotiability is limited to the Payee and it ceases to be transferable. The Banker, therefore, must be satisfied that the presenter is the Payee; and in cases where such Cheques are presented to the Drawee by another Bank, the amount is not paid to the presenting Bank unless the endorsement is guaranteed.

(VI.) **On Demand and Unconditionally.**—A Cheque, in pursuance of the Stamp Act, 1870, must be payable on demand, and payable unconditionally. If an instrument be drawn, not payable on demand but at a future time, no matter how soon, it is not a Cheque. **At sight**, is now equivalent to *on demand*. It is not essential that the actual words "on demand" should be expressed. For instance, a Cheque drawn "Pay Bearer Fifty Pounds" is, in law, a Cheque payable on demand, and any expression equivalent to "on demand" is valid. A Cheque must also be payable unconditionally. If there be any condition attached to the payment of the amount the Banker can refuse to negotiate the Cheque, as it is no part of his business to observe the fulfilment of any duty imposed by the Drawer on the Payee as a condition precedent of payment.

(VII.) **The Drawer.**—**Drawer's Signature.**—The signature of the Drawer is the authority to the Banker, and is therefore essential. As we have seen, it is not absolutely necessary that the signature should be subscribed at foot of the order, but the instrument must bear the Drawer's name in his own handwriting somewhere on the face of it, and be his order to pay. A **marksman**, if the mark be duly attested, may draw a Cheque. A Banker is not *bound* to honour his customer's signature if it should be signed in a manner different from his usual or specimen signature, no matter how clear the evidence is that it is the writing of the customer. For example, if a person who has given his Banker a specimen signature "J. Smith" should sign his Cheque "John Smith," the Banker is not bound to pay it, as the signature differs from that which his customer has instructed him to honour. But if a Banker has evidence that it is, *bona fide*, his customer's signature, and is satisfied therewith, he may pay it on his own responsibility. Should he not pay it, he should be careful to supply the proper motive of refusal, *i.e.*, that the Drawer's subscription differs from his usual signature.

An Infant—that is a person under 21 years of age—cannot

keep a Bank account, or draw valid Cheques. A Banker who cashes a Cheque drawn by an infant is not thereby discharged, that is to say, an infant can make him account for the funds paid away on such document. A **married woman** can keep a Current Account, (1) of her separate moneys (which are defined below); (2) by the permission and authority of her husband, which may be implied as well as written;* and (3) as her husband's agent. A married woman's separate estate is defined in the Married Woman's Property Act thus:—"The "wages and earnings of any married woman acquired or gained "by her after the passing of this Act in any employment, occu-"pation, or trade, in which she is engaged or which she carries "on separately from her husband, and also any money or "property so acquired by her through the exercise of any "literary, artistic, or scientific skill, and all investments of such "wages, earnings, money, or property, shall be deemed and "taken to be property held and settled to her separate use, "independent of any husband to whom she may be married, "and her receipts alone shall be a good discharge for such "wages, earnings, money, and property." A Banker, who is the Drawee, is not entitled to dishonour the Cheque of an **idiot** or **lunatic** because the Drawer is believed by him to be an idiot or lunatic. Nor is a **Drunken man's** Cheque invalid.

Cheques drawn on a Current Account which stands in the Banker's books in **joint and several names** (such as "John "Smith and Thomas Brown"), be they Trustees or otherwise, must be signed by both, or all, parties individually. If an account be held in joint names of **trustees**, and one of the parties absconds, the Court of Chancery must be applied to to appoint another in his place, or to authorise and make valid the Cheques by the remaining Trustee. In a **joint**

* See Appendix for form of authority.

account in the names of A. and B., the Drawer's signature "for self and A.—B." will not discharge the Banker unless he has A's. authority for such a signature. In a **partnership** account, the signature or act of one of the known and authorised partners will bind all. In the case of an **executors'** account, it has been held that the signature of one of the executors will be a sufficient authority to the Banker, but this is not so in the case of an account in the names of **administrators or assignees in bankruptcy.** The Cheques of a **Company** are signed by one or more officers of the company, under the written authority of a quorum of the directors. The Cheques of a **Corporation** are usually signed by some of the members and officials of the Corporation; but the authority to the Banker to honour Cheques so signed must be under the Corporate Seal. The Cheques of a **Firm** are signed in the name of the Firm by any one of the authorised partners or members, and such signature is binding on the other partners. The cheques of a **limited company** must be signed for the Company by one or more authorised officials. We have seen cheques signed *in manuscript*, "Johnson & Co., Limited"—an entirely irregular subscription; a Limited Company has no individuality or personality, and cannot sign its name at the foot of a cheque in this fashion. The Bankers of a duly constituted Joint Stock Company, where the Cheques on the Company's account purport to be signed by the **Directors,** or any of them, are not bound to ascertain that such purporting Directors have been legally appointed as Directors, or legally authorised to draw Cheques, provided there is nothing on the face of the Cheque in violation of, or inconsistent with, the Articles of Association of the Company, or nothing to excite suspicion. This was laid down in an action by the East Holyford Mining Company against the National Bank.

Endorsement.—A Cheque payable to a person "or order" must bear his endorsement. Endorsement signifies literally a signing on the back, but as applied to Cheques it has the wider signification of discharge or receipt, for the signature of a Payee of a Cheque drawn to order, may be on the face of the Cheque, or anywhere upon it, as long as it operates as a discharge to the Banker. A Cheque payable to "*bearer or order*" requires the endorsement of the Presenter. It has been pointed out that a Cheque made payable by the Drawer to the bearer, and remaining so, cannot be efficaciously or validly endorsed payable to the order of a further party by the Payee, or any subsequent holder. A Cheque drawn payable to "order," must be endorsed, or purport to be endorsed, by the person in whose favour it is drawn; and he, in his turn, can make it payable to the order of a third party, and so on.* It is obvious that if the spelling of the surname in the endorsement differs from that of the Payee, the Cheque is not endorsed by the party to whom it is payable. For instance, *John Smith*, an endorser, is not the same person as *John Smyth*, the payee. Therefore any variation in the spelling of the surname constitutes an irregularity, and the Banker is not discharged in paying such an irregularly-endorsed order upon him. A variation in the spelling of a common Christian name does not constitute an irregularity. A Cheque drawn by an illiterate

---

* The 16 & 17 Vic., c. 59, says:—Provided always that any Draft or Order drawn upon a Banker for a sum of money payable to order on demand, which shall, when presented for payment, *purport to be endorsed by the person to whom the same shall be drawn payable*, shall be a sufficient authority to such Banker to pay the amount of such Draft or Order to the bearer thereof; and it shall not be incumbent on such Banker to prove that such endorsement, or any subsequent endorsement, was made by, or under the direction or authority of the person to whom the said Draft or Order was or is made payable, either by the drawer or any endorser thereof.

party, and payable to "Gorge Smith," and endorsed "George Smith" is correctly and regularly discharged. As long as the necessary endorsement is regular, the Banker is not bound to ascertain that it is *bona fide*. The Banker is discharged if the Cheque *purports to be endorsed* by the Payee. If Thomas Brown fraudulently writes "John Smith" on a Cheque payable to "John Smith or order," the Banker is not liable for the mispayment, as the Cheque purports to be endorsed by John Smith, and it is no part of a Banker's business to ascertain the genuineness of the endorsement. Even should he surmise from a knowledge of the Payee's signature that the endorsement is a forgery, he is protected in paying it, because there may be more John Smiths (or any other name) than one. Where, however, the Payee is a person of whom, at the time, there could be no other person of the same name, and that his signature is known to the Banker, and that the endorsement is manifestly a forgery, the Banker would be deemed guilty of negligence if he paid the amount, and, presumably, would not be held discharged. For example, if a Cheque is payable to the Duke of St. Albans, and the Banker is acquainted with the Duke's signature, and the endorsement is not, to the Banker's knowledge, in the Duke's handwriting, and does not purport to be done by his authority, therefore, as there is only one Duke of St. Albans, and only one endorsement possible, the Banker is entitled to decline payment of the Cheque, as the endorsement is to his knowledge not the endorsement of the Payee; and if he does pay it he will be held guilty of negligence. An **endorsement in pencil** is a sufficient discharge. Bankers, as a rule, on the ground of the non-permanency of such writing, require that the Payee should endorse his name in ink, and of course he complies with such a rational request. But in the case of a

Payee endorsing in pencil, and transferring the Cheque to a third party, the Banker cannot dishonour the Cheque because the first Payee has given his order in a perishable writing. As has been said by a great authority, the law does not prescribe the material with which a Payee is to write his name, and it is his order equally in perishable pencil-writing as in imperishable ink. If a Payee write **Mr.** or **Mrs.** before his or her name, it is an irregular endorsement, for such an addition changes the endorsement from a signature to a mere address. The same rule applies to a title written before the name. A Payee, however, can write Esquire *after* his name, as it is but a description of himself sub-added to his signature.* The same applies to titles, such as Knight, Baronet, &c., and Academical Degrees, &c., &c. An endorsement **per procuration** (pp. John Smith, Henry Brown) is regular in law, as it has been laid down† that it purports to be endorsed by the Payee. Some Bankers require per-procuration endorsements to be guaranteed by the presenter, but such guaranty is not necessary, as the Banker is fully and legally discharged by a per-procuration endorsement. However, such an endorsement as "**For** John Brown, John Smith," is not regular, as in this case John Smith is not empowered, and does not purport to be empowered, to give a discharge for John Brown, whereas in the former he alleges a procuration power, which has been held sufficient for the Banker. In 1868, after the judicial decision as to the validity of per-procuration endorsements, the London Banks agreed amongst themselves to accept such endorsements without a guaranty from the presenting Bank. The Irish Banks, since the publication of the first edition of this work, have

---

* This opinion has been contested, but we see no grounds to alter it.

† In Cookson *v.* Bank of England, in Hare *v.* Copland (the Royal Bank), and in Charles *v.* Blackwell.

come to the same understanding. A Cheque payable to "John Smith, **Senior**," is correctly discharged "John Smith," for Senior is a superfluous designation. But one to "John Smith, **Junior**," must be endorsed "John Smith, Junior." A Payee does not invalidate his endorsement by writing the word "Lodge" over his name; but the words "Lodged to Account of" will invalidate the discharge, for then the endorsement *in toto* is but a memorandum, and does not *per se* purport to be a discharge by the Payee. A Cheque payable to **Messrs**. Smith is correctly endorsed "A. and B. Smith," but not correctly if endorsed "Smith and Co." A Cheque payable to "Messrs. Smith and Co." is said to be incorrect when endorsed "John Smith and Co.," or "John and James Smith and Co.," but it seems to us that these are both "Messrs. Smith and Co.,' and the Cheque purports, therefore, to bear the Payee's endorsement.* A Cheque endorsed by an alleged **executor** or **administrator** of the Payee is a sufficient discharge to the Banker; but it is the usual, but totally needless, custom with some Banks to require a guaranty to such an endorsement. The Banker, however, is apparently protected by the same rule

* It is proper to point out that the Council of the Institute of Bankers (London), and the Editor of the *Bankers' Magazine*, are of the former opinion on this point, on the ground that the endorsers *John Smith and Co.*, may not be the Payees, *Messrs. Smith and Co.* There is no legal decision to guide us, and we can rely alone on common sense, and the custom of Bankers. It seems, however, that if this argument were to rule the Practice of Bankers, it would invalidate an endorsement *J. Brown*, on a Cheque payable to *John Brown*, as the endorser might be James, or Joseph, or Jeremiah, and not John, the Payee. The broad test in these matters, however—seeing that Bankers should act amongst themselves, so as to facilitate and not obstruct every day business—is whether the Drawee is himself protected and his customers' interests guarded by law in paying on such endorsements, and we doubt if a Court would decide that an endorsement such as that in question would be an incorrect, irregular, and insufficient discharge.

of law as applies in a per-procuration case. A Cheque drawn payable to **two or more** several individuals must be endorsed severally by each of the parties; but on a Dividend Warrant so drawn the discharge of one of the payees is sufficient. The endorsements of **Companies** and **Corporations** must purport to be by some authorised officer; but it is not the Banker's duty, when such Cheques are presented by a Banker, to acquaint himself with the genuineness of the purported authority. For example, in case of a Cheque payable to a Bank, and endorsed for the Bank "John Brown, pro Mgr.," it does not devolve on the Banker to ascertain that John Brown, or any other signatory, whose name, perhaps, he never heard, is a person duly authorized to sign for the Bank. But it would be his duty to satisfy himself as to the endorser's powers in a case where a Cheque is presented for payment through a channel that he is unacquainted with, or under circumstances reasonably to excite suspicion. This does not apply where a Cheque payable to a Company, purports to be endorsed by a quorum of Directors, or in the case of a Corporation, by a member or members under the Corporate Seal. An endorsement purporting to be by an **Agent** of the Payee has been held to be a sufficient discharge. An endorsement, merely by way of acknowledgment to the Drawee, of the receipt of the amount in no way creates a liability on the part of such endorser. But where a Cheque is endorsed by the Payee and transferred for value, and endorsed by the transferee, and dishonoured, the transferee's recourse is against the previous endorser. A Cheque to "bearer" passes by delivery, as one to "order" does by the endorsement of the Payee.

IV.

CROSSED CHEQUES.

A CHEQUE is said to be crossed when it bears on the face two parallel transverse lines. When it bears the parallel lines only, or the lines with the words "and Company," or some legible contraction of those words between them, it is said to be **crossed generally.** When within the lines it bears the name of a Bank, it is said to be **crossed specially.** If a Cheque is an open Cheque a crossing can be added by any *bona fide* holder. Crossing operates as a direction to the Banker on whom the Cheque is drawn, to pay the amount in case of a Cheque crossed generally to a Banker only, and in the case of a Cheque crossed specially to the Banker designated in the crossing only. The development of the system and principles of Crossed Cheques will be readily understood from a brief history of the legislation on the question.

The Origin of Crossed Cheques is to be found in the custom, which obtained amongst those Bankers who were members of the London Clearing House, of writing or stamping the name of their Bank across the face of the Cheque for purposes of identification and reference. The custom came to be regarded as a safeguard, as it operated by way of notice to the Bank on whom the Cheque was drawn that it was the property of the Bank whose name was across the face of it; and it thus came to be recognised as the Drawee-Bank's duty to negotiate it for that Bank and for no other. After a while the London merchants and large firms adopted the plan, and crossed the Cheques they sent for lodgment with the name of the Bank where the lodgment was to be made.

The next development was the introduction by the merchants, when Cheques became a more general mode of payment, of the practice of crossing the Cheques which they remitted to their friends and creditors with the name of that creditor's or friend's Banker, and where the name was not known, of crossing it with two parallel tranverse lines, with the words "and Company" between them, to enable the parties to whom the Cheque was remitted to adopt the safeguard of putting their Banker's name between the lines. The words "and Company" were used, presumably, because the generality of country Banks were, at the period referred to, private firms or companies. If the person in whose favour the Cheque was drawn inserted his Banker's name in the crossing, it was an indication to the Bank on whom the Cheque was drawn that the amount was to be paid only to such Banker whose name was therein, and if no Banker's name was inserted, and that merely the words "and Company," or a contraction of them, were between the lines, it was regarded as an indication to the Drawee to pay the amount to a Banker only, as it was evident that such was the intention of the Drawer. The object and effect of this safeguard are evident. However, where the Drawer had inserted the Payee's Banker's name in the crossing, it was found that such Payee could not transfer the Cheque to a party having a different Banker, and hence it became competent for a subsequent holder to erase the Banker's name with which it was originally crossed, provided he substituted the name of another. This course was, however, found to be inconvenient, and it led to the general crossing "and Company" being adopted more usually; as thus, without obliteration or erasion, the Cheque's transferability was not destroyed, and the Payee was apparently protected.

It is to be understood that this custom of crossing, at this period, found no recognition in the Statute Law. On the contrary when the Courts came to deal with the subject it was decided (in the case of *Bellamy* v. *Majoribanks*,) that the crossing of a Cheque *payable to bearer*, with a Banker's name, did not restrict its negotiability to that Banker—that in fact it did not restrain its negotiability at all, as it was no more than a mere memorandum to the holder that he was to present it through that Banker; and to the Drawee it was but a mere direction to pay it to such Banker, but a direction which it was not legally incumbent on him to follow, and which his not following was no more than a proof of negligence to which no penalty attached, and for which, even in case of fraud, he, the Banker on whom it was drawn, could not be held liable. To make the Drawee liable in such a case, a specific agreement between him and the Drawer of the Cheque to the effect that such crossing with a Banker's name would be regarded as a direction to pay only to that Banker, was necessary.

The effect of this judgment was the passing of the 19 and 20 Victoria, c. 25, which briefly enacted that the crossing of a Cheque, whether payable to bearer or order, should be a direction to the Banker on whom it was drawn to pay it to a Banker only. When the enactment came to be considered by the Judges, it was held that it affected the Drawee-Banker only where the crossing appeared on the face of the Cheque when it was presented for payment, and that he was not liable for mispayment when the crossing had been obliterated; and there was no law to prevent any person, whether a fraudulent holder or not, erasing or obliterating any cross-writing on a Cheque. This judgment, which was pronounced by the Common Pleas and confirmed by the Court of Exchequer, amounted to a ruling that the crossing was not a material or integral portion of the Cheque, but a mere addition, which any person so disposed could remove with impunity.

In consequence of this case it was enacted (21 and 22 Victoria, c. 79, s. 1), in 1858 that the crossing was to be deemed a material part of the Cheque, and the Banker on whom it was drawn should not pay it to other than the Banker whose name was so crossed, and any person obliterating, altering, or adding to, a crossing on a Cheque or Draft, with intent to defraud, shall be guilty of felony. A *bonâ fide* holder of a Cheque crossed with the words "and Company," or any abbreviation thereof, could, however, add the name of a Banker ; or a holder of an uncrossed Cheque or Draft might cross it, either specially or generally. But (by the 4th Section) it is provided that a Banker (unless he has acted *mala fide* or been guilty of negligence) shall not be in any way responsible, or incur any liability, in paying to other than a Banker a Cheque bearing an altered or obliterated or added-to crossing, if the Cheque does not at the time when it is presented for payment plainly appear to be or to have been, crossed, or to have been obliterated, added-to, or altered.

It was imagined that the law on the subject was set at rest and permanently defined in these Statutes and judgments of the Courts, and, consequently, the public were somewhat astonished by the further definition of the law, which the celebrated case of *Smith* v. *Union Bank of London* occasioned. The facts of this case were as follows : A firm named Mills and Co., being indebted to Smith (the Plaintiff), gave him a Cheque on the Union Bank of London (the Defendants) in his favour, and payable to his order. Smith duly received it, and endorsed it, and crossed it with the name of his Bankers, the London and County Bank. The Cheque was stolen from Smith, but it ultimately came into the possession, *bonâ fide* and for value received, of a person who was a customer of the London and Westminster Bank. He, in the ordinary course, paid it into his Bankers, the London and Westminster Bank, who presented it duly to the Drawees, the Union Bank of London—the Defendants. The Union Bank of London paid it, although, being crossed to the London and County Bank, it was presented by the London and Westminster Bank. Smith, the original Payee, from whom it was stolen, then brought this action against the Union Bank of London, treating himself as the rightful owner of the Cheque, and charging the defendants with having wrongfully converted it, and claiming the amount on the ground that the defendants had infringed the 21 and 22 Vic., c. 79, above quoted, which enacted that the Banker upon whom a crossed Cheque is drawn shall not pay it to any other than the Banker named in the crossing; and that by their infringement of the Act he (Smith) had suffered loss. The action was tried in the Court of Queen's Bench, in April, 1875, and judgment was given in favour of the defendants. It came on for appeal subsequently and the decision of the Court below was confirmed — Lord Cairns pronouncing the judgment of the Court. The judgment rested chiefly on the ground that the right of action lay not in Smith but in the Drawers of the Cheque, to whom alone the Union Bank was answerable. Smith had endorsed in blank the Cheque—a very material point — and thereby had made it a negotiable instrument payable to bearer, and it does not appear he took the precaution of acquainting the Drawers—Mills & Co.—that it had left his possession fraudulently, and requiring them to stop payment of it at the Drawees and give him a duplicate. The right of action against the Union Bank lay only with the Drawers of the Cheque. They could refuse to have their account debited with the amount of a document which was irregularly paid through the oversight or negligence of the Drawee. But again, the mere fact alone of the payment of the Cheque could not in itself damnify or cause a loss to Smith, because the holder could have easily devised means o have it passed through the crossees, the London and County Bank, to the Drawees, who would be bound to pay it, or stand the liability of an action by the Drawers for dishonouring their draft. The crossing operated only as a caution to the Drawees to be circumspect in the paying of it; they paid it to the London and Westminster Bank—through oversight, no doubt—but their doing so, did not, in itself, necessarily inflict a direct loss on Smith.

This judgment caused the passing of a further enactment on the subject of Crossed Cheques—39 & 40 Vic., c. 81, known as "The Crossed Cheques Act, 1876,"—and it is supposed to have settled the law on the question,—as it doubtless has, until some other unforeseen decision or unexpected exposition of the existing Acts. This Act defines a general crossing and a special crossing, and creates a new species of crossing which is to be effected by the addition to either a general or a special crossing of the words "**not negotiable.**" The 4th section explains general and special crossings. It enacts: "Where a " Cheque bears across its face an addition of the words 'and " Company,' or any abbreviation thereof, between two parallel "transverse lines, or of two parallel transverse lines simply, " and either with or without the words 'not negotiable,' that " addition shall be deemed a crossing, and the Cheque shall be "deemed to be crossed generally. Where a Cheque bears "across its face an addition of the name of a Banker, either "with or without the words 'not negotiable,' that addition shall "be deemed a crossing, and the Cheque shall be deemed to be "crossed specially, and to be crossed to that Banker." The 12th section enacts: "A person taking a Cheque crossed "generally or specially, bearing in either case the words 'not "'negotiable,' shall not have, and shall not be capable of giving, "a better title to the Cheque than that which the person from "whom he took it had. But a Banker who has in good faith "and without negligence received payment for a customer of a "Cheque crossed generally or specially to himself, shall not, in "case the title to the Cheque prove defective, incur any "liability to the true owner of the Cheque by reason only of "having received such payment."*

* The construction of sect. 12 was brought before the Court of Common Pleas Division in the case *Matthiessen and Buck* v. *The London and County Banking Company* (41 L. T. Rep. N. S. 35) upon a demurrer to the statement of defence. It was an action by the Payee of three Crossed Cheques against the defendants for a conversion by receiving the proceeds of three Crossed Cheques which had come into their hands with forged endorsements. The statement of claim alleged that the Cheques in question were given to one of their travellers by certain customers of the plaintiffs for goods; that they were drawn payable to plaintiffs or their order; that two of them were crossed with the words "and Co."; that they were stolen by their traveller, who forged their name on the back of each of them, and were then paid into defendants' bank; that defendants received payment of them from the Bankers on whom they were drawn, and that by so receiving and dealing with the said Cheques the defendants converted them to their own use, and wrongfully deprived the plaintiffs of the possession of the same, and that by the Act they could not have a better title to them than the person from whom they were received, *i.e.*, the traveller who forged the endorsements, and obtained the amount by fraud. The defendants relied for protection on sect. 12 of the Crossed Cheques Act, 1876, above set out. In the course of the argument the plaintiffs contended that the protection given to Bankers by sect. 12 is only given with respect to Cheques bearing on them

The development in the legal aspect of Crossed Cheques has thus been very gradual, and each successive enactment has been the result of a legal judgment which showed that the law was not in accord with the views accepted by the general public. The habit of crossing was in vogue for many years before it obtained legal recognition. The **first Act** was passed in 1856, and it was to the effect that a Cheque or Draft crossed with a Banker's name was payable only to, or through such

the words "not negotiable," and that the section had therefore no application to the case before the court. "It is true," they said, "that this condition is not expressly mentioned in the latter part of the section on which the defendants rely, but the first part of the same section deals with Cheques crossed generally or specially, bearing in either case the words 'not negotiable.' Then comes the word 'but,' introducing the provision which was intended to afford a protection to Bankers. This word 'but' shows that the two clauses of the section deal with the same subject matter. The second clause is in the nature of a provision, and must be confined to those Cheques only with which the first clause deals." The plaintiffs contended this construction would violate the plain language of the Act, and this was the opinion of the court. In giving judgment for the defendant, Mr. Justice Grove said—"Taking these two clauses as they "appear, by the plain reading and grammatical construction, they apply to "different states of things. The first clause applies to Cheques limited by "the words 'not negotiable'; the second clause, omitting these words, gives "protection to Bankers with regard to Cheques crossed generally or specially. "The second clause says nothing about the words 'not negotiable.'" With regard to the effect sought to be put on the word "but," he observed that to adopt the construction of the defendants "would be forcing the "words of the Statute, and virtually making a new section by interpolating "words into the second clause which do not occur there, and which he could "not suppose to have been otherwise than intentionally omitted. . . . "It is not irrational to suppose that the Legislature wished to give to collect-"ing Bankers that protection which it was supposed that a previous Statute "(16 & 17 Vic., c. 59, s. 19) had already given, but which turned out in "fact, according to the decision in *Ogden* v. *Benas*, not to have been given." Mr. Justice Lindley's judgment was to the same effect. He thought that "but" is far too loose a word to control the plain meaning of a section of an Act of Parliament.

Banker. This Act was the result of the judgment in the case of *Carlin* v. *Ireland*, delivered on 12th December, 1855, which declared the law to be, that a general crossing did not affect the negotiability of a cheque, and that any person taking such crossed Cheque, *bonâ fide*, for value, was entitled to payment by the Drawees. **The next enactment** on the subject was with a view to remedy the defect which the case of *Simmonds* v. *Taylor* discovered. In this case the crossing had been obliterated, and there was no remedy against the offender, and consequently, in 1858, it was enacted that the crossing was a material part of the Cheque, and a fraudulent alteration or obliteration was constituted a felony. And **finally**, owing to the decision in *Smith* v. *Union Bank of London*, the Act of 1876 was passed, defining the two forms of crossing in existence: a *general* crossing (which consists of two parallel lines alone, or with the words "and Company," or any abbreviation thereof, between them), and a *special* crossing (which consists of a name of a Bank between the lines); and creating the new species, "not negotiable." The words "not negotiable" do not signify that the Cheque cannot be negotiated or transferred; they operate merely as a warning or direction to any person who receives it, that he, even though he should have received it for value and *bonâ fide*, has yet not any better title to it than any previous holder, negotiator, or transferee. Thus, if a Cheque so crossed be stolen by A., it is obvious that the wrong-doer has no *bonâ fide* title to it, and should he negotiate the Cheque with a further party B., that further party B., even though he receives it for value, *bonâ fide*, and without any notice or suspicion that it has been wrongfully obtained, can yet have no better title to it—no truer ownership in it, than A. who obtained it fraudulently, and who has therefore no title at all to it.

It is always to be borne in mind, however, that a Banker, although he may have made payment of a "not negotiable" Cheque drawn upon himself, which some previous transferror has wrongfully obtained, is, nevertheless, protected, unless fraud, complicity, or negligence, can be brought home to him. The remedy against the Banker is, in all cases, in the hands of the Drawer of the Cheque, and not of the Payee or any holder; for as has been said, the Banker has no privity except with the Drawer. There is, however, an exception to this rule, that the Drawer *only* can have a right of action against the Drawee. A Cheque is an order payable on demand *without acceptance*, but if the Banker on whom it is drawn, initial it for future payment, such an initialing is held to amount to an acceptance, and the holder has a remedy against the Banker in case of dishonour or want of funds of the Cheque so initialled when presented at the appointed time.

V.

PRESENTATION, PAYMENT, AND DISHONOUR, OF CHEQUES.

Time of Presentation.—The strict legal rule as to the time of presentation of a Cheque is, that it must be presented as soon as possible after it has been issued. The ordinary rule is that it must be presented within a reasonable time, and as circumstances contribute to define what this is, the question whether the presentation has been effected within a reasonable time is, in a law suit, one for the jury. The holder of a Cheque defers its presentation for payment at his own risk. This does not convey that the Drawer's liability is voided by any such delay, for unless presentation is delayed for six years or more (when the Statute of Limitations terminates the liability), there is remedy against the Drawer by the Payee or any lawful holder, by an action at law for the amount; but a Banker will not pay a Cheque, presentation of which has been delayed for a longer period than six calendar months. It means that in the event of the Drawer's death or bankruptcy, the holder may not be allowed to claim under the estate, as he had been negligent in obtaining payment during the lifetime or solvency of the Drawer. Again, in case of the insolvency of the Banker on whom the Cheque is drawn, where the Holder of a Cheque did not present it within a reasonable time, the Drawer would be discharged and the Holder would have no recourse to him, or to any previous Endorser, for the amount. By the Law

Merchant and the custom of Bankers, a Cheque becomes **stale** after six months from the date of issue, and payment, as has been said, is refused by the Drawee, on the grounds that it is a Stale Cheque. The reason of non-payment of a Stale Cheque is, that the delay in presentation raises a presumption of defect or infirmity of the Presenter's title, and the Banker is entitled to act on the doubt this presumption creates. If, however, it is proven to a Banker that a *stale* Cheque is *bonâ fide*, *e.g.*, that it is presented by the Payee in person, who explains the delay satisfactorily, and that there are sufficient funds to pay it, the Banker is empowered to honour it, and protected in so doing.

A Banker (A.) is not entitled to **delay presentation** of a Cheque on another Bank (B.) lodged by a Customer. The custom of Bankers decides what would or would not be a delay; and in case the Banker (A.) has been guilty of negligence in presenting the Cheque, and that the Drawer die, or be in default; or that the Drawee fail, and the Customer who lodged it is damnified by such default or failure, the Banker (A.) is liable. Presentation by post, or through one's own Banker is a good presentation. Where the holder is a third party he must not fail to present the Cheque within reasonable time in order to maintain an action against the primary Payee in case of dishonour. Likewise, failure on the part of the last holder to make due presentation, will absolve the previous endorsers from liability. The legal rules of presentation have regard chiefly to the failure of the Drawees, and most of the cases are on this point. In all instances a Cheque must be presented on business days - (not holidays*)—and during business hours, in order to be a valid presentation.

* The Bank Holidays Act (25th May, 1871), *created* the following holidays for English and Irish Banks :—Easter Monday, the Monday in Whitsun week, the first Monday in August, and the 26th day of December if a week-

Payment of Cheques.—In practice, a Banker generally extends to the Presenter of a Cheque the courtesy of consulting his wishes as to the manner in which he desires to receive payment, and acceding to these wishes if practicable. But such a course is entirely a courtesy on the part of the Banker, because his legal duty is discharged if he makes or offers payment in what is known as Legal Tender. **Legal Tender** is defined by the Coinage Act, 1870 (33 Vic., c. 10, s. 4). It consists of Bronze to the limit of one shilling, Silver Coins to the limit of forty shillings, and Gold to any extent. In England payment of sums over £5 can be legally tendered in Bank of England Notes, except by the Bank of England itself (3 & 4 William 4th, c. 98, s. 6). But special Acts declare that Bank of England Notes are *not* to be deemed legal tender in Scotland or Ireland. If a Banker pays a Cheque **in forged or worthless Notes,** or in **spurious or counterfeit Coin,** and that the person to whom the payment is made, accepts such Notes or Coin and makes no objection at the time of the payment, he has, upon discovery of the worthless nature of the Notes or Coin, no recourse against the Banker, except he can prove fraud on the Banker's part, or prove that he (the Banker) was cognisant of the fact that the Notes or Coin he disbursed were worthless.

If a Payee consents to accept payment in certain Bank Notes, other than the issue of the paying Bank, and that the

---

day. And a subsequent Act (13th May, 1875) provided that "whenever "the 26th day of December shall fall on a Sunday, the Monday immediately "next following, that is to say, the 27th December, shall be a holiday." Christmas Day and Good Friday have always been holidays. The Queen's Birthday (24th May), was observed as a Bank holiday in England and Ireland, before the passing of the above Act. It is still a holiday in the Isle of Man.

Bank whose notes he has thus accepted, stop payment, even on the following day, he cannot hold the Banker from whom he received and accepted the notes liable; nor can he compel him to change them for other notes of full value, as he took them voluntarily, and at his own risk. As in Ireland and Scotland, the only Legal Tender for sums beyond £2 in silver and 1s. in bronze, is gold, and a Payee is entitled to legal tender; therefore, if he dispenses with the legal tender and elects to accept payment in Bank Notes of any establishment, he does so entirely at his own peril and must abide the consequences. If he receives **gold** in payment, he is bound to satisfy himself of its currency and genuineness immediately on payment, and if he neglect so to do, the Banker is free from any liability under a subsequent discovery of a spurious coin. The Banker is bound to pay the Cheques drawn on him in the order in which they are presented—the only **priority** is the priority of presentation: presenting for initialing or acceptance, is a presentation for payment, because the promise or undertaking to pay amounts to a present withdrawal of funds from the Drawer's account.

Once a payment is tendered by a Banker, and accepted by the Presenter of the Cheque, **the money when paid** becomes the Presenter's property and ceases to belong to the Banker. So that should a Banker pay a Cheque drawn by A., and immediately after payment discover that A. had not sufficient funds, or that the Cheque had been stopped, or that it was specially crossed, or some such circumstance—nevertheless the money paid having entered into the possession of the Payee cannot be recalled by the Banker, even though the party receiving the payment had not moved from the Bank counter; but if the Banker should discover that he had **overpaid** the Presenter of the Cheque, he could recall the money to the extent of the overpayment. If, however, a Banker takes from his Customer in lodgment, a Cheque drawn on himself by another Customer, for which Cheque there are not sufficient funds, the non-refusal by the Banker of the Cheque is not a guaranty to pay the amount, and he can return it unpaid on the following day to the Customer who lodged it, provided he (the Banker) did not receive funds from the Drawer before it was returned dishonoured and apply them in payment of subsequently presented Cheques. If it is a Banker's regulation to require his Customer to draw Cheques exclusively on the **engraved or printed form** of Cheque which he supplies, and that the Customer is made aware either expressly or constructively of the regulation, the Banker is justified in refusing to pay orders drawn otherwise than on the form. The Bank of England, for example, will not honour Cheques which are drawn on a form other than that supplied by the Bank, and the restriction, being of a protective nature, should be enforced by all Bankers.* If payment be refused on this ground, the reason should be explicitly stated. If a Banker, or any authorised official of a Bank, or any official purporting to be authorised, should **initial a Cheque** for subsequent payment—that is to say, where another Banker presents a Cheque avowedly to be marked for payment upon the following day, the Drawee is bound by the initials. He is bound also by a verbal or written promise to pay. Such marking or initialing, or promising, though it does not amount to a legal acceptance, nevertheless, by the custom of Bankers, which is a portion of the Law

* The following notice is printed on the covers of the Cheque Books issued by some Banks:—" In consequence of forgeries and other frauds it is "particularly requested that under no circumstances whatsoever are Cheques "to be given to unknown parties in exchange for cash; that no blank "Cheques be given to strangers upon any plea; and that no Cheque be "drawn on blank paper or on any form other than that supplied by the Bank. "The Bank does not undertake to pay any Cheques so drawn without "special advice from the Drawer."

Merchant, it operates to bind the Banker who so marks or promises to pay the amount on the following day. But if the holder neglects to present the Cheque so marked on the ensuing day, he is guilty of unreasonable delay, and the Banker's engagement to pay is rescinded by such delay. Even should the Drawer die after the initialing or promising, and before presentation for payment, though death under ordinary circumstances invalidates a Cheque, yet the Banker who has initialed it is bound to pay it, and protected in so doing.

A Cheque is transferable by delivery, and *bonâ-fide* delivery of it passes the rights and equities in it. A Cheque is not money; but the amount of unnegotiated Cheques, if in order, may be admitted as money to Probate or Letters of Administration of the effects of a *bonâ-fide* holder. As a Cheque is not money, a Banker is not bound to surrender, or justified in surrendering, a Bill entrusted to him for collection, unless the Cheque is drawn on himself and he has funds of the Drawer to pay it, in which case it is equivalent to money. If a Banker surrender a Bill or documents upon a Cheque, he does so at his own risk; and if the Cheque is received from a person other than the Drawer, it is questionable whether he would have recourse except to the Drawer, in the event of dishonour.

Stopping Payment of Cheques.—As a Cheque is an order to a Banker to pay, the maker of that order, *i.e.*, the Drawer, can of course rescind it, and instruct the Banker not to pay a certain Cheque which has been issued by him. This act of countermanding is called **stopping the payment.** The order to stop payment is an executory order. It should be in writing and signed, and it is as binding on a Banker as the order to pay; so that if a Banker pay a Cheque drawn on him, after the payment thereof has been stopped, he is not discharged, and the Drawer's account cannot be debited with the amount. A Drawer is entitled to stop his Cheque if he wishes, and he is not bound to give the Banker his reasons for so doing. The ordinary motives for stopping payment of a Cheque are, that the Cheque has been lost, or stolen; or fraudulently obtained; or obtained on certain conditions which are unfulfilled or violated. If payment of a Cheque is refused to the Payee on the ground that it has been stopped, the Payee's remedy is solely against the Drawer, who can remove the stop and withdraw his countermanding order.

Dishonour.—As a Banker is said to honour a Cheque when he obeys the order or command of the Drawer to pay the amount specified on demand, he is said to dishonour it when he refuses to obey. The motive for refusal may be some irregularity in the Cheque itself, such, for instance, as an unconfirmed alteration, a variance in the Drawer's signature, or a post-dating; or it may be because the Cheque is incomplete, by not being dated for instance; or it may have been mutilated; or the Banker may refuse payment because the Cheque is crossed. But what is generally understood by the expression **dishonouring a Cheque** is the refusal to pay the amount, because the Banker has not sufficient funds of the Drawer's in his possession to enable him to pay it in full. A Banker is not empowered to make a **part payment** on a Cheque: for instance, if A. draws a Cheque for £50, and his balance at the Drawee's is but £30, the Drawee is not entitled to pay the £30 on account.

It has been argued, that a Banker who did so pay on account the Drawer's balance in his hands, that balance being insufficient for the full discharge of the amount of the Cheque, would be protected in any action by the Drawer on the payment; but it appears to be the better opinion that, in adopting such a course, the Banker was not complying with the Drawer's order, which was to pay £50; and there is no middle course between compliance and non-compliance. Neither is a Banker empowered to disclose to the Presenter the balance at the credit of the Drawer's account in his hands, thereby to enable the Presenter to lodge to the Drawer's credit the amount deficient, and so provide sufficient funds to meet the Cheque and obtain payment. Making a part payment on a Cheque, as above, would be a disclosure of the Customer's account, and, on no occasion or under no circumstances—except as a witness in some of Her Majesty's Courts of Law or Equity—can a Banker disclose the state of his Customer's account. If he should do so, and that Customer is thereby damnified, an action lies against the Banker by the Customer.

A Banker is bound to give verbally a reason for dishonouring his Customer's Cheque. Merely saying he **cannot pay** it, is not a sufficient answer to a Presenter. Nor is the answer "**present again**" (which some Banks are in the habit of making), a sufficient answer, unless the reason for requiring the future presentation is given, as for instance, that the Banker has not had time to realize the funds the Drawer had lodged, which is a justifiable reason for refusing to pay. The usual words of dishonour are "**Refer to Drawer.**" These generally mean that, as the Banker has not sufficient money of the Drawer's to pay the amount, the holder must present it to the Drawer for redemption. "Refer to Drawer" is usually equivalent to saying there are not enough funds to meet the Cheque, though this is sometimes more plainly expressed by "**not Sufficient Funds,**" or shortly, "**N. S.,**" which is also a general dishonour. This implies that the Drawer has some funds at the Banker's; whereas "**no funds**" and "**no account**" are unequivocal forms. "Refer to Drawer" is a comprehensive answer of dishonour, and may mean merely that there is an irregularity in the Cheque, or that the payment has been stopped ; it does not *necessarily* convey or imply that there are insufficient funds, though it is the answer usually given in case of absence of funds or of credit.

If a Banker **wrongfully dishonour** his Customer's Cheque, *i.e.*, refuse to pay it while there are sufficient realized moneys of the Drawer in his hands—no matter if such refusal arise through some error in the Bank Books, whereby the Drawer's balance is erroneously stated,—an action by the Drawer will lie against the Banker, and damages be obtainable. Dishonour is, *per se*, a wrong to the Drawer, and, in case of its being wrongful, entitles him to damages in an action against the Banker. But special damages must be proven. The extent of these damages is therefore gauged by the injury done to the Plaintiff's credit and commercial and financial reputation. A Banker is not bound to give notice to the Drawer of a Cheque upon him that the Cheque has been refused payment, for non-compliance with the order to pay is sufficient notice. It is stated by Mr. Macleod that, if through the wrongful dishonour of a Cheque the Drawer becomes bankrupt, his assignees in bankruptcy have a right of action against the Bank. If a Cheque is imperfect, *i.e.*, that a material portion is **mutilated**—even though the pieces be fastened together—the Banker is bound to refuse to negotiate it, because the presumption is that the fact of its having been torn is *prima facie* evidence that the Drawer intended to cancel it. If a Banker pay such a mutilated Cheque on him, and that the Drawer or rightful owner is damnified by such payment (even assuming the mutilation to be unintentional), an action will lie against the Banker for the amount. A Banker, however, is justified in refusing payment of a Customer's Cheque, even though he have funds to pay it, if he have positive knowledge that it is for an **illegal and fraudulent purpose**, such as the corrupt procurement of a government appointment. Bankers should in all cases keep a record of the Cheques they dishonour, in order to be in a position to refute a false allegation by the Drawers of such Cheques, that they were wrongfully dishonoured. The **death** of a Drawer is reason for non-payment of his Cheque. A Banker cannot pay the Cheque of a Customer who has since died, if he has knowledge of the death, unless, as has been stated, he has previously initialed it for payment. In this case the initialing amounts at the time to a withdrawal from the Drawer's account of funds to the amount of the Cheque so initialed. Upon the death of an individual, his personalty immediately vests in his executors or administrators, and the Banker is accountable to them for the moneys of the deceased. But the death of an Endorser does not affect the negotiability of a Cheque, for the Banker has privity only with the Drawer. The **Bankruptcy** of the Drawer is also reason sufficient for non-payment of his Cheque; because on a person's Bankruptcy all his property vests, in the first instance, in his creditors, and subsequently in trustees or assignees, and his Cheque, if paid, would be paid to the detriment of creditors. The Banker, however, must have knowledge of the Death or Bankruptcy of his customer. The knowledge may be by formal notice, in which case it is an *actual knowledge;* or, by general report, as in a case such as that of the death of a notable individual, in which case the knowledge would be assumed against him, and it would rest with him to prove that he was not aware of what was a common topic of news. An announcement of death in the newspapers is sufficient notice to the Banker; and if such announcement is *untrue,* the Banker is protected if he acted upon it *bonâ-fide* in belief of its truth. If a Cheque be notified to the Banker

The Law and Practice of Banking. 171

on whom it is drawn, and that after notification, and before presentation, the Drawer die, the holder is entitled to payment.

Cheques Incapable of Dishonour.—The Cheque Bank.—An entirely new principle in banking was introduced in 1873 by an establishment called "The Cheque Bank." It was formed "to carry on business not in opposition to, but in "co-operation with, existing Bankers. It was to undertake no "financial business, to discount no bills, and to allow no in- "terest upon deposits." The principle of its operations was that for every sum lodged with it, a number of Cheques available at most for that amount and for no more would be given to the Depositor. Thus for a lodgment of £100, a party obtained, for instance, one hundred Cheques, each printed and perforated, as being available for one pound or under. The Cheques could be filled in with the name of the payee and with the amount, which could not exceed £1. Such instruments would obviously be a great convenience to those who had numerous small payments and remittances to make, and fraud was precluded by the form and structure of the Cheque. Furthermore, there was no possibility of dishonour, and the documents could be accepted and negotiated without fear of risk; for, should the Cheques be filled in for Sums under that for which they were available, the balance then lying at the credit of the depositor was not refunded to him until all the Cheques had been presented and paid. There were thus no overdrafts, and no losses incurred. The profits of the Bank were to be derived from the interest on the securities representing its capital and on the balance of deposits in its hands. It issues guaranteed Cheques for even amounts, from £1 to £10, to the full amount of every deposit lodged.* The

* The same principle of issuing guaranteed cheques for amounts of from £1 to £10 was also adopted by the Commercial Bank of Manchester, which was founded in 1875, and has since gone into liquidation.

Bank incurred exceptionally heavy outlay in advertising and other similar expenses during the first few years of its existence, and did not meet with support sufficient to cover them. It was, therefore, reconstructed in 1876, since which time it has progressed somewhat more satisfactorily, although it has not yet realised the hopes of the Founders. The apparent reason why the Cheque Bank has not obtained that wide support and exhibited that progress to which it seems to be entitled, is that in the event of the loss and non-presentation of any of the Cheques the amount of such lost Cheque was forfeited by the Depositor. The Cheque would be outstanding, and, as long as it was outstanding, the utmost amount it could represent would be retained by the Bank.

Lost Cheque.—If a Cheque be lost, the Drawer can be compelled to give a duplicate, under proper and sufficient indemnity.

Knowledge of Fraud on part of Customers.—If a Banker has actual knowledge, that his Customer has drawn a Cheque for a fraudulent purpose, he is not only entitled to refuse to honour it, but also liable if he does honour it, because in honouring it he would be abetting a fraud. But the knowledge must not be of a speculative kind, it must be such as does not necessitate any enquiry into the action of the Customer, for a Banker is not entitled to enquire; and if he is without such positive knowledge, he is bound to perform his obligations to the Drawer and cannot refuse to pay his Cheque. A Banker cannot, knowingly, hold money to be disposed of for **illegal or immoral purposes.** If he assents to so hold money, which he knows to be illegally applied, he can be indicted for conspiracy.

Criminal Offences.—If a person draw a Cheque on a

Bank where he has no account, and obtain money or goods for uch Cheque, and that the reason given for the dishonour be "*no account*," the Drawer of it can be indicted by the Holder for obtaining money (or goods) under false pretences—the false pretence being, that he had an account at the Bank. It is not a false pretence, however, if the Drawer really have an account but not sufficient funds, because he can plead that he expected to have funds, &c. To obtain money on a forged Cheque, knowing it to be forged, is to obtain it under a false pretence. To write the endorsement of a Payee to whose order a Cheque is made payable, with the intent to defraud, is forgery. By Statute, it is forgery to alter the crossing, as it is to alter fraudulently any material part of a Cheque.

Paid Cheques.—A Cheque when paid must be cancelled by the Drawee under a penalty of £50 (by the Stamp Act, 1870). It is the property of the Drawer, though it remains in the possession of the Banker on whom it is drawn, until it is delivered to him. As the Cheque is to the Banker the proof that he has paid the money, and is both his authority to debit the Drawer's account and evidence of his having done so, and as, in case of overdraft, it is his right of action to recover the debt, he is not bound to surrender it to the Drawer without a written acknowledgment (*see page* 178). Some Banks return to the Customer his paid Cheques at the termination of each half year when the Bank's accounts are made up and the Books closed, obtaining a receipt acknowledging the correctness of the balance as stated in the Customer's pass-book, and also acknowledging the receipt of the paid Cheques. Others pursue the course of surrendering the paid Cheques at those intervals during the progress of the Customer's account when he obtains his pass-book, written up to date, and of requiring his initials by way of a receipt for the Cheques paid during the time embraced in this periodical writing up. If on this periodical delivery the Bank obtained from the Customer a written acknowledgment that the Cheques surrendered were correctly debited to his account, it would be a safe and serviceable proceeding, for thereby the Bank would not only obtain a concurrent ratification of its book-keeping, but it would get rid of those vouchers, the accumulation of which is so undesirable. But, when the Customer's initials in the pass-book are only by way of acknowledgment of the receipt of such a *number* of paid vouchers, it cannot be considered a perfect system.

The Cheques, when paid, are to the Drawer *prima facie* proof of payment to his Creditor, the Payee, if endorsed by him. But it is only a proof of *payment*, and not a sufficient or final proof of a *debt*.

Banker's Books as Evidence.—Formerly (in compliance with the rule of Law that where primary evidence was obtainable it alone would be admitted in Court), in order to prove an entry in a Banker's Ledger, the Book itself should be produced. The manifest inconvenience and inexpedience of this course was obviated by an Act, passed in 1878 (amending one of 1876), through the exertions of Sir John Lubbock, to the effect that a copy of an entry in a Banker's Book, verified by an authorised official of the Bank, shall be received in evidence. And the Act has since been so construed that such copy is evidence even against a person not a Customer of the Bank from whose Books the copy has been made.

VI.

PASS BOOK—OVERDRAWN CURRENT ACCOUNT—RIGHT TO SUE ON CHEQUES.

Pass Book.—THE part occupied by a Pass Book in Banking practice is thus exhaustively defined by Grant:—" A " book called a *pass book*, is delivered by the Bankers to the " Customer, in which at the head of the first page and there " only, the Bankers by the name of their firm are described as " the Debtors, and the Customer as the Creditor in the ac- " count; on the Debtor side are entered all sums paid to or " received by the Bankers on account of the Customer, and " on the Credit side all sums paid to him or on his account; " and these entries being summed up at the bottom of each " page, the amount of each, or the balance between them is " carried over to the next folio without further mention of the " names of the parties, until the book being full, it becomes " necessary to deliver a fresh one to the Customer. For the " purpose of having the book made-up by the Bankers from " their own books of account, the Customer returns it to them " from time to time; and the proper entries being made by " them up to the day on which it is left for that purpose, they " hand it again to the Customer, who thereupon may examine " it, and if there appears any error or omission, it is his busi- " ness to send it back to be rectified; if he does not, his

"silence is regarded as an admission that the entries are
"correct: but no other settlement, statement or delivery of
"accounts, or any other transaction which can be regarded as
"the closing of an old, or the opening of a new, account,
"or as varying, renewing or confirming (in respect of the
"persons or the parties mutually dealing) the credit given on
"either side, takes place in the ordinary course of business,
"unless when the name or firm of one of the parties is altered,
"and a new account thereupon opened in the new name or
"firm."

An **entry in a Pass Book** of an amount to the credit of the Customer, is evidence, *prima facie*, of such a lodgment having been made, and the entry binds the Banker unless he can prove that it was made in error. The burden of proof will generally lie on the Banker, and the question at issue is one to be decided by the jury. The difficulty of disproving such an entry is apparent, and a verdict may depend on the relative credibility of the plaintiff and defendant. Making a false entry in a Pass Book with the intention to defraud, is forgery, and punishable as such.

Interest on Current Account.—Banks, as a rule, allow interest on the credit balances of their Customers at Deposit rates, when the balance is maintained for a given time at a certain figure, or upon the lowest balance of the period, or upon the average balance—according to the practice of the Bank, or according to special arrangement. In Ireland this practice does not obtain. Generally speaking, however, it is a recognised rule there that all accounts of a charitable or benevolent nature, and those of bodies or societies whose object is to benefit—intellectually, morally, or socially—their members or the public, are accorded the privilege of receiving interest on their daily balances, usually at Deposit rates. Some public accounts, and private accounts which show a continuous very large credit balance, are also favoured, but in these cases it is a matter of arrangement with the Bank and not a recognised right as in the case of charities.

Overdrawn Current Account.—An account is said to be overdrawn when the Account-holder has drawn more than the amount of his balance. The relations between the Banker and his Customer are then reversed, for the Banker becomes the Creditor, and the Customer the Debtor. The remedy for recovery of the amount is simply a common-law action for debt. A Banker, in his own protection, generally requires a deposit of securities or a guaranty sufficient to cover the amount he allows his Customer to overdraw, and he charges interest on the actual daily balance owed. An agreement, express or implied, on the Banker's part, to allow his customer a stated overdraft, is considered as binding on the Banker, unless there is a failure of the conditions under which such agreement was made, or that the aspect of the position and business of the Customer has altered. If securities are deposited with a Banker, and the Customer is permitted to draw against them in the recognised manner, the Banker cannot dishonour his Customer's Cheque which does not overdraw beyond the value of the securities, without giving notice to that effect; unless the Customer by so drawing violate an agreement or understanding, or exceed the limit placed on his overdraft by the Banker.

An **agent** cannot overdraw his principal's account so as to render the principal liable to the Banker, unless knowledge of such overdrawing can be traced to the principal, for knowledge implies consent.

If a Banker, holding **securities** for an overdraft, realise such securities, he is only entitled to the amount due with reasonable simple interest thereon, and any surplus after payment of the amount due to himself, must be held by him for the benefit of the Debtor. In case of overdraft, the interest thereon is computed on the daily balance of the debt. A question arose in one of the Colonies as to whether a Bank was entitled to interest on such a balance, after the death of the Debtor, and was decided in favour of the Bank (S. Australian Bank *v.* Horner). But the right to charge compound interest, *i.e.*, interest on interest already charged, ceases with death of the debtor.

The **Paid Cheques** of an Account-holder who maintains a Credit Balance at his Banker's, belong to the Account-holder, and though he may allow them to be retained by the Banker nevertheless they are in his (the Customer's) constructive possession, as he can claim and obtain them at any time; but, in the case of an overdrawn account, the Banker need not restore the Paid Cheques as long as the Drawer is his Debtor, as they are his vouchers of the payments, and his evidence of the Drawer's indebtednesss; and, in an action for the balance due, are his proof of the debt.

Lodgment for Special Purpose.—If one who is a Debtor on foot of an overdrawn account, give money to the Banker with instructions to apply the amount in payment of specified acceptances falling due, or to obtain a Bank Order, or for any purpose other than the credit of his overdraft, the Banker is bound to apply the money as directed, and he cannot apply it in reduction of the Debtor's overdraft.

Two Accounts.—It has been laid down and can be accepted as law, that where a person has accounts at two branches of the same Bank, one of which accounts is Debtor and the other Creditor, the Manager of the Branch where the Credit Balance is held can refuse to pay a Cheque on such

Credit Balance as long as the Customer is indebted to another branch to the amount of the Credit Balance or more. For this purpose branches of a Bank are considered as the same Bank. Further, by law, the Credit Balance at one branch can be applied in reduction or discharge of the Debit Balance at another branch, even without notice to the Customer.

Right to Sue on a Cheque.—The right to sue on a Cheque is in the Holder of the Cheque. His remedy is against the person from whom he received it; against the previous endorser, if there be such; and if the Holder be the first Payee, against the Drawer. In the case of a **free gift of a Cheque,** however, the Payee, in case of its dishonour, has no action against the Drawer, and cannot enforce the payment of the amount. No right of action against the Banker is in any holder, unless the Banker have actually or constructively promised the Holder to pay the amount to him. If a Cheque is wrongfully dishonoured, the Payee has recourse to the Drawer, and the Drawer only can recover damages from the Banker. The reason of this is, that there is no privity except between the Drawer and Drawee, and the Banker owes no duty to the Payee.

The principle of **privity** is well defined in the legal decisions. In a case where A. lodges a sum of money at a Banker's to be paid in specified portions to B., C., and D., in case the Banker refuse to honour the Cheque of B., C., or D., for payment of the amounts, *they* have no action against him—the right of action is in A. But if the Banker had informed B., C., and D., that he held, at their disposal, the amount lodged by A., this would create a privity, and give them a right of action against him in case of dishonour. **Assent** by a Banker to perform certain duties, although those duties be outside his ordinary business as a Banker, binds him, and in case of failure in the performance he is liable to his Customer. Assent may be either actual or constructive. If a Banker undertake to make investments, or to collect the coupons or interest due on securities deposited with him for safe custody, he is bound to do so, and can be made liable if he neglect and loss ensue.

VII.

BILLS OF EXCHANGE AND PROMISSORY NOTES.

The Chief Business in Banking is lending out a certain proportion of the moneys held on Deposit Receipt and on Current Account. These loans are mostly by way of Bills of Exchange and Promissory Notes, and are called Discounts.

Bills of Exchange are generally believed to have been introduced into Commercial dealings by the Italian Merchants. They were known and in use throughout Europe in the 14th Century, and the origin of them is traced by Montesquieu to the Jews and Lombards, who having been banished from France and England in the 13th Century, invented them as a means of receiving value for the goods and property they had to relinquish in these countries. Blackstone, however, points to their earlier use by the Moguls, and another writer* strives to prove that such an instrument was known to the Athenians. Though there is no reference to them in the Roman code, yet, as we have shown, they appear to have been used by the ancient Romans, but the earliest mention of them in modern times occurs in the middle of the 12th Century. The first case relating to them in the English Law Courts was that of Martin *v.* Boure, decided in the reign of James the First. At this

* Depauw.

period, however, their use was restricted to the purposes of foreign commerce, and as inland bills they did not obtain till the Reign of Charles II. Evelyn, in his Diary, under date May 6th, 1645, being in Rome, writes, "The Bills of Exchange "I took up from my first entering Italy till I went from Rome, "amounted but to 616 *Ducati di Banco.*" The privilege of using Bills of Exchange was then confined to merchants, and there is a record of an old case tried by the Court of King's Bench in the reign of William and Mary, where it was decided that an action on one could not be maintained, because the defendant was a *gentleman* and not a *merchant.* An act of the Scottish Parliament, passed in 1696, placed inland and foreign Bills of Exchange on the same footing; and the advance of commerce, the exigencies of trade, the wants of intertraffic, and the convenience of the people, gradually obliterated all restrictions, and now any person capable of contracting can be a party to such an instrument.

The importance and utility of Bills of Exchange in Commercial transactions are paramount. Blackstone's illustration of the practical advantage of the system is as follows :—Let us suppose that B., residing in Liverpool, wishes to receive £1,000, which awaits his orders in the hands of F. at New York. He applies to D., going from Liverpool to New York, to pay him the above amount, less the usual rate of Discount, and to take his Draft or Bill on F. for the £1,000 payable at sight. Now, this arrangement may, in truth, accommodate both B. and D., for B. receives the amount of his debt on transferring it to D., and D. carries his money across the Atlantic in the shape of a Bill of Exchange, without danger or risk in the transportation, and, on arriving at New York, he presents his Bill to F. and is paid. The Bill of Exchange operates then in this way, that, if *accepted*, it effects a transfer of the right of action, as against F. (the party originally indebted), from B. to D.

A Bill of Exchange is "a document purporting to be an "instrument of pecuniary obligation for value received, and "which is employed for the purpose of settling a debt in a "manner convenient to the parties concerned." It is a negotiable unconditional written order from A. who is called the Drawer, to B. who is called the Drawee, to pay him, or a third party C. who is called the Payee, a stated sum of money specified therein, "absolutely and at all events." A Cheque is legally and technically an inland Bill of Exchange payable on demand; but the Bills of Exchange we now deal with are those which are drawn payable at a future stated time. They differ from Cheques in many respects. A Cheque is due whenever it is presented to the Drawee—a Bill is due on a certain day. The Drawer of a Cheque must have money or credit with the Drawee—the Drawer of a Bill need not. The death of a Drawer of a Cheque rescinds the order to the Drawee to pay—not so with a Bill. The Drawer of a Cheque is not discharged to the Payee by want of presentment of the Cheque to the Drawee—the Drawer of a Bill is discharged. The Drawee of a Bill usually gives an undertaking to pay the Bill when it becomes due—this is effected by his writing his name upon it, and when this is done he is called the **Acceptor** and his act an **Acceptance**;—the Drawee of a Cheque does not accept or undertake to pay the amount drawn on him. A Cheque is due when demanded from the Drawee, but the Drawee of a Bill is allowed three days in addition to the date upon which the Drawer orders him to pay (unless it be stated on the Bill that it is drawn "without grace"); these days are called the **days of grace**, and though originally allowed to the Drawee as a favour, they are now settled as his legal right.

A Bill, like a Cheque, must be dated and located; must have a Drawee; must have the amount of money set out in writing; must be stamped as directed by the Statute. And further, it must be payable "absolutely and at all events," without conditions, and independent of contingencies. It must be payable at a certain time which must inevitably come to pass. For instance, a Bill drawn "three months after the death of A. B." is a good Bill, because its term is one that must be fulfilled. But a Bill drawn "three months after the realization" of certain goods, is not a good Bill, for the realization is but a contingency, and by no means an inevitable occurrence.

A Bill passes by delivery if payable to *bearer*, and by endorsement and delivery if payable to *order;* but whereas the right of action against the Drawee for non-payment in the case of a Cheque lies solely in the Drawer—in the case of a Bill the right of action is alone in the *holder*—but he must be a *boná-fide* holder. A Cheque by being crossed "not negotiable," as has been shown, can be so drawn as to destroy the title of a holder for value, where a previous holder's title has been fraudulent or infirm. But there is no similar provision in respect to the negotiators of Bills of Exchange. A *boná-fide* holder of a Bill can compel payment, no matter what the infirmities in an antecedent holder's title may be. A Bill of Exchange further differs from a Cheque on a Banker, in that if the Drawee, being the Acceptor, pay the amount on an endorsement forged by the Holder, he is not discharged or exonerated, as the Drawee of a Cheque is.

Endorsement.—A Bill is endorsable similarly as a Cheque—in blank or specially—and, as in the case of a Cheque, in the first instance it becomes payable to the bearer—if a *boná-fide* holder; and in the second, only to the special Payee, or to his further order; and it can be endorsed in blank by any further endorsee. The essence of a Bill is, that it is assignable—it is a Bill *of Exchange*—and the assignability is unlimited, just as the assignability of a Cheque is.

A Bill of Exchange is a simple contract; but it differs from all other simple contracts, in that it is assignable, and does not require a **consideration**, as a consideration *prima facie* exists, and is therefore presumed by law until such a presumption is disproved. But if the acceptance is proved to have been for an immoral or illegal consideration, the instrument is void as against the Acceptor. An acceptance for a **gambling debt**, for instance, is for an illegal consideration, and though an innocent Endorsee can recover from the Drawer, he cannot from the Acceptor; and if the Acceptor pay the Bill to the Transferee, he can recover the amount from the Drawer. **Stockjobbing** is a species of gambling, and an acceptance to a Broker for a debt contracted by gambling in Stocks is for an illegal consideration. But *except* in cases of an acceptance for an illegal or immoral consideration, the Acceptor cannot plead in defence to an action by an Endorsee that there was no consideration—that is, that he got no value for the acceptance, and the onus lies on him to prove that the acceptance was actually and absolutely given for an illegal or immoral consideration.

Promissory Notes seem to have had their origin in the "Goldsmiths' Notes," of which mention is made in the Introduction.* They are not as ancient an instrument as Bills of Exchange, and do not seem to have been regarded as a negotiable security until about the middle of the 17th century. And though at that period they were so recognised by the merchants, the Statute Law did not place them on the same footing as Bills of Exchange till Queen Anne's reign (3 & 4

---

* Lord Holt says they were "an invention of the Goldsmiths in Lombard "Street."

Anne, c. 9); and not till the time of Lord Kenyon was it judicially fixed that Promissory Notes, like Bills, should be entitled to the three days' grace.

A Promissory Note, or note of hand, is a writing, wherein the maker, (*i.e.*, the person who signs it) promises to pay a certain person, or his order, or the bearer, a certain stated sum of money, at a certain time, absolutely and at all events. That time may be upon demand, or at sight (which is equivalent to on demand), or upon a specified date, or a specified number of days or months after sight. There are no fixed forms of words in which either a Bill of Exchange or a Promissory Note must be drawn. The usual form of a Promissory Note is as follows :—

[£50.] London, 1st *November*, 1881.

[*Three*] *months (or on demand, or*..............*days after sight)*

I (or we, or we jointly and severally), promise to pay A. B.,

or his order, [*Fifty*] *Pounds Sterling.*

The promissor or promissors sign at the foot. But any writing that contains a promise as above stated is valid in law, and is a legal instrument if duly stamped. In a Promissory Note, the Maker or Promissor occupies the same position in contemplation of the law as does the Acceptor in a Bill of Exchange —that is to say, he is the *primary* Debtor, and all the other parties are but collaterally liable—that is, liable in the event of the Promissor's default. A note drawn, "we promise to pay," is called a **Joint Note,** in which the promissors are liable jointly; one drawn, "we jointly and severally promise to pay," is a **Joint and Several Note,** in which the promissors are liable jointly and individually.

A Bank Note is a Promissory Note, unstamped by Statute, but it differs from an ordinary Promissory Note in that it is considered in law as actual money; whereas an ordinary personal Promissory Note is deemed a security for money only. A person cannot make a **Promissory Note to himself,** or to himself and another person; but he can make one to himself *or his order* and it becomes a negotiable instrument when endorsed by him. A note signed by two or more, and drawn "I promise," is a joint and several note: and in a joint and several note, as has been said, all the promissors are principals, and individually liable. If one of the promissors to a joint or to a joint and several note, pay the entire amount, he may maintain an action against his fellow promissors for their individual contributory share. A Promissory Note can be drawn payable by **instalments,** but it must bear the stamp duty of the gross amount, and although a Cheque payable "on demand" must be presented for payment without any unreasonable delay, nevertheless, a Promissory Note so drawn may lie out unpresented for any length of time—even for years, as it is an instrument intended only as a continuing security. A Promissory Note, however, is presumed at law to have been discharged if not presented or renewed during twenty years after the making or maturing of it.

An Accommodation Bill is one which has been signed by a party, without a consideration, and merely as an act of accommodation to enable the person accommodated to obtain money on the Bill. The peculiarity of it is that it is accepted under an express or implied undertaking that the Acceptor will be indemnified by the Drawer against any claim under it —that the Drawer, not the Acceptor, will provide the funds to meet it. The Drawer is understood to be primarily liable, but the accommodating party, whether Acceptor or not, cannot divest himself of his liability to a *bonâ fide* holder. Even a person who has been induced to accept through fraud, is liable to an innocent holder. Accommodation Bills have been called the "plague spot of Commerce," and the successful negotiation of them to an unlimited extent has been the cause of several commercial catastrophes. They are one of the Banker's greatest dangers. They bear all the appearance of reality—*i.e.*, that they represent an actual and *bonâ fide* commercial transaction. But not only are they deceptive in this respect, but they deceive in that there is no means of ascertaining what party to the bill is the real Debtor. No value has passed between the parties; the Acceptor does not prepare to meet the Bill—he is impliedly indemnified by the Drawer whom he accommodates with his signature; and the Drawer, from the mere fact of his resorting to this device, is presumably of no solvency. No Banker will therefore discount a Bill that he knows to be an Accommodation Bill.

The usual form of words used in a **Bill of Exchange** is as follows :—

[£50.] *London*, 1st *November*, 1881.

(Three) months [or days] after date* [or after sight] pay to my order [or to bearer, or to a third party] the sum of [Fifty] Pounds Sterling, value received.

To Mr. William Smith,
10, Tipton Street,
Liverpool.   [*John Brown.*]

---

* If such an instrument is drawn "on demand," or "at sight," it is known as a CASH ORDER, and is payable without acceptance on presentation.

The Bill must bear the Statutory Stamp Duty detailed subsequently. Mr. William Smith, in this case, would accept the Bill, by writing upon it his name, which is generally written across the face of the Bill, but not necessarily, as a Bill can be accepted on the back or at the foot. He probably makes it payable at his Bankers, by writing over or under his name "Payable at the ———— Bank," and such an acceptance amounts to a direction to these Bankers to pay it when it matures or becomes due, which in the above case would be on the 4th of February, 1881, being three months—*i.e.*, calendar months—after the date, the 1st November, 1880, together with three days of grace added. A Bill can be drawn "after demand" or "after notice."

Acceptance.—There are three forms of acceptance—(1) **general acceptance**, which is an undertaking to pay the amount, not at any Bank, or elsewhere than at the Acceptor's address as named on the Bill and when presented to himself or his representative there; (2) **a special acceptance**, which is where the Acceptor makes it payable at a Banker's or some specified place, in which case it is incumbent on the Holder —in order to maintain his recourse against previous Endorsers, but not absolutely incumbent, in order to maintain recourse against the Acceptor—to present it at the Banker's, or the place specified, and not to the Acceptor, or at his address; and (3) **a particular acceptance**, which is in this form,—*e.g.*, "accepted payable at the Anglo-Indian Bank only," or— "and not elsewhere or otherwise," in which case the Holder is limited in his powers of presentation and is bound to present it at the Bank named, and that within Banking hours on the day the Bill matures. In **suing** an *Acceptor* who has accepted in the first or second forms, it is not necessary to prove presentation either to the Acceptor or at the Bank named, for an

Acceptor is bound to discover where his acceptance is, and to pay it. But in suing the *Drawer or an Endorser*, presentation at the place specified must be proved. But in the case of a particular acceptance (3), in order to sue the Acceptor for non-payment, it is necessary to prove that the Bill of Exchange was presented where only payable, that is, in this case, at the Anglo-Indian Bank.

If an Acceptor make a Bill **payable at his Bankers**, and they have sufficient funds of his in their hands to pay it, when it is presented at its maturity, such acceptance is sufficient authority to them to charge it to his account, and no direction or authorization beyond the terms of the acceptance is necessary; and if the Banker, having funds, neglect to pay it, he is liable to an action by the Acceptor for dishonour. But if the Banker pay on a **forged** endorsement,* he cannot charge the Acceptor's account, and, obviously, if he pay an acceptance which is a forgery, he cannot debit the party whose acceptance it purports to be. Should he pay a Bill bearing a forged endorsement, or a forged acceptance, his remedy is against the party to whom he has made the payment.

If an Acceptor make a Bill **payable at a Bank where he has no account**, he cannot compel the Banker to receive money to pay the acceptance; nor, if at the maturity of the Bill he remit the amount to the Banker, in the absence of assent by the Banker to receive and hold the money and to pay the Bill, the Acceptor cannot make the Banker liable in case of dishonour. Assent, however, may be constructive as well as express. For instance, if the Banker has been in the habit

---

* When there are several Endorsers on a Bill *payable to bearer*, a *bonâ fide* Holder is *not* affected by an intermediate fraud of which he has no cognizance; nor is he bound to make inquiry as to the validity or *bonâ fides* of any preceding endorsements.

of receiving money from the Acceptor for such a purpose and applying it as directed, that will be deemed a constructive assent on his part, in the absence of notice to the contrary, to do so again.

A **differing acceptance** is where the Acceptor accepts for an amount, or for a term, differing from the amount or term as directed by the Drawer, and the holder can only charge the Acceptor with the amount he has accepted for, and the maturity to bind the Acceptor is the maturity named in the acceptance. However, in a case where a Bill was dated September the 8th, and drawn at four months, and the Acceptors wrote over the acceptance, "due 11th Dec.," it was held that these words did not qualify the acceptance, but were at most an inaccurate description of the date of the Bill; but if the Acceptors had written, "due 11th Feb.," and thereby extended the time, it is probable that such date would be a material part of the Bill. An acceptance must be by the Drawee, and the Drawer himself may be the Drawee.

If there are **several Drawees**, the Bill must be accepted by all; but the fact of its not being accepted by all, does not relieve those who do accept. If a person write his name by way of acceptance upon a blank or **unfilled stamp**, and *deliver it*, he is bound by such acceptance; but if a blank stamp so accepted be stolen or obtained fraudulently, he would not be bound, for liability attaches only on delivery. The Statute Law, before the 41 Vict., c. 13 (1878), declared that an acceptance should be "in writing and signed by the Ac-"ceptor," which necessitated some **words of acceptance** in writing. But by that Statute the signature alone of the Drawee was declared to be sufficient.* If an unaccepted Bill

---

* The words of the Statute, after declaring that doubts have arisen as to

be left with the Drawee for acceptance, and that he consent to accept it, and that subsequently he destroy the Bill or lose it of malice, it is probable he could be made liable to a Holder for value. But if he had, *ab initio*, refused to accept, then in the event of the loss or destruction of the instrument he could not be liable.

Qualified or Conditional Acceptance.—If a Drawee accept a Bill qualifiedly, and that the Holder agree to such acceptance, he can only charge the Acceptor upon nonpayment after the fulfilment of those qualifying conditions; but to charge the Drawer and previous Endorsers, he is bound to notice them of the nature of the acceptance, and if they object to the qualified terms of it, they can refuse to be charged in the event of dishonour. An acceptance is said to be **conditional** when it is an engagement to pay upon the fulfilment of conditions named therein. For example :—" accepted payable on " surrender of Bill of Lading"—"accepted payable when goods " now consigned to me are sold"—and such like, are conditional acceptances, and if the Drawer or Holder consent to such an acceptance, he can only institute an action for the amount when the conditions of the acceptances are exhausted. Though an *acceptance* can be conditional, an *endorsement* cannot, or rather, a conditional endorsement is not usual in practice, as it tends to restrict the negotiability of the Bill, and an

---

the true effect and intention of the Mercantile Law Amendment Act (1856), are— 1. An acceptance of a bill of exchange is not and shall not be deemed to be insufficient under the provisions of the said Statute by reason only that such acceptance consists merely of the signature of the drawee written on such bill.

2. Nothing in this Act shall affect the validity or invalidity of any verdict or judgment recovered before the passing of this Act.

3. This Act may be cited for all purposes as the "Bills of Exchange Act, 1878."

endorsement cannot be restrictive. As a Bill drawn **after sight** begins to run from the time it is sighted or confirmed by the Acceptor, it is therefore necessary that the date of the acceptance should be set forth on the Bill. A Bill **"at sight"** is payable on demand, whether accepted or not, but the Drawee is bound only in case of acceptance.

What Acceptance Admits. — The Acceptor is the primary Debtor to the Holder; but the other parties to it are regarded as securities—to one or any of whom the Holder has recourse. By his act of acceptance the Drawee admits that he is indebted to the Drawer, and he cannot subsequently plead that the Drawer or Payee was a person incapacitated, or that the Drawer's signature is a forgery. But acceptance is no admission in respect to the endorsers, and if an endorsement is known to him to be a forgery he can refuse payment. Where the Drawer's name is signed " **per-procuration,**" acceptance is an admission of debt to the principal, and consequently the principal's endorsement is necessary, and the Acceptor can refuse to pay on the agent's endorsement "per-procuration," even though it be so endorsed at the time of acceptance. Therefore, in a Bill drawn payable to the Drawer's order, where his signature, as Drawer, is "per-procuration," some Bankers require that it be endorsed by the *Drawer himself* and not by the agent who signed as Drawer.

Bills of Exchange or Promissory Notes need not be **on paper**; they are valid on any substitutionary substance except metal. Nor need they be written **in ink**, as a bill drawn and signed in pencil is legal and valid.* Nor need they be in any **precise form of words** as long as the intention to promise

---

* We believe a County Court Judge in Ireland a short while ago dismissed an action on a Bill of Exchange because it was drawn on the *wrong side of the stamp*, and was, according to him, therefore an illegal document.(!)

or to accept is apparent on the face of the instrument. The **constituent features** of a Bill of Exchange are — (1) the Date, (2) the Amount, (3) the Time when Payable, (4) the Payee, (5) the Drawer's Signature, (6) the Drawee, (7) the Place where payable.

The Date.—Though the place where drawn and the date when drawn, are usual and proper in a Bill of Exchange, they are not necessary or essential to its validity. Evidence as to the time of making will fix the date. A Bill, like a Cheque, may be post-dated, but if *a Banker* issue a Bill under the provisions of 9 Geo. IV., c. 23, and post-date it, he is liable to a penalty of £100.

The Amount.—It is necessary that the amount should be specifically stated. The remarks as to the amount as in Cheques apply equally to Bills.

The Time when Payable.—If no time is stated, the Bill is payable on demand. "*At sight*" and cognate expressions are equivalent to "*on demand.*"* *After sight* on a Bill of Exchange means after acceptance by the Drawee, and not merely after he has seen it; but the same expression on a Promissory Note necessitates no more than exhibition or presentation to the maker. A Bill or Note may be payable at any time, no matter how distant, provided that the time is definite and inevitable; but it must be payable at some time or other, and that time must be specified.

The Payee.—A Payee must be particularised. It may be the bearer, or some person specially; or a person or his order; or persons jointly; or a Company or a Corporation. The Payee can be the Drawer himself. But there must be a Payee. A Bill payable to "—— or order," and so negoti-

* Formerly, "at sight" was considered a term entitled to three days' grace after acceptance.

ated, was held not to be a Bill of Exchange, as there was no Payee. But if a space is left for the Payee's name, it can be filled in by a lawful Holder with his own name, but he must prove authority from the Drawer so to do. If a Bill is payable *specially*, that is, to a Payee without the alternative words "or order" or "or bearer," it is not negotiable to other parties, but, like a Cheque, must be paid by the Drawee to the Payee alone. A Bill, like a Cheque, is transferable. If payable to order it passes by endorsement and delivery; if to bearer, by delivery.

The Drawer's Signature.—The signature of the Drawer of a Bill or maker of a Note is usually at the foot, but not necessarily, for a note drawn: "I, William Jones, promise to "pay, &c.," is a good note. A marksman can be a Drawer.

The Drawee.—The Drawee must be particularized. His surname must be spelt correctly, for if there is a divergence between the spelling of the names of the Drawee and Acceptor, it may be pleaded that they are not the same person, and therefore that the Bill is invalid.

The Place where Payable.—The Acceptor has the power of locating or domiciling a Bill, but if the place is stated in the body of the instrument, and it be accepted generally, it is a part of the contract. It has been the opinion of some Judges, that if a *Drawer* make a Bill payable at his own place, such an act is evidence that the Bill was an Accommodation Bill.

"Value Received."—These words are not necessary in a Bill. They are either superfluous as between Drawer and Drawee, or ambiguous where the Payee is a third party.

Bills of Exchange, because of their paramount utility and necessity in trade and commerce, have been so highly favoured by the law, that a **special means of recovering** on them has been provided by the Legislature. An action on a Bill or Note, instituted within six months after it shall have become payable, may be commenced by a writ, which instead of ordering the defendant to appear, etc., gives him notice that if within twelve days he do not obtain leave to appear and do appear, judgment will be registered and execution follow. Upon the defendant's appearance he must, if he intends to defend the action, obtain the leave of the Court to defend it ; and this leave will not be granted unless it be made to appear to the Court that the defence is in its nature reasonable and *bonâ fide*. A defendant, however, is not, by the Court's refusal, deprived of the right to bring his case before a jury. The object of this special procedure in the case of Bills of Exchange, is to prevent defences of a vexatious and frivolous character being entered upon with the object of obtaining a delay, or defrauding a plaintiff—to the ultimate restriction of the free negotiability of these instruments and the consequent injury to commerce.

VIII.

PERSONS INCAPACITATED TO BE PARTIES TO A BILL OF EXCHANGE.

An **agent** cannot endorse or accept Bills so as to bind his principal unless with the special authority of the principal. Ratification by the principal of the agent's acts, or of similar acts in the past, will bind the principal. The words "per procuration," are an express declaration of a specialty authority, and a person who takes a Bill so accepted, drawn, or endorsed, is bound to inform himself of the truth and extent of the declared authority. An agent so appointed incurs no personal responsibility in connection with the instruments he so signs under his authority. But if an agent implies an authority which does not exist, he is personally liable.

Partners.—" Partners not in trade cannot bind each other " by Bills. Therefore, an attorney who is partner with another, " has not, *from that relation alone*, power to bind his co-partner, " by a Bill or Note. No more have partners carrying on business " as brokers by getting orders on commission and dividing the " expenses."* If a partner act outside his partnership powers, to the knowledge of the other contracting parties, they cannot hold his co-partners liable for the deeds of the one who exceeded his authority. Or where a party takes a Bill with notice that it was

* Byles.

accepted in a firm's name, by one partner, but without the sanction or knowledge or authority of the other partners, he cannot charge the other partners, although it be for value received. But the other partners would be liable to an innocent *bonâ fide* holder for value. If a person be a sleeping or **secret partner** and unknown to a creditor, he is yet liable to that creditor on the partnership transactions; and on the other hand, if a person be an ostensible partner, *i.e.*, that his name appears publicly as a partner, though he derive no benefit from the partnership, he is also liable to a creditor who believed him to be, and treated him as, an active partner, even although a deed of dissolution which had not been published or notified may have been executed. If dissolution is effected by the death of one of the partners, no notification is necessary.

Infants.—By the Infants' Relief Act (37 & 38 Vict., c. 62) all contracts by Infants (*i.e.*, persons under the age of twenty-one), to repay money lent, or to be lent, or for goods supplied, or to be supplied, *other than contracts for necessaries*, are made absolutely void, and, being absolutely void, no action can be brought upon a ratification made after full age of any promise or contract made during infancy; a contract that is *void* cannot be ratified, though a *voidable* one may. An Infant's promise by way of note of hand, or otherwise, to pay **for necessaries** can be enforced, the jury answering whether the articles were necessaries or not; but such a note of hand, to be recoverable upon, must be for the exact sum due for the necessaries, and not a note bearing interest or a penalty. Though he should represent himself as of full age, an Infant is not liable on a Bill of Exchange; still he can endorse a Bill, and give a good title to the Transferee, but the Transferee or Endorser has no right of action against the Infant. An Infant may sue and recover payment through his guardian. The following case, though not strictly dealing with Infants' Contracts, may yet well be included under this head. It was one where a Banker discounted a Promissory Note to the Bank, signed by A., who had just ceased to be an Infant, and gave the proceeds unreservedly to B., who represented that it was given in payment of necessaries supplied to A., and though the Bank had such knowledge of the relative position of the parties that it warranted their belief in these representations, yet—B., having misappropriated the money—the Bank was restrained from suing on the note, and the note was declared to be invalid.* It is, however, to be remembered that Infants, though incapable to contract on their own account, may be agents of others who are capable, and as such can bind those others.

Lunatics, Idiots, and a Person non compos mentis. —Contracts by a Lunatic, an Idiot, or a person *non compos* through infirmity or age, are absolutely void. But if the contract be a fair contract, whereby the Lunatic or infirm person has derived benefit, and one where the other contracting party had no notice or knowledge of the incapacity, the contract could not be voided by the Lunatic on the ground of his lunacy.

Married Women.—The contracts of a married woman are void, unless she contracts under the Married Women's Property Act (33 & 34 Vict., c. 93). Without her husband's authority (express or implied) she cannot render either him or herself liable, not even though she represent herself as unmarried. In the latter case an action would lie, not on the contract, but for obtaining under a false pretence. She is liable if she have a separate estate ; or if her husband be transported, or unheard of for seven years ; or if he be an alien who never

* Dettmar *v.* Metropolitan and Provincial Bank.

resided in the Kingdom. A Bill drawn payable to a single woman vests in her husband on her marriage, and his endorsement alone is a discharge. But since the passing of the Married Women's Property Act, the husband is not liable on a Bill or Note given by the wife during her spinsterhood.

Undue Influence.—If a person give a Bill or Note under the exercise of undue influence, he cannot repudiate the liability to an innocent *bonâ fide* holder. His remedy is in a Court of Equity.

Drunkenness.—*Total Drunkenness*, amounting to a perversion or deprivation of mental power, incapacitates a man from contracting, and it is a good defence to an action on a Bill of Exchange, or Promissory Note. "It is just the same," said Baron Alderson, "as if the defendant had written his name on "the Bill in his sleep in a state of somnambulism." But if an act done during total drunkenness is ratified at a subsequent sober and lucid period, the ratification makes the contract valid.

Partial Drunkenness.—It may also be a defence on an action that the defendant signed the Bill or Note while partially drunk. But a defence of this nature differs from the preceding case, inasmuch as it should be proved that the drunkenness was the result of an intentional act or contrivance on the part of him who obtained the signature to the Bill; or else that the defendant was induced to sign by a person who had knowledge, and took advantage of, his drunken condition.

Convicted Felons.—A convicted Felon during the period of his sentence cannot be a contracting party to, or bring an action on, a Bill of Exchange. But he can, through an interim administrator, receive as Endorser the benefit of a Bill maturing during his term of sentence, or take action on one dishonoured. A contract also in favour of an **alien enemy**, and against a British subject in the British Isles, is void as against the subjec

Corporations and Companies.—"Without a special "authority, express or implied, a Corporation has no power to "make, endorse, or accept Bills or Notes;"* and it was decided in a case of Overend, Gurney and Co., against the Mid Wales Railway Company, that a **Railway Company** can neither accept, draw, nor endorse a Bill of Exchange. A **Joint Stock Company,** however, can accept by the hands of the Directors, or a quorum of them, and each individual member of the Company will be bound by their act. But if they accept personally in their own names, and not as Directors of the Joint Stock Company, the liability will not extend beyond them personally. Directors of a Joint Stock Company cannot bind the Company *as Drawers*, unless there is a special authority to that effect. A joint *and several* Note signed by Directors will bind only the Directors signing. By the 25 & 26 Vic., c. 9, s. 47, and the 30 & 31 Vic., c. 131, if any person on behalf of a Limited Company registered under these ("the Companies") Acts, signs or endorses a Bill, Cheque, or Note on which the name of the Company is not duly mentioned, he is not only made personally responsible to the holder, but liable to a penalty of £50.

Societies.—The contracting powers of Societies, such as Loan and Building and Co-operative Societies and the like, are generally defined in the deeds incorporating them.

* Byles.

IX.

THE STAMP DUTIES.

The Stamp Act of 1870 now regulates the mode of writing and stamping, and the duties on, Bills of Exchange.

The following are the provisions contained in the Act and Schedule thereto, which relate to Bills of Exchange and Promissory Notes :—

By sect. 7 (1), Every instrument written upon stamped material is to be written in such manner, and every instrument partly or wholly written before being stamped is to be so stamped, that the stamp must appear on the face of the instrument, and cannot be used for or applied to any other instrument written upon the same piece of material.

(2) If more than one instrument be written upon the same piece of material, every one of such instruments is to be separately and distinctly stamped with the duty with which it is chargeable.

By sect. 8, Except where express opinion to the contrary is made by this or any other act—

(1) An instrument containing or relating to several distinct matters is to be separately and distinctly charged as if it were a separate instrument, with duty in respect of each such matters.

(2) An instrument made for any consideration or considerations in respect whereof it is chargeable with ad valorem duty, and also for any further or other valuable consideration or considerations, is to be charged with duty in respect of such last-named consideration or considerations, as if it were a separate instrument made for consideration or considerations only.

By sect. 9 (1), A stamp which by any word or words on the face of it is appropriated to any particular description of instrument is not to be used, or, if used, is not to be available, for an instrument of any other description.

(2) An instrument falling under the particular description to which any stamp is so appropriated as aforesaid is not to be deemed duly stamped unless it is stamped with the stamp so appropriated.

By sect. 11, Where an instrument is chargeable with *ad valorem* duty in respect of any money in any foreign or colonial currency, such duty shall be calculated on the value of such money in British currency according to the current rate of exchange on the day of the date of the instrument.

By sect. 12, Where an instrument is chargeable with *ad valorem* duty in respect of any stock or of any marketable security, such duty shall be calculated on the value of such stock or security according to the average price thereof on the day of the date of the instrument.

By sect. 13, Where an instrument contains a statement of current rate of exchange, or average price, as the case may require, and it is stamped in accordance with such statement, so far as regards the subject-matter of such statement, to be deemed duly stamped, unless or until it is shown that such statement is untrue, and that the instrument is in fact insufficiently stamped.

By sect. 15 (1), Except where express provision to the contrary is made by this or any other Act, any unstamped or insufficiently-stamped instrument may be stamped after the execution thereof, on payment of the unpaid duty and a penalty of ten pounds, and also, by way of further penalty when the unpaid duty exceeds ten pounds, of interest on such duty, at the rate of five pounds per centum per annum from the day upon which the instrument was first executed up to the time when such interest is equal in amount to the unpaid duty.

And the payment of any penalty or penalties is to be denoted on the instrument by a particular stamp.

(2) Provided as follows:
  (a) Any unstamped or insufficiently stamped instrument, which has been first executed at any place out of the United Kingdom, may be stamped, at any time within two months after it has been first received in the United Kingdom, on payment of the unpaid duty only:
  (b) The commissioners may, if they think fit, at any time within twelve months after the first execution of any instrument, remit the penalty or penalties, or any part thereof.

By sect. 17, Save and except as aforesaid, no instrument executed in any part of the United Kingdom or relating, wheresoever executed, to any property situate, or to any matter or thing done or to be done, in any part of the United Kingdom, shall, *except in criminal proceedings*, be pleaded or given in evidence, or admitted to be good, useful or available in law or equity, unless it is duly stamped in accordance with the law in force at the time when it was first executed.

By sect. 23, Except where express provision is made to the contrary, all duties are to be denoted by impressed stamps only.

By sect. 24 (1), An instrument, the duty upon which is required, or permitted by law, to be denoted by an adhesive stamp, is not to be deemed duly stamped with an adhesive stamp unless the person required by law to cancel such adhesive stamp cancels the same by writing on or across the stamp his name or initials, or the name or initials of his firm, together with the true date of his so writing, so that the stamp may be effectually cancelled, and rendered incapable of being used for any other instrument, or unless it is otherwise proved that the stamp appearing on the instrument was affixed thereto at the proper time.

(2) Every person who, being required by law to cancel an adhesive stamp, wilfully neglects or refuses duly and effectually to do so in the manner aforesaid, shall forfeit the sum of ten pounds.

By sect. 36, The duty of sixpence upon an agreement may be denoted by an adhesive stamp, which is to be cancelled by the person by whom the agreement is first executed.

By sect. 45, The term "banker" means and includes any corporation, society, partnership, and persons, and every individual person carrying on the business of banking in the United Kingdom.

The term "bank note" means and includes—

(1) Any bill of exchange or promissory note issued by any banker, other than the Governor and Company of the Bank of England, for the payment of money not exceeding one hundred pounds to the bearer on demand :

(2) Any bill of exchange or promissory note so issued which entitles or is intended to entitle the bearer or holder thereof, without indorsement, or without any further or other indorsement than may be thereon at the time of the issuing thereof, to the payment of money not exceeding one hundred pounds on demand, whether the same be so expressed or not, and in whatever form, and by whomsoever such bill or note is drawn or made.

By sect. 46, A bank note issued duly stamped, or issued unstamped by a banker duly licensed or otherwise authorized to issue unstamped bank notes, may be from time to time re-issued without being liable to any stamp duty by reason of such re-issuing.

By sect. 47 (1), If any banker, not being duly licensed or otherwise authorized to issue unstamped bank notes, issues, or causes or permits to be issued, any bank note not being duly stamped, he shall forfeit the sum of fifty pounds.

(2) If any person receives or takes any such bank note in payment or as

a security, knowing the same to have been issued unstamped contrary to law, he shall forfeit the sum of twenty pounds.

By sect. 48 (1), The term "bill of exchange" for the purpose of this act indicates also draft, order, cheque, and letter of credit, and any document or writing (except a bank-note) entitling or purporting to entitle any person, whether named therein or not, to payment by any other person of, or to draw upon any other person for, any sum of money therein mentioned.

(2) An order for the payment of any sum of money by a bill of exchange or promissory note, or for the delivery of any bill of exchange or promissory note in satisfaction of any sum of money, or for the payment of any sum of money out of any particular fund which may or may not be available, or upon any condition or contingency which may or may not be performed or happen, is to be deemed for the purposes of this Act a bill of exchange for the payment of money on demand.

(3) An order for the payment of any sum of money weekly, monthly, or at any other stated periods, and also any order for the payment by any person at the time after the date thereof of any sum of money, and sent or delivered by the person making the same to the person by whom the payment is to be made, and not to the person to whom the payment is to be made, or to any person on his behalf, is to be deemed for the purposes of this act a bill of exchange for the payment of money on demand.

By sect. 49 (1), The term "promissory note" means and includes any document or writing (except a bank note) containing a promise to pay any sum of money.

(2) A note promising the payment of any sum of money out of any particular fund which may or may not be available, or upon any condition or contingency which may or may not be performed or happen, is to be deemed for the purposes of this Act a promissory note for the said sum of money.

By sect. 50, The fixed duty of one penny on a bill of exchange for the payment of money on demand may be denoted by an adhesive stamp, which is to be cancelled by the person by whom the bill is signed before he delivers it out of his hands, custody, or power.

By sect. 51 (1), The *ad valorem* duties upon bills of exchange and promissory notes drawn or made out of the United Kingdom are to be denoted by adhesive stamps.

(2) Every person into whose hands any such bill or note comes in the United Kingdom before it is stamped, shall, before he presents for payment, or indorses, transfers, or in any manner negotiates, or pays such bill or note, affix thereto a proper adhesive stamp or proper adhesive stamps of sufficient amount, and cancel every stamp so affixed thereto.

(3) Provided as follows :

(a) If at the time when any such bill or note comes into the hands of any *bonâ fide* holder thereof there is affixed thereto an adhesive stamp effectually obliterated, and purporting and appearing to be duly cancelled, such stamp shall, so far as relates to such holder, be deemed to be duly cancelled, although it may not appear to have been so affixed or cancelled by the proper person.

(b) If at the time when any such bill or note comes into the hands of any *bonâ fide* holder thereof there is affixed thereto an adhesive stamp not duly cancelled, it shall be competent for such holder to cancel such stamp, as if he were the person by whom it was affixed, and upon his so doing such bill or note shall be deemed duly stamped, and as valid and available as if the stamp had been duly cancelled by the person by whom it was affixed.

(4) But neither of the foregoing provisoes is to relieve any person from any penalty incurred by him for not cancelling any adhesive stamp.

By sect. 52, A bill of exchange or promissory note purporting to be drawn or made out of the United Kingdom is, for the purpose of this Act, to be deemed to have been so drawn or made, although it may in fact have been drawn or made within the United Kingdom.

By sect 53 (1), Where a bill of exchange or promissory note has been written on material bearing an impressed stamp of sufficient amount but of improper denomination, it may be stamped with the proper stamp on payment of the duty, and a penalty of forty shillings if the bill or note be not then payable according to its tenor, and of ten pounds if the same be so payable.

(2) Except as aforesaid, no bill of exchange or promissory note shall be stamped with an impressed stamp after the execution thereof.

By sect. 54 (1), Every person who issues, indorses, transfers, negotiates, presents for payment, or pays any bill of exchange or promissory note liable to duty and not being duly stamped shall forfeit the sum of ten pounds, and the person who takes or receives from any other person any such bill or note not being duly stamped, either in payment or as a security, or by purchase or otherwise, shall not be entitled to recover thereon, or to make the same available for any purpose whatever.

(2) Provided that if any bill of exchange for the payment of money on demand, liable only to the duty of one penny, is presented for payment unstamped, the person to whom it is so presented may affix thereto a proper adhesive stamp, and cancel the same, as if he had been the drawer of the bill, and may, upon so doing, pay the sum in the said bill mentioned, and charge the duty in account against the person by whom the bill was drawn, or deduct such duty from the said sum, and such bill is, so far as respects the duty, to be deemed good and valid.

(3) But the foregoing proviso is not to relieve any person from any penalty he may have incurred in relation to such bill.

By sect. 55, When a bill of exchange is drawn in a set according to the custom of merchants, and one of the set is duly stamped, the other or others of the set shall, unless issued or in some manner negotiated apart from such duly stamped bill, be exempt from duty; and upon proof of the loss or destruction of a duly stamped bill forming one of a set, any other bill of the set which has not been issued or in any manner negotiated apart from such lost or destroyed bill may, although unstamped, be admitted in evidence to prove the contents of such lost or destroyed bill.

By sect. 96 (1), The duty on a contract note may be denoted by an adhesive stamp, which is to be cancelled by the person by whom the note is first executed.

(2) Every person who makes or executes any contract note chargeable with duty, and not being duly stamped, shall forfeit the sum of twenty pounds.

(3) No broker, agent, or other person shall have any legal claim to any charge for brokerage, commission, or agency, with reference to the sale or purchase of any stock or marketable security of the value of five pounds or upwards mentioned or referred to in any contract note, unless such note is duly stamped.

By sect. 2 of 34 Vic., c. 4, The term "foreign security" means and includes every security for money by or on behalf of any foreign or colonial state government, municipal body, corporation, or company, bearing date or signed after the third day of June, one thousand eight hundred and sixty-two, except an instrument chargeable with duty as a bill of exchange or promissory note—

(1) Which is made or issued in the United Kingdom;
(2) Which, the interest thereon being payable in the United Kingdom, is assigned, transferred, or in any manner negotiated in the United Kingdom.

By sect. 3 of the same act, every person who in the United Kingdom makes, issues, assigns, transfers, or negotiates, or pays any interest upon any foreign security not being duly stamped, shall forfeit the sum of twenty pounds.

By sect. 115, The commissioners may at any time, without reference to the date thereof, allow any foreign security to be stamped without the payment of any penalty, upon being satisfied, in any manner that they may think proper, that it was not made or issued, and has not been transferred, assigned, or negotiated within the United Kingdom, and that no interest has been paid thereon within the United Kingdom.

By sect. 116, The duty upon a notarial act, and upon the protest by a notary public of a bill of exchange or promissory note, may be denoted by an adhesive stamp which is to be cancelled by the notary.

By sect. 120, The term "receipt" means and includes any note, memorandum, or writing whatsoever, whereby any money amounting to two pounds or upwards, or any bill of exchange or promissory note for money amounting to two pounds or upwards, is acknowledged or expressed to have been received or deposited or paid, or whereby any debt or demand, or any part of a debt or demand, of the amount of two pounds or upwards, is acknowledged to have been settled, satisfied, or discharged, or which signifies or imports any such acknowledgment, and whether the same is or is not signed with the name of any person.

By sect. 121, The duty upon a receipt may be denoted by an adhesive stamp, which is to be cancelled by the person by whom the receipt is given before he delivers it out of his hands.

By sect. 122, A receipt given without being stamped may be stamped with an impressed stamp upon the terms following; that is to say—

(1) Within fourteen days after it has been given, on payment of the duty and a penalty of five pounds;

(2) After fourteen days, but within one month, after it has been given, on payment of the duty and a penalty of ten pounds;

and shall not in any other case be stamped with an impressed stamp.

By sect. 123, If any person—

(1) Gives any receipt liable to duty and not duly stamped;

(2) In any case where a receipt would be liable to duty refuses to give a receipt duly stamped;

(3) Upon a payment to the amount of two pounds or upwards gives a receipt for a sum not amounting to two pounds, or separates or divides the amount paid with intent to evade the duty;

he shall forfeit the sum of ten pounds.

SCHEDULE to the above Act.

	£	s.	d.
AGREEMENT, or any MEMORANDUM of an AGREEMENT, made in England or Ireland under hand only, or made in Scotland without any clause of registration, and not otherwise specifically charged with any duty, whether the same be only evidence of a contract, or obligatory upon the parties from its being a written instrument	0	0	6

Exemptions.

(1) Agreement or memorandum the matter whereof is not of the value of 5*l*.

(2) Agreement or memorandum for the hire of any labourer, artificer, manufacturer, or menial servant.

(3) Agreement, letter, or memorandum made for or relating to the sale of any goods, wares, or merchandise.
(4) Agreement or memorandum made between the master and mariners of any ship or vessel for wages on any voyage coastwise from port to port in the United Kingdom.

				£	s.	d.
BANK NOTE—						
For money not exceeding 1*l.*	...	...	...	0	0	5
Exceeding 1*l.* and not exceeding 2*l.*	...	...	...	0	0	10
,, 1*l.* ,, 5*l.*	...	...	...	0	1	3
,, 5*l.* ,, 10*l.*	...	...	...	0	1	9
,, 10*l.* ,, 20*l.*	...	...	...	0	2	0
,, 20*l.* ,, 30*l.*	...	...	...	0	3	0
,, 30*l.* ,, 50*l.*	...	...	...	0	5	0
,, 50*l.* ,, 100*l.*	...	...	...	0	8	6
BILL OF EXCHANGE—						
Payable on demand	...	...	...	0	0	1

BILL OF EXCHANGE of any other kind whatsoever (except a bank note) and PROMISSORY NOTE of any kind whatsoever (except a bank note)—drawn, or expressed to be payable, or actually paid, or endorsed or in any manner negotiated in the United Kingdom :

			£	s.	d.
Where the amount of value of the money for which the bill or note is drawn or made does not exceed 5*l.*	...	...	0	0	1
Exceeds 5*l.* and does not exceed 10*l.*	...	...	0	0	2
,, 10*l.* ,, 25*l.*	...	...	0	0	3
,, 25*l.* ,, 50*l.*	...	...	0	0	6
,, 50*l.* ,, 75*l.*	...	...	0	0	9
,, 75*l.* ,, 100*l.*	...	...	0	1	0
,, 100*l.*—					
for every 100*l.* and also for any fractional part of 100*l.* of such amount or value	...	...	0	1	0

Exemptions.

(1) Bill or note issued by the Governor and Company of the Bank of England or Bank of Ireland.
(2) Draft or order drawn by any banker in the United Kingdom, upon any other banker in the United Kingdom, not payable to bearer or to order, and used solely for the purpose of settling or clearing any account between such bankers.
(3) Letter written by a banker in the United Kingdom to any other banker in the United Kingdom directing the payment of any sum of money, the same not being payable to bearer or to order, and such letter not being sent or delivered to the person to whom payment is to be made, or to any person on his behalf.
(4) Letter of credit granted in the United Kingdom authorising drafts to be drawn out of the United Kingdom payable in the United Kingdom.

(5) Draft or order drawn by the Accountant General of the Court of Chancery in England or Ireland.
(6) Warrant or order for the payment of any annuity granted by the Commissioners for the Reduction of the National Debt, or for the payment of any dividend or interest on any share in the Government or Parliamentary stock or funds.
(7) Bill drawn by the Lords Commissioners of the Admiralty or by any person under their authority, under the authority of any Act of Parliament upon and payable by the Accountant General of the Navy.
(8) Bill drawn (according to a form prescribed by her Majesty's orders by any person duly authorised to draw the same) upon and payable out of any public account for any pay or allowance of the army or other expenditure connected therewith.
(9) Coupon or warrant for interest attached to and issued with any security.

	£	s.	d.
PROTEST of any bill of exchange or promissory note:—			
Where the duty on the bill or note does not exceed 1s. the same duty as the bill or note			
In any other case	0	1	0
RECEIPT given for or upon the payment of money amounting to 2l. or upwards	0	0	1

Exemptions.

(1) Receipt given for money deposited in any bank, or with any banker, to be accounted for or expressed to be received of the person to whom the same is to be accounted for.
(2) Acknowledgement by any banker of the receipt of any bill of exchange or promissory note for the purpose of being presented for acceptance or payment.
(3) Receipt given for or upon the payment of any parliamentary taxes or duties, or of money to or for the use of her Majesty.
(4) Receipt given by the Accountant General of the Navy, for any money received by him for the service of the navy.
(5) Receipt given by any agent for money imprested to him on account of the pay of the army.
(6) Receipt given by any officer, seaman, marine or soldier, or his representatives, for or on account of any wages, pay, or pension, due from the Admiralty or Army Pay Office.
(7) Receipts given for the consideration money for the purchase of any share in any of the Government or Parliamentary stocks or funds, or in the stock of the East Indian Company, or in the stocks or funds of the Secretary of State in Council of India, or of the Governor and Company of the Bank of England, or

of the Bank of Ireland, or for any dividend paid on any share of the said stocks or funds respectively.

(8) Receipt given for any principal money or interest due on an Exchequer Bill.

(9) Receipt written upon a bill of exchange or promissory note duly stamped.

(10) Receipt given upon any bill or note of the governor and company of the Bank of England or the Bank of Ireland.

(11) Receipt endorsed or otherwise written upon or contained in any instrument liable to stamp duty, and duly stamped, acknowledging the receipt of the consideration money therein expressed, or the receipt of any principal money, interest, or annuity thereby secured or therein mentioned.

(12) Receipt given for drawback or bounty upon the exportation of any goods or merchandise from the United Kingdom.

(13) Receipt given for the return of any duties of customs upon certificates of over entry.

(14) Receipt endorsed upon any bill drawn by the Lords Commissioners of the Admiralty, or by any person under their authority, or under the authority of any Act of Parliament, upon and payable by the Accountant General of the Navy.

" It appears," says Byles, " that the following instruments are free from duty under this and previous Statutes :

(a) Bills and Notes of the Bank of England and Bank of Ireland.

(b) Notes for one pound, one guinea, two pounds or two guineas, payable to bearer on demand issued by the Bank of Scotland, Royal Bank of Scotland, and British Linen Company.

(c) Bills or Notes issued by Bankers paying a composition in lieu of stamps.

(d) Bills drawn for the expenses of the Navy and Army.

(e) Notes of Loan, Friendly and Building Societies.

A Bill or Note which is **unstamped** or **stamped imperfectly or improperly** cannot be recovered upon; nor can it be admitted in evidence, except in criminal cases. A

Bill " drawn or made " out of the United Kingdom, requires an *ad valorem* Foreign Bill Stamp; but an Inland Bill which has been negotiated abroad does not require a Foreign Bill Stamp. Thus, a Bill drawn in Manchester on a London Bank or Firm is an Inland Bill, and if it be sent to New York, for instance, and bears evidence of having been negotiated abroad, it does not require a Foreign Bill Stamp in addition to the impressed stamp duty it of necessity bears. A Bill Stamp cannot be used except for the one transaction; therefore, having been filled on one side and negotiated as a Bill or Note, it cannot be filled for the same purpose on the reverse side, as the stamp duty is exhausted by the one transaction. Nor can a Bill be re-issued and circulated after it has been paid at maturity.

The stamp duty on Foreign Drafts payable *at sight* or *on demand*, was reduced, in 1870, to a uniform tax of one penny, to be represented by an adhesive inland revenue stamp, thus superseding the previous duty, which was one *ad valorem*. In 1871 an Act was passed abolishing days of grace on Foreign Drafts at sight, and it is a matter of general regret amongst Bankers that the useless and anomalous days of grace on Bills of Exchange of all descriptions have not also been abolished.

By the 44 Vict., c. 12, s. 47, the penny postage stamp was made available for a penny inland revenue duty, and *vice versâ;* and since the passing of that Act a penny stamp has been issued which is common to both imposts.

X.

THE TRANSFER OF BILLS.

Bills of Exchange are transferable and assignable as Cheques are. One payable to "order" passes by endorsement and delivery; one payable to "bearer" by delivery alone; mere endorsement without delivery does not pass a Bill drawn to "order." But one drawn payable *specially*, *i.e.*, "to A. B." and not to "A. B. or order," or "A. B. or bearer" is not assignable as against the Drawee, that is to say, that the Drawee is not bound to pay the amount to a Transferee. If a Bill, thus specially payable, be transferred by the Payee, he (the Payee), is liable to all subsequent Endorsers, even though they took it with notice of its un-assignable nature. But in the case of a **promissory note** thus specially payable the endorsement on it by one to whom it has not been transferred, and who has not transferred it, will not make him liable on the note. There is no limit to the transferability of a Bill of Exchange. Any Holder can transfer it by endorsement, and each Endorser stands in the position of a new maker. But in a *promissory note* this is not so, as there is no relation between the positions of the Maker and the Endorsers. If there be not space on a Bill of Exchange for the endorsements, a slip of paper can be attached to it to bear them. This slip of added paper is then part of the Bill, and it requires no additional

Stamp Duty. It is technically called an *allonge*—(from the French). Every Endorser on a Bill of Exchange is as a new Drawer, and he is liable to the subsequent Endorsers in case of dishonour by the Drawee, but (as will be shown hereafter), due notice of the dishonour is necessary to the Endorsers.

There are, however, some ways in which an Endorser, without forfeiting his title, can transfer a Bill of Exchange, and yet **divest himself of liability** to subsequent Holders and Endorsers:

(1.) By writing over his endorsement the words *sans recours*, or "without recourse to me." For in this case, subsequent Transferees take the Bill with notice that that Endorser has declined to guarantee the validity or value of the Bill, and that they must take it at their own risk for what it is worth.

(2.) By means of a special agreement of immunity entered into with the Transferee. But such a special agreement, while valid as against the party to it, will not avail him or protect him against subsequent Holders who are innocent of the agreement.

(3.) Where a transferee B., writes over an endorsement in blank of a former payee A., words transferring it to a subsequent Holder D. In this case the intermediate Endorser avoids incurring a liability to D., as the endorsement by its nature effaces, as it were, those interposing between A. and his direct Transferee D.

(4.) Where a Bill is transferred, and re-endorsed to a previous Endorser, the intermediate Endorsers are not liable.

A Bill of Exchange can also bear a **restrictive endorsement** which will not bind the persons making it. For instance, if a Payee endorse a Bill "Pay A. B. *for my use*, C. D.," or some equivalent expression, the endorsement by A. B. does not bind him in regard to subsequent Holders, for by the terms of the writing they have notice that he is but a channel and not a Holder for value. But of course A. B. in case of his default, or fraud, or breach of trust, is liable *to the Transferor* C. D.

If a Holder transfer, without his endorsement, a Bill of Exchange, he cannot be made a party to an action *on the Bill* by a Subsequent Holder; and the un-endorsing Transferor—in the event of the Bill proving worthless—being, for example, a forged or a fraudulent instrument—cannot be held liable, except it be proved that he had knowledge of the worthless nature of the Bill—for the Transferee receives it at his own risk. If such knowledge be proven, he, in suppressing the truth, is guilty of a fraud, and so liable. **Non-endorsement** amounts to a refusal to guarantee the value of the instrument, that is, to guarantee that the parties to it are solvent. But the mere act of *delivery*, though without endorsement, amounts to a guarantee that the Bill or note is genuine—that is, that it is what it purports to be. A Bill or note once duly **paid** is extinguished, and no longer a transferable Document. But if it be paid before its maturity by a Drawer or Endorser, or even by the Acceptor, it is not an illegal act to put it again into circulation, or assign it before it becomes due. A Bill or Note **partly paid** can be assigned for the residue. A Bill or Note can now be taken in execution, and to steal or embezzle one is a felony. As with Cheques, so with Bills, an **endorsement in blank** by a Payee makes the Bill payable to Bearer. But a *bonâ fide* holder can convert a blank endorsement into a special one, by writing words of transfer to himself or to a third party over the endorsement in blank. The omission of the words "or order" in a transferring endorsement does not restrict the transferability of a Bill of Exchange, because negotiability is its essence, and a subsequent holder cannot thus destroy the essence of a Bill. A **misspelling** will not necessarily avoid an endorsement.

XI.

PRESENTATION OF BILLS.

Presentation for Acceptance.—As a rule it is unusual for a Banker to discount a Bill which is unaccepted, unless it be one which has been drawn on some Bank by a foreign agent which is also a Bank. Bankers' Bills drawn "after date" are usually paid when due without acceptance, and Bank of England Post Bills drawn "after sight" are accepted when issued, and thus the term runs from the day of issue. If, however, he do discount an unaccepted business Bill, it is his duty to present it for acceptance without delay, not only for his own security but for his Customer's protection. If it be drawn payable many days "after sight" it is manifest that no matter how undoubted the Bill is, it is his interest to have it accepted as soon as possible, for the term will only run from the date of acceptance.

A Banker is justified in leaving a Bill for acceptance with the Drawee for a day, to give him time to examine the document and, as has been said, " to deliberate whether he will accept or " not." If, having been discounted unaccepted, the Drawee refuse to accept, or if he retain it in his possession for a longer period than twenty-four hours, the Banker should notify to the parties to the Bill that it is unaccepted. If the Drawee has moved from the address stated on the Bill it is incumbent on the Holder to use "due diligence" to ascertain his whereabouts. A Holder's duty in case of a conditional acceptance has been already stated. It is a usual practice of Banks to send Bills of Lading accompanying Bills sent for acceptance. The party accepting is entitled to an examination of the documents, and to possession of them *unless there are instructions to the contrary given to the presenting Banker.* Possession of the Bill of Lading is, of course, a title to possession of the cargo, and if the Drawer of the Bill permits a surrender of it to the Drawee upon acceptance, he is satisfied with the solvency of the Acceptor, and content with the acceptance as payment. Frequently, however, the Bill of Lading is to be surrendered only upon payment of the Draft. The following case quoted by Grant is on the subject of surrender upon acceptance:—"A Bill of "Exchange was sent by a Bank in the United States to a Bank "in Toronto for collection and remittance, accompanying which "was a Bill of Lading for 10,000 bushels of wheat, which, on "the Bill of Exchange being accepted by the Drawees, was "delivered over to them, they being the consignees named in "the Bill of Lading; and it was held that it was *not* the duty of "the Bank in Canada, as the agent of the American Bank, *in* "*the absence of special instructions*, to retain the Bill of Lading "until the Bill of Exchange was paid." And this was the decision of the highest Court of Appeal in the Dominion, and would presumably rule a judgment under similar circumstances in this country.

Presentation for Payment.—In calculating the maturity of a Bill, "months" are counted as calendar months, and in all cases whether drawn "after date" or "after sight" three **days of grace** are added. Thus a Bill drawn on the 4th January, at one month after date, matures on the 7th February. So, a Bill drawn on the 31st January, at one month after date, becomes due on the 3rd March. The custom of allowing days of grace exists in almost all mercantile countries, but the number of days varies in different States. When a Bill is due, and not specially or particularly domiciled, it must be presented at the Acceptor's address as on the Bill; or if he has left that address, at the place which is his address at the time of maturity, and to discover this, "due diligence" is expected from the Holder. If the Acceptor be dead it must be presented to his representatives. It is not necessary to present the Bill to the Acceptor *in person*. Presentment to any person at the address is deemed sufficient, as it is the Acceptor's duty to take care of his Bill, and leave provision for it when it shall have been presented where payable. But to charge the Endorsers and Drawer, the Bill must be presented. The Bankruptcy or Insolvency of the Drawee does not absolve the Holder from his duty to present; neither is an intimation or declaration by the Drawee to the effect that he won't pay, any excuse for non-presentation. A Bill or Note must generally, but not necessarily, be presented during the Drawee's or Promissor's business hours. If it be presented at a reasonable time (and 7 or 8 o'clock in the evening has been ruled to be a reasonable time), it is sufficient to bind the parties.

The Presenter is bound to accept money in payment. If he accept a Cheque and surrender the Bill he does so at his own risk, and his doing so discharges the Endorsers and the Drawer. Money lodged in a Bank by an Acceptor for the expressed object of taking up his acceptance, is money paid to the use of *the Holder* of the Bill, and cannot be otherwise employed than in payment of that Bill. Even if the person so lodging should be indebted to the Bank where he made such lodgment, the Bank is not empowered to appropriate the money so paid in reduction or payment of the indebtedness of the party lodging it.

When it is said a Bill must be presented to the Acceptor, it is not to be understood that failure to present will discharge the Acceptor. It is an Acceptor's duty to find out where his acceptance is and to pay it, and non-presentation to him does not discharge his liability—except the Bill be *particularly* domiciled, that is, payable at a certain place "*and there only.*" But non-presentation on the Holder's part will discharge the Endorsers and the Drawer, and in order to charge them in an action on the Bill, presentation at the place where payable must be proved, provided that place is specified *in the Acceptance*, and not merely in the body of the Bill, or as a memorandum on it. A Promissory Note, however, must be presented at the place mentioned in the body of the Note. The neglect to duly present a Bill of Exchange or Promissory Note operates to discharge all the *antecedent parties*, but the Acceptor is, and continues, liable notwithstanding non-presentation.

If a Bill is payable generally in a certain town, presentation at all the Banking houses in the town is sufficient, in order to charge the Endorser and Drawer. A Bill can be paid at any time on the day it is due, and thus a refusal to pay when presented does not disentitle the Acceptor to make payment subsequently on the day of maturity; and a Bill is not therefore strictly a dishonoured Bill until the termination of the day on which it is due.

Part Payment by Drawer.—If a Banker hold a Bill on which a part payment has been made *by the Drawer*, he can proceed against the Acceptor for the full amount of the Bill, and if he recover the entire amount, he is bound to hold the previous payment in trust for the Drawer who made it.

The Order of Liability.—As has been said, the Acceptor is the primary, and therefore the principal, Debtor on a Bill of

Exchange, and the Drawer and the previous Endorsers are, in one sense, sureties for the Acceptor. The effect of this is that they are secondarily liable, that is, liable in case of default by the Acceptor. Each Endorser is liable to a subsequent Endorser, and the Drawer is liable to the first Endorser or the Payee. An Endorser may be a surety merely, and not a Transferor or a Debtor for value, but the extent of his liability to subsequent Endorsers is the same as if he were an Endorser for value. In a Promissory Note the maker or promissor is the Debtor-in-chief, and the position and liabilities of the Endorsers on a Note are the same as those of the Endorsers on a Bill. The Acceptor's liability does not lapse except by operation of the Statute of Limitations, and therefore the Holder can take his own time in suing him on the Bill, but the Drawer and Endorser, in order to maintain a remedy against them, must have been duly noticed of the dishonour or non-payment by the Acceptor. What constitutes a due notice of a dishonour will be explained subsequently. There are cases where a Bank cannot enforce duly made and executed Promissory Notes. A person gave a Promissory Note to a Bank to satisfy a claim for a liability, for which he *had been* liable, but was discharged at law, but in ignorance of the facts constituting such discharge, and the Bank could not enforce the note, although the maker had means of becoming acquainted with the facts.*

* Bell *v*. Gardiner.

XII.

NOTING AND PROTESTING.

Noting on an inland Bill of Exchange is a mere memorandum on the Bill by a notary-public, consisting of the date, his initials, and his charges; and its object seems to be to afford satisfactory evidence to the parties to the Bill, that the Bill is unaccepted, or dishonoured, as the case may be. A **protest** is superfluous on an Inland Bill and is unknown to the Common Law. A Foreign Bill, however, requires, by the custom of Bankers, to be protested for non-acceptance or non-payment, in order to retain the right to charge the Drawer and Endorsers. The protest is made by a Notary. It is, in form, "a solemn declaration written by the Notary, under a fair "copy of the Bill, stating that payment (or acceptance) has "been demanded and refused, and the reason, if any, assigned; "and, that the Bill is, therefore, protested." In Scotland a **Registered Protest** is a judgment or decree of registration under the Scottish system of summary diligence on Bills of Exchange and Promissory Notes. Thus—When a person signs a Bill or Note in Scotland, the law assumes, for the purpose of summary execution, that he has executed a warrant of attorney to sign judgment at its maturity, if not then paid; and the registration in the books of the proper Court of Notarial Protest, certifying the dishonour, is itself a judgment or decree of registration. But execution may be stayed, and often is, on cause shown to the satisfaction of a Judge at Chambers. In this respect alone a registered protest differs from a judgment in an ordinary action at law.

In addition to a protest for non-acceptance or non-payment, there is a further form known as "**protest for better security.**" It is not in general practice, and its advantages are problematical. The words "*sans frais*" (without charges) or "*sans protet*" (without protest), on a Bill of Exchange, are sufficient authority from the Drawer or Endorsers, to the Holder, to dispense with a protest in case of non-payment or non-acceptance. If there be no Notary in the locality where a Bill is payable, a protest can be made by an inhabitant, in the presence of two competent witnesses.

There is a species of acceptance which, though known to the Law, is not usual in these countries, called an acceptance "**supra protest,**" or an acceptance by some person not a party to the Bill, who accepts for what is called "the honour" of the Drawee, or perhaps of the Drawer. It is an undertaking to pay if the Drawee do not honour the Bill, and consequently at maturity the amount is first demanded from the Drawee. Payment "supra protest" is a proceeding also known to the Law.

Notice of Dishonour.—The duty to give notice of dishonour of a Bill of Exchange is a most important one, as the neglect to do so operates as a dispensation or discharge of liability as far as those legally entitled to such notice are concerned. Notice of dishonour to the previous Endorser is essential. But it is the usual and more proper course for a Holder for value of a Bill to give notice of dishonour to all the antecedent parties, as the proper sending of such notice will prevent their liability being discharged. There is no particular form of words necessary in such a notice, and Bankers have usually a printed form for the purpose ; but it must be an unequivocal notice of dishonour, and it must contain a demand for payment, and convey that the Holder looks to the party so noticed for payment. It must be explicit and describe the dishonoured Bill in such terms that the person receiving it may not be misinformed or misled.

The following examples of notices of dishonour—valid and invalid—are quoted from Mr. Justice Byles' work on " Bills of " Exchange," and will exemplify the legal requirements of this important department of Banking.

The following have been held *insufficient*:

(1) "The Note for 200*l*., drawn by H. H., dated 18th July last, payable " three months after date, and endorsed by you, became due yesterday, and " is returned to me unpaid. I therefore request you will let me have the " amount forthwith." "These facts," says Tindall, C. J., "are compatible " with an entire omission to present the Note to the maker." *Boulton* v. *Welsh*, 3 Bing, N. C. 688 ; 4 Scott, 425, S. C.

(2) "Sir, A Bill for 30*l*., dated the 18th August, 1837, at three months, " drawn and endorsed by R. Everett upon and accepted by W. Tuck, and " indorsed by you, lies at my office due and unpaid. I am, &c., S. J. " SYDNEY." *Phillips* v. *Gould*, 8 C. & P. 355.

(3) "Messrs. Strange & Co. inform Mr. James Price that Mr. John " Betterton's Acceptance for 87*l*. 5*s*. is not paid. As endorser, Mr. Price " is called upon to pay the money, which will be expected immediately. " Swindon, Dec., 1836." *Strange* v. *Price*, 10 Ad. and El. 125 ; 2 Per. & Dav. 278, S. C.

(4) "Sir, This is to inform you that the Bill I took of you, 11*l*. 2*s*. 6*d*., " is not took up, and 4*s*. 6*d*. expenses ; and the money I must pay imme- " diately. My son will be in London on Friday morning. WM. MES- " SENGER." *Messenger* v. *Southey*, 1 Man. & Gr. 76; 1 Scott, N. R. 180, S. C.

The following notices of non-payment of six Bills of Exchange were also held insufficient :

(1) "Sir, A Bill for 29*l*. 17*s*. 3*d*., drawn by Ward on Hunt, due yester- " day is unpaid, and I am sorry to say the person at whose house it is made

"payable don't speak very favourably of the Acceptor's punctuality. I should like to see you upon it to-day."

(2) "Mr. Maine, Sir, This is to give you notice that a Bill drawn by you and accepted by Josias Bateman for 47*l.* 16*s.* 9*d.*, due July 19th, 1835, is unpaid, and lies due at Mr. J. Furze's, 65, Fleet Street."

(3) "Sir, Mr. Howard's Acceptance for 21*l.* 4*s.* 4*d.*, due on Saturday, is unpaid. He has promised to pay it in a week or ten days. I shall be glad to see you upon it as early as possible."

(4) "Sir, This is to give you notice that a Bill for 176*l.* 15*s.* 6*d.*, drawn by Samuel Maine, accepted by G. Clisby, dated May 7th, 1835, at four months, lies due and unpaid at my house."

(5) "P. Johnson, Esq., Sir, This is to give you notice that a Bill, 20*l.* 17*s.* 7*d.*, drawn by Samuel Maine, accepted by Richard Jones, dated May 21st, 1835, at four months, lies due and unpaid at my house."

(6) "P. Johnson, Esq., Sir, This is to give you notice that a bill for 148*l.* 10*s.*, drawn by Samuel Maine, and accepted by G. Parker, dated May 22nd, 1835, lies due and unpaid at my house." *Furze* v. *Sharwood and Others*, 11 L. J., Q. B. 19; 2 Q. B. 388, S. C.

But the following have been held to be *sufficient* notices of dishonour :

(1) "Sir, A Bill drawn by you upon and accepted by Mr. Joshua Watson for 31*l.* 3*s.*, due yesterday, is dishonoured and unpaid ; and I am desired to give you notice thereof to request that the same may be immediately paid. I am, &c., H. D. RUSHBURY." *Woodthorpe* v. *Lawes*, 2 M. & W. 109.

(2) "Sir, The Bill for £——, drawn by you, is this day returned, *with charges*, to which your immediate attention is requested." (Signed by Endorsee.) *Grugeon* v. *Smith*, 6 Ad. & Ell. 499 ; 2 Nev. & P. 303, S. C.

(3) "Sir, I am desired by Mr. Hedger to give you notice that a Promissory Note for 99*l.* 18*s.*, payable to your order two months after the date thereof, became due yesterday, and has been returned unpaid, and I have to request you will please remit the amount thereof, *with* 1*s.* 6*d. noting*, free of postage, by return of post. I am, &c., JONES SPYER." *Hedger* v. *Stevenson*, 2 M. & W. 799 ; 5 Dowl. 771, S. C.

(4) "Your bill is unpaid ;" "*noting* 5*s.*" *Armstrong* v. *Christiani*, 5 C. B. 687 ; 17 L. J., C. P. 181.

(5) "Your note has been returned dishonoured," is sufficient, without the words "your note has been presented for payment." *Edmonds* v. *Cates*, 2 Jurist, 183.

(6) "Messrs. Houlditch are surprised that Mr. Cauty has not taken up

"Chaplin's Bill according to his promise; are also surprised to hear that Mrs. Gib's Bill was returned to the Holder unpaid."

This notice was followed by a visit from the Endorser to the Holder on the same day, in which he promised to write to the other parties, by whom, or by himself, the Bill shall be paid. *Houlditch* v. *Cauty*, 4 Bing, N. C. 441; 2 Scott, 209, S. C.

(7) "Mr. Gompertz, Sir, The Bill of Exchange for 250*l.* drawn by S. Kendall, and accepted by Charles Stretton, and bearing your indorsement, has been presented for payment to the acceptor thereof, and returned dishonoured, and now lies overdue and unpaid with me, as above, of which I hereby give you notice. I am, &c., C. LEWIS." *Lewis* v. *Gompertz*, 6 M. & W. 400.

(8) "I beg to inform you that Mr. D.'s Acceptance for 200*l.*, drawn and indorsed by you, due 31st July, has been presented for payment and returned, and now remains unpaid." *Cooke* v. *French*, 10 Ad. & Ell. 131 ; 3 Per. & D. 596, S. C.

(9) "Dear Sir, To my surprise I have received an intimation from the Birmingham and Midland Counties Bank that your draft on A. B. is dishonoured, and I have requested them to proceed on the same." *Shelton* v. *Braithwaite*, 7 M. & W. 436.

(10) "Sir, I am instructed by Mr. Molineaux to give you notice that a Bill (describing it) has been dishonoured," &c. *Stocken* v. *Colin*, 9 C. & P. 653; 7 M. & W. 515, S. C.

(11) A party sent by the holder of a dishonoured Bill of Exchange, called at the drawer's house the day after it became due, and there saw his wife, and told her that he had brought back the Bill that had been dishonoured. She said that she knew nothing about it, but would tell her husband of it when he came home. The party then went away, not leaving any written notice: held sufficient notice of dishonour. *Housego* v. *Cowne*, 2 M. & W. 348.

(12) "James Court's Acceptance, due this day, is unpaid, and *I request your immediate attention to it*," was held sufficient. *Bailey* v. *Porter*, 14 M. & W. 44. See the observations on this case in *Allen* v. *Edmundson*, 17 L. J., Exch. 293; 2 Exch. 819, S. C.; and see *Paul* v. *Joel*, 3 H. & N. 455; 28 L. J., Exch. 143; H. and N. 355, affirmed in error.

(13) "Your draft upon C., for 50*l.* due 3rd March, is returned to us unpaid, and if not taken up this day, proceedings will be taken against you for the recovery thereof," was held sufficient. *Robson* v. *Curlewis*, 2 Q. B. 421.

(14) Where the Holder, when the Bill became due, said to the executor of the Acceptor, who was also Indorser, "I have brought a bill from the plaintiff; you know what it is;" and the defendant said, "I am executor

"of the Drawee, you must persuade the plaintiff to let the Bill stand over a few days, because the Acceptor has been dead only a few days. I shall see the Bill paid." Notice of dishonour was held to be proved. *Caunt* v. *Thompson*, 18 L. J., C. P. 125 ; 7 C. B. 400, S. C.

(15) "We beg to acquaint you with the non-payment of William Miles's "Acceptance to James Wright's draft of 29th December last, at four "months, 50*l*., amounting, with expenses, to 50*l*. 5*s*. 1*d*., which remit us in "course of post without fail, to pay to Messrs. Everards & Co., Lynn," was held sufficient. *Everard* v. *Watson*, 1 E. & B. 801. In this case Lord Campbell expressed his regret at the decision of *Solarte* v. *Palmer ;* and see *Paul* v. *Joel*.

It is conceived, continues Justice Byles, that the following is the full Form of Notice to be given by the Holder to an Indorser. It may be easily altered and adapted to circumstances :

"*No.* 1, *Fleet Street, London,* 26*th Sept.,* 1842.—*Sir, I hereby give you "notice that the Bill of Exchange, dated* 22*nd ult., drawn by A. B. of* ——, "*on C. D. of* ——, *for* 100*l., payable one month after date to A. B. or his "order, and indorsed by you, has been duly presented for payment, but "was dishonoured, and is unpaid. I request you to pay me the amount "thereof. I am, Sir, your obedient servant, G. H.—To Mr. E. F., "of* ——, *(Merchant)*."

The notice must be sent to the places of business or residences of the parties, within a reasonable time after dishonour, which, in the case of Bankers, means the day after. Sundays and Bank Holidays are *dies non*.

It is general and most satisfactory, though not necessary, to post the notice of dishonour, for though the posting must be proved in an action on the Bill, it is not incumbent to prove the receipt by the noticed party of the letter containing the notice. A notice need not absolutely be in writing ; an oral notification will be sufficient, if it be capable of being proved to have been given.

An Acceptor is not entitled to any notice—that is to say, he is not discharged by reason of not having been noticed. In the event of the **Bankruptcy** of a party to whom notice was necessary, a notice to his Assignees is sufficient; and, if **dead**, a notice to the representatives of the deceased. A party who has signed a Bill as a mere **guarantor** is not discharged by reason of not having received a notice of dishonour, unless he can prove that he has been damnified thereby. If the residence of a party requiring notice, be unknown, and cannot be discovered by the exercise of due diligence, the necessity of notice is dispensed with; but in the event of the address subsequently becoming known, notice must be sent without delay. A promise to pay made by a Drawer or Endorser after a Bill has arrived at maturity is presumed to be an acknowledgment on his part that he has received the notice legally requisite, even though such notice may not have been sent, —for the promise acts by way of condonation of the omission.

Remedy for Dishonour.—The remedy for dishonour of an acceptance is by an action *on* the Bill. The Holder, or the person lawfully entitled to the amount, is the only person who can sue. If several parties, as Drawer and Acceptor and previous Endorser for example, are liable, the Holder can select the person against whom he will proceed; or he can sue all the parties individually in separate actions; but payment or discharge by any one will discharge all and terminate the suits. If the Holder obtain judgment against all the parties, he can elect which he will execute upon, but he can only execute against one of the parties. The legal procedure on a Bill is defined by the recent Judicature Act, and the writ of summons is to be in a form which is prescribed by the Act.

Bankruptcy.—Upon an Act of Bankruptcy by a party, all Bills of Exchange current, though not yet matured, as well as those overdue—in fact all debts, can be proved against his estate. But only the one proof on the one debt is admitted; thus a Bill which has been proved-on against an Acceptor by a Holder, cannot be again proved-on by an Endorser who may have paid it to the Holder. If a Bill which has been proved-on against a Bankrupt Acceptor, be nevertheless paid at maturity by the Drawer, the dividend on the Acceptor's estate received by the Holder, is in trust with him for the payer of the Bill. If more than one of the parties to a Bill, or all of them, be Bankrupt, the Holder can prove under all who are Bankrupt and receive a dividend out of the estates of all. In case of the Holder of a Bill becoming Bankrupt the Bill vests in his Trustees or Assignees, and he must Endorse it to them as portion of his assets.

Overdue Bills.—The question whether a Banker, in the absence of an express authority to that effect, is entitled to debit, or justified in debiting his Customer's account with acceptances made payable at his Bank, but not presented till they have been overdue, has never been, so far as we know, raised in England, though there is a Colonial decision (Wine *v.* Bank of New South Wales) upon it which has not commended itself to the commercial community there.

XIII.

DISCOUNT. — REBATE. — BILLS FOR COLLECTION. — FOREIGN BILLS, etc., etc.

Discount is, as the word implies, an amount deducted or *counted off* a sum advanced. It is defined to be a "deduc-"tion made for interest, in advancing money upon a Bill or "Note not due; payment in advance of interest upon money "loaned. It is equal to the interest which would be acquired "at the given rate for the given time, either by the whole sum "specified to be paid, or by that sum after it is itself deducted; "in the former case it is called *bank discount*."

The rate charged is regulated by the Bank of England rate, and is computed for the number of days the Bill has to run. It is dependent on the nature and class of the Bill discounted, Accommodation Bills being charged a higher rate than true business Bills, and those for a long term higher than those for a short one. The usual course adopted by a Banker in discounting approved Bills for his Customer is either to place the entire amount of the Bills to the credit of his account, debiting him with the discount, or else to place the proceeds to his credit. In either case it is manifest that the apparent rate charged is below the real rate, because the customer is charged a percentage on the full amount of the Bill, as if the full amount had been advanced, whereas it is the amount less the discount that the Customer receives, and upon which, therefore, he pays interest. Thus, for example, in the case of a Bill drawn at 12 months, for £1,000, and discounted at 5 per cent., the Customer is paid £950, and the Banker, therefore, receives £50 on an advance of £950 for 12 months, and this in reality represents somewhat over 5¼ per cent. The Banker charges not on the amount actually advanced, but on the amount repayable, and the Banker is by custom, entitled to the advantage of the transaction.

A Banker who discounts a Bill, becomes, as it were, the purchaser of the Bill, but the rule *caveat emptor* does not apply to him, as he has recourse against the Endorser, *i.e.*, the seller of it. But when a Bill is discounted and the proceeds held as cash at the disposal of the Customer, the Bill is purchased to this extent by the Banker, that it becomes his entire and absolute property and he can dispose of it as he wishes.

There is, however, a difference between giving a **Loan on Bills** and discounting them. In the former case the Bills are not discounted, they are held as security for the loan made, and only become negotiable by the Banker, and his property, in case of default by the borrower. The Banker has thus a qualified property in such Bills: he shall not surrender them until the loan be satisfied, and if they mature in his hands and be paid, he holds the proceeds for the benefit of his Customer, though he is entitled to apply the amount in payment of the loan should the Customer be in default. But the Banker cannot transfer Bills deposited against a loan in this manner, as his title to them is not absolute. They remain in the constructive possession of the Customer.

Rebate.—Rebate or rebatement can be briefly defined as "a deduction of interest allowed on account of a prompt pay-"ment, or upon a payment made before a debt is due, or has "been stipulated to be paid." In City Banking this allowance is an everyday occurrence. Frequently an Acceptor pays his acceptance before its maturity, generally because of the circumstance that a Bill of lading or a delivery order, authorising the possession of the commodities for which the acceptance is payment, is attached to the Bill, and obtainable only upon payment; and thus, to obtain his goods, the Acceptor pays before the Bill is due, and claims " Rebate " for the unexpired term. In this case the rate allowed is not always the rate charged ; it generally is the current Bank rate. The " Rebate," which figures in the balance sheet of some Banks, and forms an important item in the profit and loss account, is something other than that claimed by a pre-payer of a Bill. It is generally supposed to be the interest which the Bank has received for that period of the Bills current, which is unexpired. For example, if a Bill for £1,000 has been discounted on 1st June for three months at 5 per cent., the discount, roughly speaking, is £12 10s.; but as at the close of the half year, on 30th June, when the balance sheet is made up, two of these three months are unexpired, the Bank debits itself with two-thirds of this discount received, *i.e.*, with about £8 6s. 8d.—that being the amount the Acceptor could claim, were he to pay the Bill on the 1st July. This, we are informed, is the general practice of Banks, and we are further informed that in few is the amount of Rebate calculated with any accuracy, or after any scientific method.

When a Banker discounts a Bill, he deducts the discount at once, and places it to his profit and loss account. He is paid in advance, and therefore at the close of his year, on those Bills then outstanding he has the payment on the use of the portion of his capital for periods ahead of the date of his balance sheet. If every Bill discounted, matured on the 31st December, then he could claim for his profit and loss account all the discount he had received, because it would legitimately and in its entirety be his. But, on the 31st December, he holds Bills maturing one, two, or three months hence, and it is obvious that the discount, which is the interest on his capital in one way, on those Bills maturing in the next year, belongs to the profits of the next year. The amount of this next year's profits should, therefore, be deducted from the apparent profits of the current year, as these apparent profits embrace payments of interest in advance.

The "adjusting account of interest," which is used to define the liability of the Bank for interest accrued and due up to the date of the balance sheet on outstanding deposits, is calculated with exactitude. Each deposit is subjected to separate calculation, and there is no lumping or guessing in this respect. It is apparent that a Bank that lumps or guesses at its Rebate, must misrepresent its liabilities somewhat, and submit an erroneous balance sheet. To present a strictly accurate balance sheet, the Rebate on each outstanding Bill should be calculated, as the interest on each outstanding deposit is calculated. What should that rate be? Should it be the rate charged upon the Bill; or the current Bank of England rate; or a rate according to the fancy or caprice of the management?

The theory, that because in case of the prepayment of a Bill by the Drawee, a deduction is allowed him at the same rate for the unexpired term, as was paid for the whole term when the Bill was discounted, therefore a Bank at the close of the year should estimate its Rebate Account on the same principle, is one which would prove to be tedious and unwieldy in execution as it would be false in principle. We will simplify our position by a popular illustration. When a trader makes up his yearly balance sheet he takes stock, and in so doing he does not value his stock at what he can sell it for, nor at what he gave for it, but at the present market value of it. A Banker is like any other trader. His Bills on hand are his stock, and his balance sheet should be framed on the stock-taking principle—that is to say, he should estimate their value at their market value, and not at their value to him, or at the price he paid for them. The value-test, therefore, is: At what rate these Bills can be converted into money; and the difference between the nominal value of them and the proceeds of them at their marketable rate, is the true Rebate which should be shown. If this market rate be higher than the rate he has charged, so much the worse for his balance sheet: if it be lower, so much the better. Undue Bills are a reversionary and not a present asset, and, therefore, a Banker in calculating his assets must bear this in mind. Rebate, therefore, in a word, is the cost of converting a reversionary into a present asset.

Bills for Collection.—A Banker generally receives from his Customers Bills which he undertakes to collect in the usual course, and to account to the Customer for the amount, if the Bills be paid. The Banker has at no time a property in the Bills, as they are not transferred to him; though if he has made an advance upon the Bills or allowed an overdraft upon the security of them, he has a lien on them. In case a Bill left for collection be unpaid, the Banker in his Customer's interest can note or protest it unless he is instructed to the contrary, and it is his duty to return it without delay to the party who lodged it for collection, provided he—the Banker—has no lien upon it. It has been decided that should such Bills, which, though in the Banker's hands, are nevertheless not his but his Customer's, be destroyed or lost by accident, and through no negligence on the Banker's part, the loss will fall on the Customer alone. In case of the bankruptcy of the Banker, Bills deposited for collection revert to the Customer, and do not pass to the Banker's assignees.

"**Short Bills.**"—The custom of receiving undue Bills, and, as it is technically called, "entering them short" (*i.e.* short of the cash or credit column of the ledger), whereby they are known by the term "Short Bills" (and by means of which the Depositor of them may obtain a quasi credit on account of them), is a convenience and facility to the Customer. The entry is a memorandum by the Banker that he holds such Bills from his Customer for collection, and that they are to be collected on a certain date. Until they are paid, the amount is not passed to the Credit of his account. The Bills, there_fore, are, until paid, exclusively the Customer's property. They do not pass into the Banker's possession, nor has he any right to them, unless they are as security for a loan. They are at the disposal of him who deposited them, unless in case of his bankruptcy, in which event the Banker can surrender them to the bankrupt's assignees alone. If the Banker should convert or negotiate "Short Bills" he is guilty of an indictable offence.

Interest on overdue Bills.—There is no limit in law to the rate of interest which can be charged on a Bill, since the repeal and entire abolition of the Usury Laws by 17 & 18 Vic., c. 90. But Equity would restrain an usurious rate. A Bill can be drawn, with the words "bearing interest" at such a rate, upon the face of it, and that interest, unless it be contrariwise expressed, begins to run from the maturity of the Bill.

Usury.—Statutes against usury were enacted in the reign of Henry VIII., who restricted the legal rate of interest to 10 per cent. and made it a penal offence to take more. Under Edward VI. the taking of any interest whatsoever was prohibited. In Elizabeth's reign a contract for the payment of more than 10 per cent. was voided as usurious; and under successive kings the legal rate was reduced gradually until it reached 5 per cent. in Queen Anne's reign. The latter Statute enacted that any person taking a larger percentage should forfeit treble the money lent, one-half of which penalty enured to the Crown, and the other to "him that will sue for the same;" and further, that all bonds or contracts whereby a rate above 5 per cent. shall be reserved or taken, shall be utterly void. The repealing enactments are of a later date. In 1834, Bills and Notes not having more than three months to run were exempted from the operation of the laws against usury. In 1837, those not having more than 12 months to run were exempted. The 2 & 3 Vic., c. 37, exempted also all contracts for the loan of money above ten pounds, but this act did not extend to loans on landed security. And the Statute now in operation is the 17 & 18 Vic., c. 90, which made a clean sweep of the usury laws altogether.

Alteration in Bill.—An alteration in a material part of a Bill or Note vitiates the instrument. But if the alteration be made to correct an obvious mistake; or if it be made in consonance with, or furtherance of, the wishes of the parties, and before the Bill be negotiated—and that such alteration be confirmed by all the parties, the Bill is not thereby voided.

Compulsory Signing.—To compel a person by threats or violence to sign a Bill or Note is a felony. To obtain a signature to a Bill or Note by false pretences or fraudulent representations is a misdemeanour.

The Statute of Limitations.—The Statute of Limitations, which was enacted in the reign of James I. (21 Jac. I, c. 16) enacts that "all actions of debt granted on any lending "or contract without specialty, must be brought within six "years of the cause of such action, and not after." A cause of action on a Bill or Note arises at its maturity, and not at its making. If drawn "on demand" the Statute runs from the date of the instrument. The Statute of Limitations is a sufficient plea in a defence to an action for debt. Its effect, in the words of an eminent judge, "is not to destroy the debt, "but only to take away the remedy." A Bill or Note can be taken out of the Statute by part payment, but such part payment must include an admission that more is due. Payment of interest will also prevent a debt lapsing, but by a Statute no part payment endorsed on a Bill *by or on behalf of the party to whom such part payment is made* shall be deemed sufficient to take the debt out of the Statute of Limitations. It is, therefore, necessary (unless unquestionable proof of the payment is readily obtainable), that a part payment or a payment of interest should be signed by the debtor, or recorded in his handwriting. **Renewal** of a Bill will take the debt out of the Statute, as will also an acknowledgment made to the plaintiff of the indebtedness. In these cases the Statute will run from the renewal, the acknowledgment, the part payment, or the payment of interest.

Lost Bill.—Formerly no action lay at Common Law on a lost Bill or Note, except perhaps on one that was particularly payable, and, therefore, not negotiable; and, when a Bill or Note, being lost, had become due, application for payment should have been made to the Drawee, and in case of nonpayment, the usual notice of dishonour should have been given to the other parties to the Bill. But an Act of Parliament (9 & 10 Wm. III., c. 17, s. 3) provided that the Drawer can be compelled by a lawful Holder, to give, under proper and satisfactory indemnity, a Duplicate of the lost Bill. Now, however, by 17 & 18 Vic., c. 125, s. 87, the loss of a Bill or

Note cannot be set up as a defence to an action on the Bill, provided a sufficient indemnity has been offered to the Acceptor or Maker. The finder of a lost Bill, has, of course, no title against the true owner.

Foreign Bills.—A Foreign Bill is, briefly, one that is drawn or payable, or purporting to be drawn or payable, abroad —*i.e.*, outside the British Isles. It is frequently drawn in what are called "**sets**." The definition given by Mr. Justice Byles of "sets" is, "exemplars or parts of the Bill, which are "made on separate pieces of paper, each part referring to the "other parts, and containing a condition that it shall continue "payable only so long as the others remain unpaid." These *sets* generally circulate together, and constitute but one Bill, one only needing to be accepted or endorsed or stamped. On one class of Foreign Bills—*i.e.*, Bills drawn or negotiated in a Foreign Independent State—the Stamp of the country where they have been made or negotiated is not required to make them valid in this country. If such a Stamp were legally considered requisite, it would entail a necessity of a knowledge of the Stamp Laws and Stamp Duties of these countries, and this necessity would operate as a restriction to the negotiability of Foreign Bills, because no one would receive them if he knew his title could be defeated and the amount lost to him because of an irregular and insufficient Foreign Stamp. But this does not apply to another class of Foreign Bills—*i.e.*, ones drawn or negotiated in some of the Colonies, where the Stamp Duties which obtain in those Colonies are the same as those of the British Isles. The Stamp Duties on Foreign Bills negotiated in this Kingdom, are denoted by adhesive stamps, and are the same as those on Bills of Exchange, as set forth in the Stamp Act *ante.*

XIV.

BANKERS' DRAFTS AND POST BILLS—LIEN—CONFIDENTIAL REPORTS, ETC.

Bankers' Drafts.—This is the term that distinguishes Drafts which are drawn by a Bank or one of its branches, upon another of its branches or upon its agents, and which are payable on demand, without acceptance, to a specified party or his order. They are a means of remitting money from one place to another, and have all the incidents of Cheques.

Bank Post Bills.—All Banks issue Post Bills, which are Bills of Exchange, or promissory notes, payable at a given period after (*post*) date or sight at one or more given places. If drawn after date they are payable when due, with or without acceptance. They are generally drawn payable at seven days after date. These are, in the majority of instances, redeemed on demand without acceptance. These instruments generally are unstamped, as the Stamp Duty is paid by composition in accordance with certain Acts of Parliament. But as the provisions of the Acts of Parliament are in respect to "Bank "Post Bills of £5 and upwards," it seems that Post Bills for less than £5, issued unstamped, would not be embraced in the Composition Duty, and would, therefore, not be legal instruments. The power to pay a Composition Duty was established by the 27 & 28 Vic., c. 86, which permitted the composition, but limited it to "a period of three years from the passing of "the Act." But the power was made perpetual by 30 & 31 Vic. c. 89 (The Stamp Duty Composition Act of 1867). The power to issue Bank Post Bills payable seven days after sight was conferred on the Scotch Banks by 5 Geo. III., c. 49, s. 20. Bank of England Post Bills issued in London are only, by law, payable in London.

Bankers in Ireland were (by 9 Geo. IV., c. 81) prohibited issuing Bank Post Bills unless the same were made payable at the place they were issued; but they might have been made also payable at several places. Bank Post Bills are an old form of remittance, having been issued by the Bank of England as long ago as 1738.

Letters of Credit.—A Letter of Credit is an instrument—not a Banker's Draft or Bill of Exchange—whereby a person is enabled to draw money lodged elsewhere for his use. It is, to use Grant's words, "an authority from the Banker who signs it "to the Banker or person to whom it is addressed, upon advice "to honour the Drafts of the person named in it, and who "produces the letter; and, consequently, he alone is entitled to "draw the Draft or to receive payment." It is adapted for persons who are travelling in continental and foreign countries, and possesses elements of security which an ordinary Banker's Draft does not possess. It is a written direction by a Banker to several correspondents to pay the Drafts on him of the person named in the letter, to a certain extent, within a given period. Each payment is entered on the Letter of Credit, and the correspondents are thus informed if the credit is exhausted before the expiration of the period named. The letter bears the signature of the party in whose favour it is issued, thus providing the identification requisite. But if the Banker on whom the Drafts in connection with the Letter of Credit are drawn, pay any Drafts on a forged signature, he, as in the case of a Cheque, is not discharged to the party whose signature it purports to be. Letters of Credit, granted in the United Kingdom, authorising Drafts to be drawn out of the United Kingdom, payable in the United Kingdom, are, as has been seen, exempt from Stamp Duty by the Stamp Act; but the Drafts drawn under it are not.

Circular Notes are instruments similar to Letters of Credit, *i.e.*, are issued for a similar purpose. They are Bills of Exchange of a certain amount, drawn in French, and accompanied by a letter called a Letter of Indication, also in French (as the most general language), which is addressed to the foreign correspondents of the issuing Banker, and which contains the signature (for identification) of the party for whose favour the notes are issued. The Drawees of these notes are the correspondents specified in the letter, and the notes are payable without acceptance to the party named in the letter.

Marginal Letters of Credit.—This is another form of instrument of a somewhat similar nature to the foregoing, but they are not in general use, as far as we are aware.

A Lien is defined to be "a right in one to hold and retain "the property of another until some claim of the former is paid "or satisfied." In a Lien, though the Holder of the securities has actual possession, he is not absolutely possessed of them, and his title to the actual possession is qualified, and lapses altogether upon the satisfaction of his claim against the real owner. A **General Lien** is where securities are deposited generally to cover an indebtedness which may fluctuate from time to time, no matter how that indebtedness may be created. **A specific Lien** is where securities are deposited to cover a specific indebtedness created in a specified manner. Thus a Lien " to cover the balance due on foot of A.'s current account, "to the extent of £500," is specific. A Banker has a general Lien upon all securities he may have in his possession belonging to the indebted Customer, which have been lodged with him as securities, actually or constructively. But a Lien does not attach to securities which have been lodged for a special purpose. For instance, a Banker has no Lien for a balance against a Customer, on (*e.g.*) Exchequer Bills lodged in order that the interest on them may be drawn, or fresh Bills obtained. So a Banker has no Lien on plate deposited with him for safe custody. Nor has he a Lien on securities left at the Bank, casually or by mistake, by his Customer. If a Customer when depositing securities with a Banker, acknowledge that they do not belong to him, the Banker can have no Lien on them; and if the Banker have made advances upon the securities without any such knowledge, but that subsequently he is informed of the fact, that information is a notice to the Banker not to make further advances, for his Lien may be altogether disputed; but it cannot be made to cover the advances made after he has had notice that the securities belong wholly, or in part, to a third person; for that is notice that the Customer had no authority to pledge the securities, or saddle them with a Lien.

As a Lien is a power of detention, supported by a power to realise in case of default, and to appropriate the proceeds of the realisation to the debt due by the Customer and interest thereupon, the duty is imposed on Bankers not to realise prematurely, or to the detriment of the Customer; and further, to hold any surplus from the realisation, after the satisfaction of the debt, for the benefit of the Customer. If a Banker, having a Lien on securities for a debt, nevertheless takes a distinct security, payable at a distant day, for the same debt, he destroys his rights of a Lien.

Liability of Bankers for the conduct of their Correspondents.—If a Banker undertake to perform for his Customer a Banking duty in a place where there is a branch of his Bank, and that the Branch office is guilty of negligence which damnifies the Customer, the Banker is liable, because his Branch Bank is, as it were, himself. And also, if a Banker A. engage to perform a duty in a place where he has no Branch of his own Bank, and employs another Banker B. as his agent to discharge that duty, and this Agent-Banker by his conduct, directly or indirectly, entail a loss, and the question arises upon whom this loss shall fall, the Banker A. is liable to his Customer, and in all such cases must suffer the loss occasioned by the act of B., the agent he employed. But he, A., will have, of course, a right of recourse to B., by whose laches he has suffered the loss.

Confidential Reports on Customers.—The custom of one Banker giving another a report in confidence of the position, means, and character of his Customer, has grown from being a matter of courtesy to be a recognised and established duty. So much has it become part of a Banker's business that Banks have usually printed forms for the purpose of asking and answering such inquiries. The form asking for the information alleges the private nature of the inquiry; and that affording the information sought, bears the avowal that it is given without responsibility on the part either of the Bank or the writer personally. Banks make these inquiries, either for their own information, or on behalf of their Customers, and the information they elicit must be taken for what it is worth. Notwithstanding the printed notice on the reply-forms, to the effect that the information is given on the understanding that no responsibility is entailed by the giver, nevertheless, if it be proved that misleading information was given by malicious design, and in consequence of such information credit was given to the party reported on, which entailed a loss, the Banker giving such deliberately wrong information will be held liable. But it would be extremely difficult to prove malice in such a case. Except in undoubted and unquestionable cases, Bankers generally reply to these queries in a somewhat ambiguous fashion; for instance, "A. is believed to be respectable, and "is considered good in a business transaction for £100." This is done, perhaps, with a view of shirking a possible responsibility—though all responsibility is patently disclaimed; but it cannot be considered a satisfactory method of answering business inquiries.

Guaranties by Third Parties.—By the celebrated Statute of Frauds passed in the reign of Charles II., it is enacted by Sec. 4: That *no action shall be brought* whereby to charge the defendant upon any special promise to answer for the debt, default, or miscarriage of another person, unless the agreement upon which such action shall be brought, or some memorandum or note thereof, shall be in writing and signed by the party to be charged therewith, or by some other person thereunto by him lawfully authorised.

A Guaranty is a special promise to answer for the payment of another's debt, and therefore must be in writing to sustain an action upon it. Formerly, to constitute a valid Guaranty, a good consideration to the Guarantor should have existed, but by the 19 & 20 Vic. c. 97, s. 3, the absence of a consideration in writing "shall not be deemed invalid to support an action." It is evident, therefore, that a mere **verbal Guaranty**, agreement, or undertaking, to be liable for the debt or default of another person is legally valueless. In addition to being in writing it is necessary also that a Guaranty should bear the statutory stamp duty requisite for an agreement.

Guaranties may be **general** or **specific**. In the latter case, the terms, amount, and duration of the Guaranty are specified, and any violation of the terms without the Guarantor's knowledge and consent, and which may be to his prejudice, or which may amount to constituting a new agreement, will discharge him. A Guaranty for a stated time lapses, of course, on the expiration of the time specified. If a Guaranty (*e.g.*, for £5,000) be given to a Banker by A., for advances made to B., "*provided they do not exceed* £5,000," and that the Banker exceeds that figure, and makes advances to the extent of £10,000 to B., the Guaranty-Bond is not vacated, but is valid to its extent, that is to £5,000. The reason of this is, seemingly, that it is not in a Guarantor's power to restrict the power of a Banker to make advances; and if a Banker do exceed the Guarantor's limit, he does so on some security and responsibility other than the Guaranty by A. A **general** Guaranty is of the nature of a collateral and continuing security for fluctuating liabilities.

A Guaranty may be **withdrawn** or determined at any time by the Guarantor, provided that, at the time, the withdrawal is not to the prejudice of the Banker, or injurious to his interests. **Giving time** to a Debtor who is guaranteed, without the assent of the Guarantor, is done at the risk of the Banker-Creditor. "Giving time" means giving indulgence more than the law and the custom of Bankers prescribes, and such undue indulgence, in the absence of an express stipulation, or of the consent of the Guarantor, will discharge him. Taking a fresh and distinct Guaranty does not absolve or discharge the old surety, unless it be made and given with that intent.

A Guarantor is **released** if the Banker is guilty of negligence or laches, which are detrimental to him, the Guarantor. Guaranties should be as simple, and general, and absolute as possible. Bankers should be careful to have no provisoes or trusts in a Guaranty, and they should remember that, in obtaining a Guaranty from a party, any suppression or misrepresentation on the part of the Banker of the real state of the affairs of the party being guaranteed—or any concealment with the intent to mislead, will render the Guaranty vitiate and invalid against the Guarantor.

In Guaranties made before the 29th July, 1856, it was legally requisite that a good consideration should appear on the face of the instrument; but since that date (by 19 & 20 Vic., c. 97, s. 3), that necessity no longer exists, provided that all such undertakings "be in writing, and signed by the party to be "charged therewith, or some other person by him thereunto "lawfully authorised."

XV.

DEPOSITS AGAINST ADVANCES, AND FOR SAFE CUSTODY.

Policies—Shares—Title Deeds—Goods—*Etc.*

The Object of deposits of securities with a Banker is to protect the Banker against advances made to his Customer. Where the security deposited is one wherein the property will not pass by mere delivery, but by assignment, the property will remain in the Depositor. The Banker will have no more than a lien upon it, unless it be duly assigned, and proper notice given of such assignment. Thus, in the case of a **Policy of Assurance,** an assignment to the Bank must be made, and the company noticed thereof in order to vest the property in the Banker—otherwise in case of the Bankruptcy of the Customer the Policy would vest in his trade assignees; and notice to an agent of the Assurance Company is not deemed notice to the company, except in special cases where the agent is employed to receive such notices. This assignment, with notice of it, is chiefly of importance in the case of the Bankruptcy of the Debtor who has deposited the Policy. In ordinary cases, the mere deposit of the Policy will give the Banker a lien upon it, because the possession of it under the circumstances will constitute him an equitable mortgagee: but it is the most approved and satisfactory course to obtain an assignment in all cases.

It is to be observed that a Policy which becomes void if the assured commit suicide, is, nevertheless, valid in the hands of an assignee, if it be assigned a reasonable time before the act of suicide. A concise and effectual form of an absolute assignment is given below.*

Shares and Stock.—In the same way, in order that the Banker should obtain a property in Shares or Stock lodged by his Customer, it is usual to have the Shares or Stock transferred into the joint names of some of the officers of the Bank; but such transfers must be in accordance with the constitution of the Bank. A mere deposit of the certificates of Shares or Stock should be accompanied by a letter from the Depositor to the effect that they are lodged as security for advances. But even with such letter of deposit there is a risk run in accepting a deposit of the scrip or certificates of Shares as a security.

* I, _____
of _____
in consideration of the sum of Five Shillings, do hereby assign unto THE _____ BANK, their Successors and Assigns, the Policy of Assurance granted by _____
on the life of _____
numbered _____ and dated _____ for the sum of _____

In WITNESS whereof, I have hereunto set my hand and seal this _____ day of _____ 18_____

_____ | SEAL |

Signed in the presence of

_____

I acknowledge to have received the Five Shillings consideration mentioned above.

The mere possession of these documents does not entitle the holder, be he a Banker or a private individual, to the possession of the Shares, that is to say, to a transfer into his own name. It is necessary, therefore, for the perfect protection of a Bank making advances on such securities, that a duly executed deed of transfer to the Bank should be completed, so that the Bank shall have absolute power of disposal in the event of the default of the Debtor. Such absolute transfer, made on the stipulation, freely given by all Bankers, that the Stock and Shares shall not be disposed of, or used, except in case of default, and that a re-transfer to the owner shall be made when the indebtedness terminates, is a complete security. A mortgage on Shares, secured by deed, is an unsatisfactory security, and only one degree better than the bare deposit of the certificates. Refusal or negligence on the part of the mortgagor in performing the covenants of a deed of mortgage will imperil the security. It may be accepted as a rule that an advance on Shares or Stock, otherwise than under a complete and absolute transfer of such Shares and Stock to the Bank, is bad Banking, for it involves a venture or a risk which no Banker, in ordinary circumstances, is bound to undertake. Even in accepting a transfer of the Shares he may become liable for future calls: so that advances should not as a rule be made on Shares other than fully paid-up Shares in a limited company of the highest standing and solvency.

Bills of Lading and Dock Warrants.—As these documents, when duly endorsed, give the holder of them the right to the goods named therein, the property passes without further assignment, and they are good securities in the hands of the Banker. The distinction between Bills of Lading and Bills of Exchange has been happily defined by Mr. Macleod: one represents goods, the other represents Debt.

Title Deeds.—A mere deposit of Title Deeds constitutes the Banker an equitable Mortgagee; nevertheless, a letter of deposit is advisable, and such letter does not require to be stamped. A deposit of a Lease conveys an equitable mortgage on all fixtures and improvements in the premises, though they be added or effected subsequently to the deposit, except they are improvements or fixtures which are the property of a Sub-Lessee. But the deposit of a Lease of a house does not carry a charge on the furniture, etc., therein; but if it be a Licensed house, the Mortgagee has a charge on the goodwill of the License. A Banker holding a Lease as a mere equitable Mortgagee is not liable for the covenants of the Lease. "Where Bankers take a mortgage as security, the principal "point to be considered," says Grant, "is that the lands, etc., "meant to be charged, shall be precisely specified or desig- "nated." It is true that the intent to give a general charge upon all the property of the Mortgagor may be explained *aliunde*, but the shortest, safest, and the least troublesome and expensive mode of effecting an arrangement of this kind is, to have care taken that the mortgage deed is made as complete as possible within itself, so as to require no subsequent propping up; and he quotes the following case to show how needful is attention to this point:—A Customer being indebted to his Bankers, sent to them certain Title Deeds, with a letter in which he stated that he thereby pledged his grant of coal under an estate, which he specified, as a security for the money advanced, and also as a general cover for his Banking Account with them. There were other estates belonging to the Customer comprised in the Deeds sent, but the Court held that the Bankers could only claim a Lien in respect to the estate particularised in the letter.

Goods Deposited.—It is not usual for a Banker in

ordinary transactions to accept a deposit of goods as security for advances, for not alone would such a practice be inconvenient and troublesome, but, further, it would degrade Banking to the low level of Pawnbroking. But in a case of necessity, where no other security is obtainable, it is possible a Banker would be bound, in order to protect himself, to take a deposit of goods as security, in preference to having no security whatsoever. In such a case, his chief care is to assure himself that the goods so deposited are really the disposable property of the Debtor or the Guarantor, otherwise the Banker can, perhaps, be compelled to surrender them to the lawful owner, for it is apparent that if the depositor had no title in them he could give no title to the Banker. And, having satisfied himself on this point, he should obtain a letter o deposit, with a power of sale if the security should be goods which are not deposited ; the deposit should be accompanied by a Bill of Sale, duly executed and registered in compliance with the Law.

A security deposited to secure a specific amount, or a specific debt, cannot be otherwise applied ; and securities must be surrendered to the Debtor or Guarantor on the quittance of the debt, and if realised, the surplus, if any, must be given over to the Depositor, or to his representatives if he be dead ; or to his Assignees if he be a Bankrupt.

Realisation of Securities.—A Banker has an indisputable right to repledge or sell any securities deposited with him against advances—but only to an amount co-extensive with his claim. The 24 & 25 Vic., c. 96, s. 75, says that nothing in the Section shall restrain any Banker "from selling, "transferring or otherwise disposing of any securities or effects "in his possession upon which he shall have any Lien, claim, " or demand entitling him by law to do so," unless such sale, etc., shall extend to a greater number or part of such securities, etc., than shall be requisite for satisfying such Lien, etc. But a Banker has no Lien on securities or effects deposited with him for safe custody; or with him as Trustee; or for purposes of realisation, or collection.

"**Safe Custody.**"—Where a Customer of a Bank gives the Banker boxes containing, or said to contain, plate, jewellery, deeds, or valuables or security of any description, not by way of security, but in order that they should be safely kept, and the Banker consents to receive them, the act is said to be a deposit for safe custody. The Banker is bound to surrender such articles on the application of the Depositor. As a rule, Bankers make no charge for thus accommodating their Customers; and though an opinion seems to prevail that the Banker should not thus give the use of his strong rooms and safes to his Customers *gratuitously*, it must be remembered that if he should undertake the custody for hire he would clothe himself with a liability not attaching to him as a gratuitous custodian. The acceptance by the Banker for safe custody of his Customer's Box being for the Customer's convenience and accommodation, and not being done for reward, the Banker is not liable for any loss occasioned by robbery, fire, destruction, etc., as long as he has taken *ordinary* care of the articles so deposited, because he is but a gratuitous bailee. **Ordinary Care** is described in a judgment by the Privy Council (England) in a safe-custody suit, as "that ordinary "diligence which a reasonably prudent man takes of his own "property of the like description." Further, if the valuables deposited should be stolen, or converted by a clerk or servant in the Bank, the Banker will not be liable, unless he has been guilty of gross and culpable negligence, or that he has retained the clerk in the service of the Bank with a knowledge that he is a dishonest servant.

Nevertheless, Byles gives it as his opinion, that in cases of deposits for safe custody, accepted by the Banker without reward, "the Banker can hardly be regarded as acting "gratuitously for his Customer, such custody being *an induce-* "*ment held out to attract Customers*, by the use of whose "balances the Banker is paid." But this reasoning could hardly be made applicable to Banks that do not invite such deposits. A Banker's liability for deposits for safe custody does not lapse by time, and in case of the death of the Depositor, the Banker becomes the Trustee (to the extent of the deposit) for the representatives of the deceased.

If a Banker, entrusted with securities deposited for safe custody, shall, in violation of good faith, and contrary to the purpose for which such deposit was made, "sell, negotiate, "transfer, pledge, or in any way convert to his own use or "benefit, or the use or benefit of any person other than the "person by whom he shall have been so entrusted," such property or security, or any part thereof, he shall be guilty of a misdemeanor, and on conviction is liable to penal servitude for a term not less than five years, and not more than seven years; or to imprisonment, with or without hard labour, for any term not exceeding two years.

XVI.

BANK NOTES.—I. O. U.

A Bank Note is a promissory note issued by a Banker and made payable to the bearer on demand, which circulates as, and is equivalent to, money. It differs from other promissory notes in that it can be re-issued, and the mere possession gives a property in it. It further entitles the Holder to the amount without endorsement. Bank Notes are the descendants of the old Deposit Notes, called "Goldsmiths' Notes," issued by the early Goldsmiths who were the precursors of Bankers in London. A Bank which issues such notes is called a Bank of Issue, and "circulation" is the term applied to the aggregate notes of a Bank in the hands of the public.

The privilege of issuing Bank Notes is not possessed by all Banks, and it cannot now be obtained by those that do not possess it, nor by any new establishment. The rights and extent of the note issues of those Banks which are entitled to make and issue Bank Notes are now defined and regulated by the Statute Law. The 3 & 4 Will. IV., c. 98, enacted that no Bank of more than six persons shall issue in London, or within sixty-five miles thereof, Bills or Notes payable on demand, saving the rights of Country Bankers to make their notes payable in London. This Act determined the issues of Bank Notes by the London private Bankers, though, as a matter of fact, they had long before ceased to circulate their notes. In the early days of Banking, there was no restriction in the individual or collective amount of the notes issued by the Bankers throughout England—private or joint-stock; and it is to be observed that the instances are comparatively few where they, by fraudulent design, over-issued their notes. Not so in Ireland. There, as has already been shown, every private firm calling itself a Bank could, and did, issue notes unrestrainedly, to an almost incredible extent, sometimes without any security or even possibility of redeeming them, and the evils wrought to the country by this unlimited issue of worthless notes by Bankrupt Firms were such, that the Legislature interfered, though tardily, to protect the public and ensure them some security that the notes which should circulate as money from hand to hand should not prove worthless.

By the 55 Geo. III., c. 184,* (an Act passed on 11th July, 1815), it was provided that Bankers, duly constituted and licensed, might issue and re-issue certain promissory notes, payable to bearer on demand, for any sum not exceeding £100, on unstamped paper. The license was granted by the Commissioner of Stamps, and was charged with a Stamp Duty of £30, and though a separate license was required for every place where notes were issued, yet no more than four licenses were needed, as the fourth embraced, as one place, all the towns over and above the three for which the three preceding licenses were issued. The license lapsed in a year, so that the duty of £30 was an annual charge. One of the conditions precedent to the obtainment of the License, was the execution of a bond by the Banker, to keep a true record of the notes issued and cancelled, and a true account of the amount of the notes in circulation. On the average amount in circulation

* *Vide* Appendix.

each six months, a duty of 1s. 6d. per £100 was payable as composition, in lieu of the duty on each note hitherto chargeable. Similar provisions in regard to Ireland were contained in the 9 Geo. IV., c. 23. The 9 Geo. IV., c. 65 (passed on 15th July, 1828), enacted that after 5th April, 1829, no Banker shall issue in England notes of an amount under £5, or any under that amount which shall have been issued in Ireland or Scotland.

But the Statute which now regulates the issue of Bank Notes in England is the 7 & 8 Vic., c. 32, commonly known as the Bank Act of 1844, and in Ireland is the 8 & 9 Vic., c. 37. The former provides for the management of the Issue Department of the Bank of England. The 13th sec. places other Note Issues on the basis on which they now stand. It is as follows : "That every Banker claiming to be entitled to issue " Bank Notes in England or Wales shall, within one month " next after the passing of this Act, give notice in writing to " the Commissioners of Stamps and Taxes, at their head office " in London, of such claim, and of the place and name and " firm at and under which such Banker has issued such Notes " during the year next preceding the 27th day of April, 1844 " and thereupon the said Commissioners shall ascertain if such " Banker was, on the 6th day of May, 1844, carrying on the " business of a Banker, and lawfully issuing his own Bank Notes " in England and Wales, and if it shall so appear, then the " said Commissioners shall proceed to ascertain the average " amount of the Bank Notes of such Banker, which were in " circulation during the said period of one year preceding the " 6th day of May, 1844, according to the returns made by such " Banker, in pursuance of the Act passed in the 4th and 5th " years of the reign of her present Majesty, intituled 'an Act " ' to make further provisions relative to the returns to be made "'by Banks of the amount of their notes in circulation,' and "the said Commissioners, or any two of them, shall certify "under their hands to such Banker the average amount, when "so ascertained as aforesaid, omitting the fractions of a pound, "if any; and it shall be lawful for every such Banker to con-"tinue to issue his own Bank Notes after the 10th day of "October, 1844, to the extent of the amount so certified, and "of the amount of the gold and silver coin held by such "Banker, in the proportion and manner hereinafter mentioned, "but not to any further extent; and from and after the 10th "day of October, 1844, it shall not be lawful for any Banker "to make or issue Bank Notes in England or Wales, save "and except only such Bankers as shall have obtained "such certificate from the Commissioners of Stamps and "Taxes."

This Statute was effectually prohibitory, and no person other than a Banker, who, on the 6th day of May, 1844, was lawfully issuing his own Bank Notes, could thereafter—unless the Law was repealed—make or issue Bank Notes in any part of the United Kingdom. It is evident the Banks then issuing notes had a prescriptive right to their issue—a vested interest of which they could not be deprived without a proper compensation.

The powers of the Bank of England in regard to its Note issue have been already described (*ante* p. 62), and the regulations under which the other Banks are entitled to issue Notes are contained in the 7 & 8 Vic., c. 32, above quoted, by which, in brief, no person, other than a Banker, who on 6th May, 1844, was lawfully issuing his own Bank Notes, shall make or issue Bank Notes in any part of the United Kingdom; and those that were then Banks of Issue, shall render an account of the amount of their notes in circulation during the twelve weeks preceding the antecedent 27th April, and the average issue shall be computed therefrom; and after the passing of the Act, if the monthly average circulation of Bank Notes of any Banker shall at any time exceed the amount which such Banker is authorised to issue and have in circulation, such Banker shall in every case forfeit a sum equal to the amount by which the average monthly circulation shall have exceeded the amount he was, under the Act, authorised to issue. The Scotch and Irish Banks do not rest under this restriction, as shall be presently shown. The Banks entitled to issue Notes under this Act were empowered to relinquish the same in favour of the Bank of England, but having once relinquished, they could not resume it.

The Acts regulating the **Scotch** and **Irish Issues** are the 8 & 9 Vic., c. 38, and 8 & 9 Vic., c. 37, respectively. By these it was enacted that from and after the 6th December, 1845, it shall not be lawful for any Banker in either of these countries to have in circulation, upon the average of a period of four weeks to be ascertained as hereinafter mentioned, a greater amount of notes than an amount composed of the sums certified by the Commissioners of Stamp and Taxes, as aforesaid, *and* the monthly average amount of gold and silver coin held by such Bankers during the same period of four weeks, to be ascertained in the manner hereinafter mentioned.

These averages were to be obtained as averages usually are —on the amounts returned weekly; and a monthly return of the monthly averages was to be supplied to, and published by, the Commissioners of Stamps. The " gold and silver " coin held," was, by the Act, to include only the gold and silver coin held at the four principal offices or depots, and not that held at *all* the Branches; and, further, if the silver coin should exceed the proportion of one-fourth the amount of gold coin, the surplus was not to be taken into account, and not to be issued against. Bank Notes under £1, or for any sum together with the fractional part of a pound sterling, were prohibited, and a penalty attached to the issue of them.

The Composition Duty now payable is 3s. 6d. (three shillings and sixpence) for every £100, and also for the fractional part of £100, of the average amount and value of the Notes in circulation during every half year.

The Banks which had then, or which subsequently opened, offices in London, were deprived of their powers of issue by the Statute; thus the National Provincial, the London and Westminster, the London and County, the Union Bank of London, and others, are without Note issues of their own. But the Scotch and Irish Banks can open, and have opened, offices in London, without any forfeiture of their rights of issue in their respective countries.

At the passing of the Irish Act of 1845, the following Banks, which are now existing, were issuers of Notes :

> The Bank of Ireland.
> The Provincial Bank of Ireland.
> The Belfast Banking Company.
> The Northern Banking Company.
> The Ulster Banking Company, and
> The National Bank.

There were before the Act other Joint Stock Banks issuing Notes, which have since collapsed—the Agricultural Bank of Ireland and the Provident Bank. And the Hibernian Bank and Royal Bank, though then established, were, nevertheless, non-issuers, and have had to remain so since. The Munster

Bank was established in 1864, and, consequently, could no issue Notes.

The average circulation at the time of the passing of this Act, of the above-named six Banks, was, respectively:

The Bank of Ireland	£3,738,428
The Provincial Bank of Ireland	927,667
The Belfast Banking Company	281,611
The Northern Banking Company	243,440
The Ulster Banking Company	311,079
The National Bank	852,269

That circulation was accordingly made the basis of the future powers of issue—whether reasonably or unreasonably, it is not our present province to discuss. For every Note issued in excess of this amount, gold and silver coin must be held at the depots of the Banks, and the silver must not exceed one-fourth part of the gold. The returns of the Bank Issues for the four weeks ending the 24th September, 1881, showed the following average circulations:

The Bank of Ireland	£2,762,650
The Provincial Bank of Ireland	750,370
The Belfast Banking Company	413,759
The Northern Banking Company	343,071
The Ulster Banking Company	556,280
The National Bank	1,347,706

And the average amount of coin held in accordance with the Statute during the same period:

The Bank of Ireland	£512,696
The Provincial Bank of Ireland	393,477
The Belfast Banking Company	298,188
The Northern Banking Company	184,528
The Ulster Banking Company	339,038
The National Bank	844,643

The corresponding figures for the Scotch Banks of Issues are as follow:

	Authorised Circulation.	Average Circulation, 27th August, 1881.	Average Coin held for four weeks preceding 27th August, 1881.
	£	£	£
Bank of Scotland	343,418	780,334	561,519
Royal Bank of Scotland	216,451	730,961	672,428
British Linen Company	438,024	608,031	308,853
Commercial Bank of Scotland	374,880	755,475	562,773
National Bank of Scotland	297,024	615,585	416,894
Union Bank of Scotland	454,346	745,923	445,813
Aberdeen Town and County Bank	70,133	192,416	165,950
North of Scotland Banking Company	154,319	320,741	239,179
Clydesdale Banking Company	274,321	525,608	330,766
Caledonian Banking Company	53,434	75,354	38,177

One pound Notes are now unknown in England, as the issue of all Notes for sums under £5 was by Law prohibited there, after the 5th April, 1829. In Ireland, Scotland, and the Isle of Man, Notes for £1 are legal and current, but no Note can be issued for a less sum than £1. Notes for 30s. were issued years ago by some of the Irish Banks, but the practice has been discontinued. In Ireland the Provincial Bank is the only establishment which circulates notes for £2. Up to the passing of the Banking Act of 1879, it was the Law (by a section of "The Companies Act, 1862"), that a Banking Company which claimed to issue Notes in the United Kingdom was not entitled to become a bank with limited liability. As we shall subsequently see, this part of the Statute is repealed by the Act of 1879.

It has been seen that while the English Banks of Issue can circulate a given amount of Notes without holding Coin against it, they cannot in any event exceed their authorised issue. But the Scotch and Irish Banks are entitled to issue a certain amount of Notes, without holding an equivalent in Coin, and can further issue over and above this authorised circulation, but the surplus may be only issued against Gold and Silver Coin held, as directed by the Statute. From this circumstance, the opinion has been entertained, that in case of stoppage of the Bank, the Notes outstanding constitute a first charge on the Gold and Silver Coin, and that the Holders of the Notes are preferential Creditors. But this is not a correct view of the Law, as the Coin forms portion of the general Assets, and the Note-holders rank but as general Creditors. The objects of the Act were to restrict the reckless and inflated Note issues which characterized the early periods of Banking, and to compel the holding in the country of a certain amount of specie, for reasons which will be understood by Students of Political Economy.

It is to be remembered that the Banks of Issue hold actual value from the public for the amount represented by the Notes in circulation, and for this value they give in exchange a piece of engraved paper, intrinsically worthless. Now, a Gold Coin is intrinsically value for what it represents, and, though a Bank Note is redeemable by gold, it is still no more than a token, and its value is dependent on the credit the issuing Bank enjoys. If that credit be injured, the value of the Notes is depreciated, and as it would be a great injury to the commerce of the country to have Notes of a fluctuating and depreciating value in circulation, the State interposed to prevent this, and passed the Acts which, by compelling a proportionate holding of Gold and Silver, compel the Bank of England and Banks of Issue in Scotland and Ireland to maintain their credit, and thus, in effect, almost ensures that the represented value of a Bank Note shall be its actual value. The Coin, however, which the

Scotch and Irish issuing Banks are bound to hold against their circulation is entirely unproductive; it is received from the public in lieu of the Notes issued; it is the real money, which is represented, to its extent, by the mock money—the promises on paper—the Notes. But, as has been seen, the amount of these Notes, the representatives of real money, in the hands of the public, exceeds the amount of unproductive gold and silver the Banks hold, and, therefore, the Banks have the use of the surpluses, without paying the public anything for the loans, so to speak, of the amounts thus used productively. From the following tables it will be seen that the amounts actually held on the given dates by the Scotch and Irish Banks of Issue from the public (as represented by the difference between the Notes in circulation and the Coin held), on which the Banks paid no interest were respectively:

The Bank of Ireland ...	£2,249,954
The Provincial Bank of Ireland	356,893
The Belfast Banking Company	115,571
The Northern Banking Company	158,543
The Ulster Banking Company	217,242
The National Bank ...	503,063

These amounts would represent at 3 per cent. an annual income of, respectively:

The Bank of Ireland ...	£67,498
The Provincial Bank of Ireland	10,706
The Belfast Banking Company	3,467
The Northern Banking Company	4,756
The Ulster Banking Company	6,517
The National Bank ...	15,091

The following table represents the corresponding figures in the Scotch Banks of Issue:

	Surplus of Circulation over Coin held, 27th August, 1881.	Interest thereon at 3 per cent.
	£	£
Bank of Scotland	218,815	6,564
Royal Bank of Scotland	58,533	1,756
British Linen Company	299,178	8,975
Commercial Bank of Scotland	192,702	5,781
National Bank of Scotland	198,691	5,960
Union Bank of Scotland	300,110	9,003
Aberdeen Town and County Bank	26,466	793
North of Scotland Banking Company	81,562	2,446
Clydesdale Banking Company	194,842	5,845
Caledonian Banking Company	37,177	1,115

But the expenses attendant on the issue of Notes is something considerable. The cost of producing them is not much, but special officers have to be employed to cancel the old Notes, to keep all the records attendant on the circulation, to deal with lost, mutilated, and halves of Notes. Nevertheless, an issue is a source of material profit to a Bank.

The Bank of Ireland is the only other Bank authorised to have its Notes signed by machinery similarly to the Bank of England. It also, like the Bank of England, manufactures its Bank Note paper and prints and numbers its Notes.

Though Bank Notes are only representatives of money, nevertheless, if they have been accepted as cash by a party, they are regarded as money by the Law, and they pass under a will as money, and are included in "goods and chattels," and can be taken in execution under a writ of *fieri facias*. A Banker must pay his Notes in legal tender if required, and if he refuse to pay the bearer on demand in accordance with the promise contained in the Note, the bearer or holder can note or protest the Bank Note so refused. This was actually done on one occasion to the Bank of Ireland, when it declined to pay one of its Notes in gold to the Provincial Bank. Refusal is an act of insolvency, and the party so refused can file a petition in Bankruptcy against the Bank, on the strength of its having dishonoured its Promissory Note. It is evident, therefore, that a Bank cannot "stop payment" of any of its Notes with impunity; should it adopt this course it should get an indemnity from the party at whose instance it stops the payment—for stopping payment is a dishonouring. A *bonâ fide* Holder of a Note is entitled to payment of the amount of it by the Bank that made it, notwithstanding fraud on the part of any previous Holder, and a Banker must pay it, unless he have *actual knowledge* that the Presenter is in the fraud, or privy to it.

A Bank Note being payable to Bearer, passes by delivery, and the person transferring it is under no liability on it, as it does not bear or require his endorsement, and the Transferee takes it at his own option and risk, it not being a legal tender. Further, a transfer of a Note for a consideration, not a debt already due, amounts to a *sale* of the Note, and such sale does not convey or imply a guarantee of the solvency of the Banker that issued it. The result, however, would be different if fraud, or knowledge of the insolvency of the Bank can be proved against the Transferor.

But in an ordinary case, where A. *gives change* to B. for a Note which proves worthless, A. can recover the amount from B., unless he is proved guilty of delay, negligence, or laches in acquainting B. of the fact that it is a worthless Note. If a Bank give a Customer a receipt for money lodged, which lodgment is composed of, or includes, forged or worthless Notes, it can debit the Customer's account with the amount of such worthless Notes, if it is in a position to prove the receipt from the Customer. Forged Notes are not money, and though the Banker give a receipt for money, if he can prove that the receipt is given under the supposition that the Notes were genuine, and on the Customer's implied representation that they were genuine, he can recover the amount from the Customer. But if the Customer pay into his Banker Bank Notes issued by a Bank which fails soon after such paying in, and that the Banker has allowed a reasonable time to elapse without presenting them to the Issuing Bank, and that when presented they are found not to be value, he cannot then recover from his Customer, for due diligence in presenting them had not been exercised.

Half-Notes. — Lost-Notes. — For convenience and security in making remittances, Notes are frequently cut in halves, the parts being remitted at different times, or by different channels. The practice of cutting is not illegal, though in Scotland it is not usual, and is discountenanced by the Scotch Banks. Where one half of a Note has been lost, the Bank will pay the full amount on the production of the other half upon affidavit and indemnity, provided the amount has not already been paid to a previous applicant. A Bank can also be compelled now to pay the amount of a lost Note upon a satisfactory indemnity being given. Thus, if a Note be totally destroyed, the lawful owner of it, knowing its number, etc., can obtain payment from the Bank, provided he tenders a satisfactory indemnity; and in an action against the Banker for the amount of such loss, he, the Banker, cannot plead the loss and non-production as a defence.

Bank Notes do not lapse, nor does the Statute of Limitations apply to them. It is specially enacted that all Bank Notes shall be deemed to be in circulation from the time they shall have been issued until they be returned to the Issuing Bank, and, therefore, as long as they are outstanding, they are

current and negotiable. In Morse's "Treatise on Banks and
" Banking," it is said on this subject: "Every time a Note is
" re-issued by the Bank, the promise is renewed, and it must
" usually be impossible in the case of any particular Bill to say
" how often it has passed into, and again has been paid out by
" the Bank, or when it was last so paid out. But even if in any
" individual case it could be shown that the last issue was at a
" time so long past that the period of the Statute has since
" elapsed, yet another objection, which goes to the root of the
" matter, still remains behind. For lapse of time, in the case of
" these instruments, affords no presumption of their having been
" paid. On the contrary, their existence in other hands than
" those of the Bank, is at least *prima facie* evidence of non-
" payment, since they are never paid, and, generally speaking,
" payment can never be enforced upon them at Law, unless
" they are surrendered to the Promissor. Further, as already
" shown, a new cause of action is created by each transfer, so
" that the Statute could begin to run only from the time when
" the last Holder came into possession." In an article in the
Money Market Review for November 9, 1867, page 482, the
following remarks occur with reference to this subject:
" Country Bank Notes, as well as the Notes of the Bank of
" England, are *promissory* Notes, *payable* to the *bearer on demand*,
" and as to them, the promise to pay may be regarded as a
" promise which is *renewed from time to time, and every time*
" *the note changes hands*, and may thus be subsisting for any
" number of years, until the Note is either cancelled or paid.
" The Statute of Limitations must be specially pleaded, and
" the Banker or maker of the Note, in pleading the Statute,
" would have to plead that he had not made the promise at any
" time within the six years, and he could not prove that plea
" against the evidence of a Note in the hands of the Bearer,

" which became a new and distinct promise to him the moment
" he became the Holder or Bearer of it."

Forgery of Bank Notes.—By the 24 & 25 Vic., c. 98, s. 12, it is enacted that to forge or alter ; or offer, utter, or dispose of ; or put off, knowing the same to be forged or altered, any Note or Bill of Exchange of any Banker, commonly called a Bank Note ; or a Bank Bill of Exchange, or a Bank Post Bill, or any endorsement or assignment of such, with intent to defraud, is a felony, and it is punishable on conviction by penal servitude for life, or for a term not exceeding five years, or imprisonment not exceeding two years with or without hard labour.

Purchasing or receiving forged Bank Notes, with knowledge that they are forgeries, is a felony equal with uttering. It is also a felony to fraudulently engrave plates of Bank Notes, or to fraudulently, or without authority, manufacture Bank Note paper, on which the watermark or other distinguishing characteristics are imitated.

An I.O.U. (a contraction for the words "I owe you") is a mere acknowledgment of a debt, without a promise expressed to pay at any specified time. If such promise be expressed, the instrument is a Promissory Note requiring the Statutable *ad valorem* stamp. An I.O.U. is generally made in the well-known form :—

John Smith, Esq.,

London, 1st Oct., 1881.

I.O.U. Twenty Pounds.

£20

John Brown.

Usually an I.O.U. expresses the date, the Creditor's name,

the acknowledgment of indebtedness, the amount, and the signature. A date is not absolutely necessary, as evidence is admissible to prove the time the I.O.U. was made. Neither is the Creditor's name now absolutely necessary, as the possession and production of the I.O.U. is *prima facie* evidence that the Possessor is the Creditor. The words (or letters) expressing indebtedness are necessary, as is also the amount; and initials may be sufficient for the Debtor's signature. As long as the instrument is no more than an acknowledgment of indebtedness, it is legally an I.O.U.

An I.O.U., therefore, being a mere memorandum, and no more than an evidence of a debt, and not coming within the scope of a Bill of Exchange or Promissory Note, or an agreement to pay, does not require any stamp. An I.O.U., though evidence of a debt, is not evidence of money lent, and if it be given for an illegal or an immoral purpose, the debt of which it is evidence cannot be recovered at law. An I.O.U. cannot be transferred, or circulated and negotiated as a Promissory Note.

The Clearing House.—The "Clearing House" was established in 1775 to meet the requirements for an organised method of interexchange of cheques, bills, etc., by the London Private Banks, whereby a saving would be effected in time and labour, but chiefly in the amount of floating capital, which, if the Banks did not act in concert, would reach a sum of great magnitude. The facilities to business, and the curtailment of money payments effected by the Clearing House, will best be shown by a description of its working. Frequently during the day, at stated times, each Bank which has the privilege of the establishment transmits to the Clearing House all cheques and bills payable at other Banks, taking into account all cheques and bills payable with itself. The accounts are closed at 4 o'clock, and each bank has up to 4.45 o'clock wherein to return dishonoured cheques and unpaid bills. The balances between all the houses are then struck, and these show who has to pay and who has to receive, by means of an account like the following:

Debtors.	Dr. Balance.	GLYN & CO.	Cr. Balance.	Creditors.
120,000		Robarts, Lubbock, & Co.	20,000	140,000
100,000	20,000	Smith, Payne, & Co.		80,000
60,000		Barclay.	20,000	80,000
200,000		Union.	20,000	220,000
180,000	60,000	London Joint.		120,000
	£80,000		£60,000	

Thus Glyns' would have to pay at the Clearing House to some Banker who claimed a balance, a sum of £20,000 to settle their day's transactions; and this payment is made by a species of cheque on the Bank of England called a transfer ticket, which is duly vouched by the Clearing House official, and is available for the next day's exchange. In this manner transactions amounting to millions are daily settled without any cash payments; and a fair estimate of what a saving this is to the Banks may be gathered from the fact that the London and Westminster Bank, before it obtained connection with the Clearing House, had to keep in hand a balance of £150,000 for the purposes of settling its exchanges. A sum of this magnitude lying unproductive was a considerable loss to the Bank. The enormous extent of the Clearing House working will be seen from the subjoined returns to the year ending 30th April, 1881, since the year 1868, when first these statistics were compiled:

	Total for the Year.	On Fourths of the Month.	On Stock Exchange Account Days.	On Consols Settling Days.
	£	£	£	£
1867-1868	3,257,411,000	147,113,000	444,443,000	132,293,000
1868-1869	3,534,039,090	161,861,000	550,622.000	142,270,000
1869-1870	3,720,623,000	168,523,000	594,763,000	148,822,000
1870-1871	4,018,464,000	186,517,000	635,946,000	169,141,000
1871-1872	5,359,722,000	229,629,000	942,446,000	233,843,000
1872-1873	6,003,335,000	265,965,000	1,032,474,000	243,561,000
1873-1874	5,993,586,000	272,841,000	970,945,000	260,072,000
1874-1875	6,013,299,000	265,950,000	1,076,585,000	260,338,000
1875-1876	5,407,243,000	240,807,000	962,595,000	242,245,000
1876-1877	4,873,000,000	231,630,000	718,793,000	223,756,000
1877-1878	5,066,533,000	224,190,000	745,665,000	233,385,000
1878-1879	4,885,091,000	212,241,000	811,072,000	221,264,000
1879-1880	5,265,976,000	218,477,000	965,533,000	233,143,000
1880-1881	5,909,989,000	240,822,000	1,205,197,000	265,579,000

XVII.

SHARES AND SHAREHOLDERS.

Though England, unlike Scotland and Ireland, still throughout its Provinces contains numerous private Banking Establishments, the majority of the Banks are Joint Stock Banks. All the Irish and Scotch Banks are likewise Joint Stock.

A **Joint Stock Company** is a certain kind of partnership entered into by a number of persons for the purpose of carrying on some trade or business for individual profit. It differs from an ordinary partnership in many respects. The Members, individually, take no part in the business; they are merely those who contribute to the Capital of the Company, or who purchase the contributions of others. The Capital is divided into a number of equal portions, which are called Stock in the case of the Bank of England and Bank of Ireland, and Shares in every other Joint Stock Bank. One or more of these Shares are held by each Member, and he is entitled to a division of the profits in proportion to his holding, but he can take no direct part in the management. The management of the Bank is vested in a limited number of Members, who are delegates of the Shareholders, and who are called Directors. These are subject to the control of the general body of Shareholders, or a certain majority of them, exercised at proper meetings. The Directors only can bind the Company, and the

Directors only are liable, should the Company engage in fraudulent transactions. Beyond the acts and resolutions passed at duly convened meetings of the body of Members in prescribed order, the Shareholders have no power to bind the Company, or even to interfere in its management. The **capital** of a mercantile firm generally means the accumulated sum with which the business is commenced. But in a Bank, or other Joint Stock Companies, this is usually but a portion of the amount that the Members have subscribed to pay, and that they may be called on to pay. The entire capital available for the business is called the **Subscribed** Capital. Of this a portion only generally is called for, in order to commence operations; this is called the **Paid-up** Capital, and on this amount only a dividend or division of profits is paid to the Members.

In the Banks and Companies called **Limited**, that is established under the Limited Companies Act, or registered under the Banking Act of 1879, the Shareholder is in no event liable to be called on for more than the amount unpaid or uncalled on each Share. Thus, if the Capital be £1,000,000, and it be divided into 100,000 parts, or Shares of £10 each, and if, of this £10, half or £5 only be paid up on each Share, in the event of the failure or Bankruptcy of the Bank, or of a further call to develop the business of the concern, the Shareholder can only be called on for the balance unpaid, that is, £5 on each Share he holds, and no more, whether the amounts so called should be enough to satisfy the claims against the Bank or not. But in an **Unlimited** Bank the case is different. A Shareholder in an Unlimited Bank is *primarily* liable for the amount remaining uncalled on his Shares, and *secondarily* for the unsatisfied debts of the Bank; and this being so, he may possibly be delivered of every atom of property he possesses. But under the **Banking Act of 1879**, an Unlimited Company can be registered as Limited, and the liability attaching to each Share can be divided —a portion of it constituted an immediate or primary liability, and the balance a deferred or secondary liability. Thus, *e.g.*, if the Share be £100, and £20 be paid up, the Company registering under the Act of 1879, limits the liability to the uncalled balance of £80 per Share. The constitution of the Company can then be altered so that of that £80 per share liability, £30 only (*e.g.*) per Share can be available for further call; except in case of the Bankruptcy or winding-up of the Establishment, when the remaining £50 per Share is available for the benefit of the Creditors. The liability, however, *in respect to Notes in circulation*, does not become limited by registration under this Act.

The Shares are transferable, and if the Bank be successful, the Shares become of more value than the amount originally paid on them. This extra value is called a *premium*, and is regulated by the public estimate of the Shares. The Shares are purchasable on the Stock Exchanges, and being freely transferable, any person who can purchase can become a Shareholder. The Company's assent or permission is not required, nor can a Company refuse to transfer Shares to any person who has purchased them.

The formation of Joint Stock Companies is regulated by Acts of Parliament,—The Joint Stock Companies Acts of 1856 and 1857. By these it is provided that any seven or more persons associated for any lawful purpose, may, by subscribing their names to a memorandum of association, and registering in the terms of the Act, form themselves into an incorporated company. A List of the Shareholders in each Company formed under these Acts, or under the Companies Act of 1862, must be furnished annually to the Registrar of Joint Stock Companies, and it is open to public inspection. The liability respectively of a Shareholder in a Limited and an Unlimited Company has been pointed out; and in case of sale or transfer of Shares, in a Limited Company, the Transferor can, in case of default or failure of the Bank without actual or callable Assets, be held liable for one year after he has transferred his Shares; and in case of an Unlimited Company, for three years after he has transferred them; but the liability does not extend to debts contracted since the transfer. The object of this law is to prevent a Member divesting himself of liability, in the presence and with the knowledge of a collapse, and transferring that liability thus knowingly to, perhaps, indigent persons, from whom, to the detriment of the Creditors, nothing could be recovered.

If a company of more than twenty persons unite for trade purposes, and do not register under the Acts of Parliament, each Member can be sued individually for the debts of the Company.

Shares in a Bank are personal property. In a Company formed under the Companies Act of 1862, they are expressly declared by the Act to be so; and in Banking Companies formed otherwise they are so at the Common Law. Subscribers to, or Members of, a Company, obtain a Certificate of the number of Shares they hold and of their name as Holder or Proprietor, and the Transferor of Shares must produce and surrender this Certificate to the Company upon the transfer of the Shares from his name to another's. Thus the possession of the Certificate is evidence of proprietorship. Such Certificate can be pledged for advances, and no notice of such pledging is necessary in order to give an equitable lien to the holder of it, *i.e.*, the person with whom it has been lodged as a pledge or security.

But in case of the Bankruptcy of a Shareholder who is indebted to the Bank wherein he is a Proprietor, the Bank has a lien on his Shares for his indebtedness, and this lien is not destroyed or alienated by the fact that the Certificate is deposited with another Creditor, whether that Creditor be a Banker or not. But a Stockbroker entrusted with Scrip or Certificates for the purposes of sale of the Stock and Shares cannot pledge it with his Banker for his own private debt: this would amount to a fraudulent conversion, and on discovery of the fraud the real owner of the Shares can recover the scrip from the Bank. Joint Stock Banks are obliged to exhibit to a Proprietor, who applies for it during business hours, the list of Shareholders, and to supply him with a copy thereof, upon his paying a prescribed fee. The Bank of England and Bank of Ireland, however, are exempt from this provision.

By the Act known as **Leeman's Act**, a Contract for the sale of Bank Shares will be null and void, unless it shall set forth the numbers of the Shares, as registered in the Bank Books, and if there be no such register, the name of the Proprietor who is the seller; and to insert false numbers or a false name is a misdemeanour. But the Act is comparatively a dead letter. Its provisions are never complied with, as compliance with them would obstruct the free sale of the Shares. But any Stockbroker purchasing Bank Shares can demand from the seller the numbers of the Shares and the name of the Proprietor. All contracts for the sale or purchase of Shares, when the value is £5 or upwards, require a penny stamp duty. Once a Purchaser has accepted a transfer, he cannot repudiate the transaction, or divest himself of his liability as a Shareholder, unless he has been induced to become a Proprietor by false or fraudulent representations, by Directors or others, as to the position, financially, of the Bank. Upon a discovery that such representations are false or fraudulent, he can recover the amount paid by him, from the parties deceiving him.

If the name of a lawful Holder has been **forged** to a transfer deed, and the transfer duly registered in the Books of the Bank, he can compel the purchaser, though he be a *bonâ fide* Purchaser, to redeliver the Shares to him, and the Bank to cancel the transfer.

Bank Directors are sometimes empowered by the Deed of Settlement to **refuse to transfer** Shares to a person who is not of means sufficient to pay any calls unpaid, which may yet be callable; but the power is not exercised, as the exercise of it would possibly involve the Bank in a suit which they could not successfully maintain, so that practically and legally there is no limit to the assignability of Shares. Transfers are effected by a Deed, in a prescribed form, the signatures of Transferor and Transferee being duly witnessed. The registered lists of Proprietors is *prima facie* evidence of proprietorship.

Shares can be held **jointly** in two or more names, but no trusts are recognised, nor are Bankers compelled to regard them. A Deed of Transfer to A. and B. as Trustees for C. makes A. and B. the legal Shareholders, with the rights and liabilities attaching thereto; and being joint Holders, survivorship operates; that is to say, if A. dies, B. becomes the Shareholder, without any act except proof of death of A. This is the case if A. and B. were wife and husband.

A **Married Woman** can purchase Shares in her own name, if out of her separate estate, but she and her separate estate are alone liable in case of Bankruptcy of the Bank. **Clergymen**, though they may be Shareholders, cannot be

Directors or Managers in a Banking Company, nor can they be Partners in a Private Bank.

It has been pointed out that a Bank has a **lien on the Shares** of a Member who is indebted to the Company, and this doctrine is so well defined that it has been ruled that it has a lien on the Dividends on such shares also; and further, that where a Shareholder was a party to a Bill, and before the maturity thereof, a transfer of his Shares was presented to the Bank for registration, it was held that the Bank was justified in refusing to register it, the Master of the Rolls (England) saying that there was a debt existing, though the remedy for its recovery was suspended until the Bill had matured and was dishonoured.

Directors are Delegates chosen from the Contributors or Shareholders, for the purpose of directing or managing the acts or transactions of the Company, or, as it is frequently expressed, "to superintend, order, conduct, regulate, and "manage all the affairs and business of the Company." A certain holding of Shares in the Company, which holding is designated in the Articles of the Company, are the usual qualifications for a seat on the Board, but a capacity to take part in the management and an attentive superintendence are requisite attributes of a Director. Directors can, at discretion, restrict the business of a Company, but they cannot extend it into paths not contemplated by, or provided in, the Deed of Incorporation. A Banking Company, though a Corporation, can contract otherwise than under its Seal. The Companies Act of 1867 provides that a Contract to bind a Company can be signed by any person acting under the authority of the Company.

A Banking Company cannot **purchase its own Shares,**

nor can it supply the Bank's Funds to parties for the purchase of them, especially if the Bank is in a critical position; because such an action would, by creating a demand for the Shares, augment their market price, and thus, the act would be one to deceive the Shareholders and the public; and "no cir-"cumstances of embarrassment, no difficulty, can excuse por-"traying in false and delusive colours the condition of the "affairs of the Bank entrusted to the charge of the Directors."* And it has been distinctly ruled that " Directors representing, " with the intent to raise the shares of the Company in price, " in their reports, and by their Agents, that the affairs of the " Company are in a very prosperous state, and declaring large " Dividends at a time when those affairs are greatly embar-"rassed, and thereby inducing a person to purchase Shares, " may be made criminally responsible for their conduct." (Grant).

Again, it is by law a gross fraud for Directors to pay a **Dividend** derived from other sources except the *bonâ fide* profits of the Company. The declaration of a Dividend is a declaration that the Company has made profits to pay it, and, therefore, if a Dividend is paid which does not come out of the profits, it is a fraud, and the Directors can be punished. And if a person buys Shares on the strength of such representations, or rather misrepresentations, he has an action against the Directors, and even if he have not legally suffered any injury, he can, nevertheless, indict them for conspiracy. But the wilful offence must be proven at the time, and a person cannot avoid his purchase or contract on such grounds because subsequently a Bank stops payment, and it is discovered that the previous Report was a misrepresentation; otherwise it would be in the power of all purchasers to repudiate liability

* *In re* Grant.

at the time of the Company's Bankruptcy, to the injury of the Creditors.

The 24 & 25 Vic., c. 69, deals with **criminal offences by Directors.** To fraudulently use or appropriate the Bank's Funds to his own use ; to make or cause to be made false entries ; to falsify Accounts or destroy Documents ; to publish Balance Sheets, false to his knowledge in a material particular, with intent to deceive, are, if fraudulently done, misdemeanours, and punishable as such.

It is further to be observed that any Bank Director who **traffics in the Shares** of his Bank, and makes a profit thereby, cannot lawfully obtain that profit, but can be compelled to apply it to the uses of the Shareholders. He is in the position of a Trustee, and profits made in this manner belong to the *cestui que trust.* Thus, if a Director, acting on special information, acquired at a meeting of his Board or otherwise, buys Shares in his Bank with the knowledge that, owing to a coming action by the Board, these Shares will increase in value, and that he sells Shares so bought, at the enhanced price, the profit he thus makes belongs lawfully not to him, but to the Shareholders, and it can be recovered from him by an Equity Suit.

XVIII.

THE BANKING ACT OF 1879.—DIRECTORS' DUTIES.

The Most Notable event in Banking Legislation since the passing of the Peel Acts, was the enactment of the statute known as "The Banking Act of 1879," the text of which will be found in the Appendix. It permitted a mild revolution in the constitution of Joint Stock Banks, and inaugurated a method whereby in Banks and all Joint Stock Companies, Shareholders with unlimited liability attached to their Shareholdings could limit their liability, and those in Limited Companies could qualify their liability. The Act is due to the failure of the City of Glasgow Bank, to the startling revelations of its management, and to the ruin occasioned by its collapse,—occurrences too fresh in the public mind to require a recapitulation of the history of the wreck of that Establishment. From a personal point of view the ruin which overwhelmed the mass of the Shareholders convinced the public that a Share proprietorship, to which possible beggary was linked, was not desirable; even a good dividend in the present was no compensation for contingent ruin in the future; and therefore wealthy Shareholders—those who had something to lose beyond their Shares—got outside the pale of a prospective calamity by selling their Shares. Their places on the register as Proprietors were filled by less wealthy classes; and thus the fact of a Bank being a company of unlimited liability, instead of making its position stronger and its solvency more impregnable, operated in the opposite direction. From a public point of view then, unlimited liability did not mean unlimited security, and thus, in a period of panic or financial uneasiness, the public and Shareholders alike were inclined to turn away from an unlimited concern. Though panics and the causes and consequences of panics pass quickly from the public mind, yet investors will not lose sight of their own responsibilities, when these responsibilities mean a possible penury. Putting aside the social aspect of the failure of an unlimited Bank, it would become a public,—indeed, a national,—calamity, if the moneyed classes should exclude themselves from a Shareholding connection with Banking Institutions. When the Proprietary deteriorates, the security to the public and the customers of the Bank deteriorates also. The Act of 1879 was designed to remedy the evils attached to unlimited liability, and it has already been adopted by many important establishments. The effect of its operations can be adjudged to be advantageous to both the Banks themselves and to their Customers. By it an unlimited Company may register itself as a limited one, and may increase its nominal Capital;—or may provide that a portion of the uncalled Capital shall be set apart, and the liability to pay it be reserved—but no part of the increased Capital or of the reserved Capital can be called up, except in the event of the winding-up of the Company; and the Company being thus limited, the Shareholders have no liability beyond the nominal Capital. Before this Act Shareholders in an unlimited Company were liable as far as their last penny. A Company already limited under previous Acts of Parliament can likewise set apart a portion of its uncalled Capital, to be callable only in the event of the Company being wound up. The limitation of the liability under this Act does not extend to the liability to the public on account of the Company's Bank Notes in circulation. The Act (*q.v.*) has further provisions for Audit, intended to be a protection to the public, but of little real value. It will be seen, then, that under this Act the Shareholders can divorce themselves from unlimited liability, while the security offered to the public is not really diminished.

The Act, which was an improved edition of one projected previously but withdrawn, though modest in aim and title, contained the germs of a complete revolution. It was not compulsory in its principal clauses, but merely provided that unlimited Banks *might* re-register themselves as limited, and it insisted on an audit of accounts of such as did register. The change to limited liability has been thus effected in a way to retain all the confidence of Depositors, since in every instance already adopted a very large reserve liability, only to be called up under the terms of the Act in the event of liquidation, remains. That the movement will become general may now perhaps be taken for granted.

The objections urged against the new Act were principally that it was Panic Legislation; that the security it offered to the public was more apparent than real, while a change in the constitution of the Bank, and the publication of the word "Limited," as a portion of the Bank's title, would disturb the public mind, that might not fully comprehend its effect; that it was impolitic to legislate for such a nervous system as the Banking public because one Bank had been proven to be fraudulently and incompetently managed. These arguments have had but little effect, and the strongest proof of the value of the Act, and of its appreciation by both Banks and public, is to be found in the number of establishments which have already adopted it.

Nevertheless, taking into consideration the different positions of the Joint Stock Banks in this country and of the Colonial

Banks which can transact business here, it is anticipated that further legislation which will tend to secure uniformity in the constitutions of the Companies is necessary.

The Chartered Banks of Scotland, which occupy an exceptional position, have petitioned for special legislation, and the Lords of the Treasury, in their reply, seem to admit that the question of the constitution of our Banks is not yet finally settled, and that it must be soon a matter for discussion in Parliament.*

Powerful and useful, however, as legislation of this character may be, yet the best safeguard to both Shareholders and Depositors in Banks lies in the appointment as Directors of men of undoubted financial ability, high character, and good position. Respectability without capacity is of little value, and capacity without character is dangerous in the extreme. The essential knowledge of Finance is not acquired in a moment, nor mastered at a glance. The responsibilities of Directorship are very grave. A Director is entrusted with the lending and disposition of other people's money, and as he can select those to whom he lends he is under the serious duty of knowing how to estimate the borrowers' characters—which enter largely into the consideration of loaning—and of being able to judge not alone of the present, but of the prospective solvency of the borrower. There is also the moral duty, of which mention

* The law relating to Banking is in a very unsatisfactory state, and it is a matter for regret that the Bill introduced recently by Sir John Lubbock, and designed to consolidate and declare the law relating to Bills of Exchange, Promissory Notes, and Cheques, did not get time for discussion and lead to a practical result. This Bill was prepared by the Association of Chambers of Commerce and the Institute of Bankers—to the latter of which, although but a young institution, the commercial public and the Banking Profession are under many obligations for the ability and intelligence with which it treats the important subjects that come within its scope.

has been made already, of employing the great sums at the command of the Board in such a manner that the industrious and honest will be encouraged and assisted, and the trade and interest of the country developed and fostered—a duty that the unwise or incompetent cannot adequately discharge. If the position of Bank Director is lightly undertaken and without a full sense of the necessary attributes and qualifications of the post, it is possible the difficult and delicate duties may be lightly discharged. The effect of the exposures of the management of the City of Glasgow Bank, and of others, has been to teach Shareholders that these duties are sometimes neglected, and the obligations of a Directorship forgotten completely. Audits and Acts of Parliament are effective as far as they go, but they do not and cannot go far enough to ensure perfect management; nor yet to secure men of perfect integrity and perfect ability as Directors. To effect this latter, Shareholders must look to themselves rather than to Parliament.

XIX.

THE STOCK EXCHANGES AND STOCK-BROKING.

THE term "Stock Exchange," from having signified a building where dealings in Stocks and Shares were transacted, has now come to be applied to an association of persons called Stock-brokers, who effect purchases or sales in these commodities, and who are governed by certain recognised usages, forms, and regulations.

A *Share* in a Joint Stock Company is one of a certain number of equal portions into which the invested capital of a concern is divided, and *Stock* is generally applied to Government Funded Debts, and to those Funds which are consolidated, and purchasable in divisible quantities. A Share is indivisible; one must purchase one or two or any given number of Shares. But of Stock one can purchase it in divided amounts, such as £20 or £30 of it. The prices quoted in Stock Lists are the prices of the individual Share, and of the Stock per £100. The word *broker* means simply an agent, and is variously derived.* The rapid and stupendous growth of enterprises and industries has opened and created

---

* The Latin *abrocator*, a negotiator; *brocarius*, a broker. From the old English word *broc*, a badger (one who buys corn in one place, and sells it in another, so called from the animal that carries away his store of corn from the cornfields), came the old English word *brogger*, one who deals in corn.

such a multitude of channels for investments, that markets for the sale and purchase of such investments are a necessity of the age ; and that these markets should be organised and conducted by fixed rules and regulations, and that the negotiators should be men of stability and reputation, are also essentials to public convenience and public safety. Hence the kingdom has various such organizations, London being the parent of the provincial bodies. In England there are Stock Exchanges at Liverpool, Manchester, Birmingham, Leeds, Bristol, Hull, and Newcastle ; in Scotland, at Edinburgh, Glasgow, and Aberdeen; and in Ireland at Dublin. These Stock Exchanges are all independent bodies, formed and governed by their own rules, and with the exception of the great London prototype, are of such recent establishment that they are almost without any history.

The public funding system which originated in Venice about 1173, and was introduced into Florence in 1340, was begun in London about 1690. Previous to this period there was practically no such thing as an investment of superfluous capital. The well-known story of Pope's father carrying £20,000 in gold—the profits of a trading life in London—in a box, from the metropolis to his country retreat, to be spent as occasion demanded, is well known. The bankers of the day, as has been already said, were safe custodians merely, who took charge of wealth and valuables, and distributed them in obedience to the written orders of the depositors. There were no public or Joint Stock Companies, and money was unprofitably stored. Such a condition of stagnation of wealth could have none other than the obvious result—that some enterprise would be discovered, some industry created, for its employment. The long period of inoperative capital was succeeded by a fever of investing-excitement, engendered and fostered by crowds of promoters of all kinds of schemes. The coffee-houses, especially Garraway's and Jonathan's, were the centres where those who had money to invest, charmed by the promises and hopes of rapid enrichment, met those who professed to invest it for them, in projects, some real and feasible, some preposterous and knavish. This occurred about 200 years ago, before the funding of the National Debt, and to this time are due those Stock-jobbers, the precursors of the Stock-brokers of to-day. The National Debt was created in 1693, and consisted then of £1,000,000 raised by means of life annuities, at 10 per cent. till 1700, and 7 per cent. thereafter; and the existence of a Government debt gave life to the Stock-jobbing trade, and gave it a *raison d'être*. Originally these agents or jobbers conducted their business in the streets near the Bank of England, and ultimately fixed on a meeting-place in the locality thence known as Change Alley. From this the body moved to Sweeting's Alley, to a building they called the "Stock Exchange," and at the beginning of this century it had risen in numbers and importance to such a degree that a new place of business was necessary. Thus, on the 18th of May, 1801, the foundation-stone of the present Stock Exchange in Capel Court was laid on the site of the residence of Lord Mayor Sir William Capel (Anno 1504). On the day of the ceremony the public debt was £552,730,924, having been increased, by the seven years' war, and the American and French wars, by over £500,000,000 during the space of a century. Beyond the celebrated hoax for which Lord Cochrane, Johnstone, and others were wrongfully convicted in 1814, no further incident of Capel Court has become a matter of history. Its daily business, though it may affect the credit of nations, and the wealth of millions, is not of a description to make history. Its constitution, and its methods of business, seeing that its members deal with the earnings and redundant moneys of the entire Kingdom nearly, should be more familiar than they are to the public.

The London Stock Exchange belongs to a Joint Stock Company, the proprietary of which may or may not be members of the Exchange. The capital is about £200,000, and the revenue is popularly believed to pay at present between 30 and 40 per cent. thereupon. The Stock Exchange is "a "voluntary association of from 1,600 to 2,000 members, sub- "ject to the committee, and responsible to each other as "amongst themselves." The committee is composed of 30 members selected by ballot annually by the body, and a five years' standing is the sole qualification for a nomination to serve upon it. The principal qualifications for membership are as follows : The applicant must be twenty-one years of age or over; must be a British subject, and if a foreigner, must have been naturalized for two years ; must not engage in any other business than that of the Stock Exchange ; if married, his wife must not be engaged in business; must not be a partner of any person except a member of the Stock Exchange ; must not be a member of any other institution where dealings in stocks and shares are negotiated.—The regulations in this regard are specially directed towards maintaining the respectability of the members. The requirements for admission as a member are more than formalities. They are of two descriptions : those for an applicant who has already been a clerk in the building, and those for an applicant who has not. In the latter case the applicant must be recommended by three solvent and reputable members of four years' standing each, who individually must undertake to pay £500 to the creditors of the applicant in case of his default within four years' from the date of his entrance, and must individually give their assurance that in case of a mulct for such default they are not in any way indemnified. These guaranteeing members are also individually required to express their readiness to take the applicant's cheque for £3,000 in the way of business. The entrance fee in this case is 150 guineas, and the annual subscription in all cases is 21 guineas. An applicant who has already been a clerk of four years' standing in the Exchange is required to produce two guarantors only, in the sum of £300 each, and his entrance fee is 75 guineas. The clerks here spoken of have a *locus standi* on Change; they are admitted by the committee, and are subject to certain rules framed to govern their conduct and to fix their responsibilities. The names of the clerks are posted in the building, and their admission has to be sanctioned by the governing body. They are not permitted to transact any business till they have had two years' experience, and have attained the age of twenty years. A clerk may be a member, but no person can become a clerk until he has obtained an engagement in the service of a member; and a member cannot apply to the committee for the admission of his clerk to the Exchange as an "authorised clerk" without first obtaining the consent of his—the member's—sureties. As a rule, those who aspire to be Brokers begin by fulfilling the duties of an authorised clerk; by this apprenticeship a knowledge of the complications and intricacies of Stock-jobbing and Stock-broking are acquired, and a personal acquaintance with the Brokers is established—two adjuncts which are essential to a successful trading as a Stock-broker in the great association which swarms daily in Capel Court.

The members of the London Stock Exchange consist of two classes—Stock-brokers and Stock-jobbers. The Broker deals with the public, and the Jobber is the intermediary between broker and broker. Jobbers can deal in Stocks on their own account; but it is supposed to be against the etiquette of the

Stock Exchange for Brokers to buy or sell for themselves. The Jobbers, therefore, are the speculators, and as speculation is attended with risk, the trade of jobbing demands more knowledge, shrewdness, and circumspection than that of broking. It is necessary that a Broker should obtain a license from the Lord Mayor and Aldermen of the City of London, which license costs £5 and is payable yearly. A Jobber requires no license, but if he transacts the business of a Broker he is liable to a penalty of £100, which can be sued for and recovered by the Chamberlain of the City of London. A Broker is remunerated according to a scale of fees authorised by the Committee of the Stock Exchange. These are as follows:

Government Funds—
    British or Foreign, ⅛th, or 2s. 6d. per cent. on the price.
    Exchequer Bills ... 1s. ,, ,,
    Colonial and American Government Stock and Railway Bonds ... 1s. ,, ,,

Shares—
    under £5 ... ... 1s. per share
    over £5 and under £10   1s. 6d. ,,
    over £10 and under £25   2s. ,,
    over £25 and under £50   5s. ,,
    over £50 ... ... 10s. per cent.

But, notwithstanding this regulated scale, a Broker can contract with his client to effect transactions at a special rate of commission, and in the event of such a contract the foregoing Stock Exchange terms are abrogated. A client's business can, therefore, be "lumped" and effected for a given fee, quite irrespective of the ordinary scales of charges. In this respect, the London Brokers have more latitude than those of some other exchanges—the Dublin, for example, where any departure from the fixed rate is not permissible. The remuneration of the Jobber, however, is not subject to any regulation scale. His legitimate business is, as has been said, to bring the buying Broker and the selling Broker together, and his remuneration is the difference between the buying and selling price. This is one-eighth per cent. in Consols, but in respect to other Stocks and Shares it fluctuates, and is not regulated by any rule.

In the old days, the line of demarcation between the two classes of members was very distinct. The Brokers alone had the *entrée* of the Stock Exchange. They alone could enter the Temple, while the Jobbers frequented and dealt in the Courts, so to speak. This distinction has, with other rights and privileges, long since been blotted out, either by express Acts or by the levelling influence of Time. Stock-broking and Stockbrokers have, from time to time, attracted the attention of Parliament. Some Acts were directed towards preventing Brokers dealing on their own account, and in 1734 a special Act was passed prohibiting jobbing in the English Funds, and in Indian Securities. The term "Sworn Brokers" that we still find appended to the names of sundry members of the Stock Exchange, refers to a restriction—now abolished—enforced by "The Lord Mayor, Citizens, and Commonwealth of London," whereby each Broker was bound to swear that he would not buy or sell on his account, and to give security for the fulfilment of his oath. Though this oath is no longer imposed, its spirit remains in the usages of the body, and it is regarded as a violation of the etiquette of the society that one should enter into speculation or any irregular dealing on his own account. Each Broker, however, is arbiter of his own business, and his own honesty and discretion regulate his actions as to such transactions. It is to be stated, that, as a rule, *noblesse oblige*, in the Stock Exchange as elsewhere, is a more effectual safeguard than any written rules and laws, and thus Stockbrokers as a body act in a manner to maintain their high and honourable reputation.

If a Broker, being possessed of private information regarding any securities, should purchase for himself such securities entrusted to him to sell by a client, he is liable to refund to the client any profit he may have netted on the transaction. If, in any case, he acts to the prejudice of the client, by concealing knowledge he is possessed of, or misleading by representations knowingly false, and becomes a purchaser or seller on his own account to the detriment of the client, he is liable on discovery to forfeit and refund any profit that may have accrued to him by his act.

Frauds by Stock Brokers are defined and punished by the 24 & 25 Vic., c. 96, s. 75. "Whosoever, having been en-
"trusted, either solely or jointly with any other person, as
"a banker, merchant, BROKER, attorney, or other agent,
"with any money or security for the "payment of money,
"with any direction in writing to apply, pay, or deliver
"such money or security or any part thereof respectively,
"or the proceeds or any part of the proceeds of such
"security, for any purpose, or to any person specified in
"such direction, shall, in violation of good faith, and contrary
"to the terms of such direction, in anywise convert to his
"own use or benefit, or the use or benefit of any person other
"than the person by whom he shall have been so instructed,
"such money, security, or proceeds, or any part thereof re-
"spectively; and whosoever, having been entrusted, either
"solely or jointly with any other person, as a banker, merchant,
"BROKER, attorney, or other agent, with any chattel or valuable
"security, or any power of attorney for the sale or transfer of

"any share or interest in any public stock or fund, whether of
"the United Kingdom or any part thereof, or of any foreign
"state, or in any stock or fund of any body corporate, com-
"pany, or society, for safe custody or for any special purpose,
"without any authority to sell, negotiate, transfer, or pledge,
"shall, in violation of good faith, and contrary to the object or
"purpose for which such chattel, security, or power of attorney
"shall have been entrusted to him, sell, negotiate, transfer,
"pledge, or in any manner convert to his own use or benefit,
"or the use or benefit of any person other than the person by
"whom he shall have been so entrusted, such chattel or security
"or the proceeds of the same, or any part thereof, or the share
"or interest in the stock or fund to which such power of
"attorney shall relate, or any part thereof, shall be guilty of a
"misdemeanour, and being convicted thereof shall be liable,
"at the discretion of the court, to be kept in penal servitude
"for any term not exceeding seven years and not less than
"three years, or to be imprisoned for any term not exceeding
"two years, with or without hard labour, and with or without
"solitary confinement; but nothing in this section contained
"relating to agents shall affect any trustee in or under any
"instrument whatever, or any mortgagee of any property, real
"or personal, in respect of any act done by such trustee or
"mortgagee in relation to the property comprised in or affected
"by any such trust or mortgage; nor shall restrain any banker,
"merchant, BROKER, attorney, or other agent from receiving any
"money which shall be or become actually due and payable
"upon or by virtue of any valuable security, according to the
"tenor and effect thereof, in such manner as he might have
"done if this Act had not been passed; nor from selling, trans-
"ferring, or otherwise disposing of any securities or effects in
"his possession upon which he shall have any lien, claim, or

"demand entitling him by law so to do, unless such sale,
"transfer, or other disposal shall extend to a greater number or
"part of such securities or effects than shall be requisite for
"satisfying such lien, claim, or demand."

A Broker cannot at law recover moneys expended in the purchase of shares in an illegal company, or in one formed for immoral purposes, and he is liable to his client for any loss or damages the client may sustain through his neglect, incapacity, or ignorance. A Broker is at law presumed to know his business, but he is not expected to depart from the ordinary course of dealings, and if a client finds that his Broker buys at the dearest and sells at the cheapest price of the day, there is no remedy for any loss sustained by such dealings, whether it arise from want of judgment or not. A Broker deals for his client or principal at the client's risk entirely, and the client is liable to him for any loss or default, unless where the transactions are of a speculative or gambling nature. Such contracts cannot be enforced at law, and the Broker, if he should undertake them, does so at his own risk, relying on his client's solvency and honour. Jobbers are liable to Brokers for the due fulfilment of their contracts, such as the proper transfer and delivery of Stocks and Shares; and thus a Jobber, in the case of a purchase, is bound to acquaint himself with the status and ability of the ostensible purchaser, and deals under the responsibility of seeing that the transferee or purchaser is not a disqualified person, such as an infant, etc. A transfer to an infant, or to a party incapacitated to be a shareholder, is not a good transfer, and in such a case the Jobber is liable to the Broker with whom he has negotiated the sale. A Jobber can deal unrestrictedly for himself, and is not bound to disclose his principal, if he has one, and he, as a rule, restricts his operations to some particular branch of securities in which he makes himself a master. Thus, Jobbers are frequently more proficient in special knowledge than Brokers. The inducements to gamble and speculate are, therefore, stronger with the Jobber, consequently they run greater risks, while they may make larger profits than Brokers, and in many instances a Jobber's career, if he be a wild dealer—a "plunger"—is suddenly cut short by some unlucky speculation, and he passes away out of the charmed body where he has shone like a meteor.

The position of the members of "the Society of the Stock "Exchange" in **Dublin** varies in many fundamental particulars from that of the London Stock Exchange. In Dublin each person seeking to be a member has to obtain from the Lord Lieutenant a license to act as a Government Stock-broker, pursuant to 39 George III., cap. 60, and 56 George III., cap. 98. The nature of this license is an authority to buy and sell Government Stock. To buy and sell and traffic and deal in every other species of Stocks and Shares requires no license in theory, but as the body of members would not negotiate with any other than a member, a person to deal in such commodities on commission must, in practice, be duly licensed. This license costs £100, and is usually granted as a matter of course, upon a letter of recommendation signed by the Secretary of the Bank of Ireland, the President of the Stock Exchange, and the President of the Chamber of Commerce. The applicant for admission must give the President of the Stock Exchange ten clear days' notice of his intention to apply to the Viceroy, and such notice is placed before the members, and posted in the Stock Exchange. The Committee report on the applicant, who, being duly qualified and approved of, obtains the recommendatory signature of the President to his letter of application to the Lord Lieutenant. The preliminaries to membership are as follows :—

1. The Applicant must provide two solvent Sureties in the sum of £1,000 each, to continue for three years from date of admission.
2. He must satisfy the Committee that he is the *bonâ fide* owner of £2,000 unencumbered.
3. He must declare he is not a member of a partnership.
4. He must not be a Bill-broker or Discounter, or engaged in any trade incompatible with Stock-broking. His wife—if he has one—must not be engaged in trade.
5. He must not have been a Bankrupt or Insolvent, or one who has compounded with his creditors, unless he have paid his debts in full.

There is a special disqualification to this effect: "No person "shall be admissible as a member if he shall have been in the "employment of any member within one year previously to "his application, unless entering into partnership with his "employer"—the drift of which is not very apparent. But the other rules for admission are necessary, like those of the London body, to assure the public of the solvency, and to maintain the respectability, of the members. The annual subscription is twenty guineas. There are no Jobbers—specially so called—as on the London Stock Exchange, on the Dublin Stock Exchange; nor is there the third class of "authorised "clerks" of which we have spoken.

Stock-broking is by some regarded as a very simple business, and one which does not demand any study or apprenticeship. But it is a science full of subtleties, and mastered only by study; it is a pursuit wherein the knowledge and wisdom, obtainable only from a pre-acquaintanceship with the methods of the money market, are needful, and have daily opportunities of being displayed.

Purchases and sales are of two descriptions—for cash or for account. For cash, means for present delivery; for account, for delivery on the day called the account day. Two such days are appointed by the committee in each month—one at the middle, and the other at the end of the month. Each account day is preceded by the name day—*i.e.*, the day upon which the name of the purchaser or seller is delivered, in order to have the deed of transfer filled. If Shares and Stock are not delivered within ten days after the time for delivery, the purchaser can buy in, at the then market price, on the eleventh day, and the defaulting member is liable for any loss contracted.

The following days are observed as holidays on both the London and Dublin Stock Exchanges:

1st January.	Whit Monday.
Good Friday.	First Monday in August.
Easter Monday.	1st November.
1st May.	Christmas Day.
	26th December.

If any of the foregoing fall on Sunday, the ensuing Monday is observed; and, in addition to these, the committee can, by giving three days' notice, appoint any day a holiday. The London Exchange is closed on the Derby Day.

The following are the technical expressions in use on the Stock Exchange which refer to the business procedure:

Scrip, is frequently but erroneously applied to certificates of shares, or any writing alleging property in Shares. It properly signifies the memorandum given to an original allottee, and is contracted from *subscription*, of which subscription the memorandum is an acknowledgment.

Contango, is the payment made, by way of fine, by a *purchaser* who is unable or indisposed to honour his contract, and requires time to complete it; in which case the delivery to him of his purchase is deferred to a further account day, and for this "carrying over" he pays a stipulated sum, called a contango. On the other hand, when a *seller* is not in a position to honour his contract, and to deliver, the purchaser sanctions the delay and exacts a "**Backwardation.**"

Options are payments made by A. for the purchase or sale of the option of buying from or selling to B. certain specified Stocks or Shares at a certain specified future time. If the movements in the prices of these Stocks would prove disadvantageous to B., he is content to lose his option money and not effect the purchase. An option to sell is a "**put.**" An option to buy is a "**call.**" An option to sell or to buy is a "**put and call.**"

Par, is the *nominal* value of Stocks and Shares. A par price in stocks is £100; in shares, a price equal to the amount paid up on each share. *Discount* is the amount below par, when the price is below the nominal value. *Premium*, the amount above par, when the price is above the nominal value.

Bear, is a speculator who operates for a *fall*—one who contracts to deliver, at a specified future time, stocks which he does not own.*

---

* The origin of this term is to be found in the proverb, "Selling the "skin before the bear was caught," and came into use in its present signification at the time of the South Sea Speculation. In a letter dated 19th June, 1714, from Thomas Harley, cousin of Lord Treasurer Oxford, to Dean Swift, this passage occurs : "You never heard such bellowing about "the town of the state of the nation, especially amongst the sharpers, "*sellers of bearskins*, and the rest of that kind." Bull seems to have been invented as a companion phrase to Bear, and to have been hit upon because of the fancied derivation of bear from the animal who pulled down—bull being an animal which sends upwards with his horns.

Bull, is a speculator who operates for a *rise* in the market price—one who contracts to take a Bear's sales.

It has been argued that in this advanced and radical age such institutions as Stock Exchanges, which are close boroughs to which few are admitted, and which make their own terms with the public, should be abolished, and the sale and purchase of Stocks and Shares be as free and unrestricted as the sale and purchase of a pound of tea. But it is to be remembered the Stock Exchange dealings fix the public estimate, and therefore the public value of the various interests which are daily sold and bought, and the community is daily apprised of the position of all investments in public opinion. Every transaction is recorded—there is no underbidding—no hole-and-corner dealing. A purchaser or seller entrusts the sale or purchase of his property to honourable, astute, and qualified men. If each man dealt with his neighbour there would not only be scope for endless over-reaching, but there would be constant anxiety that the buyer could not consummate his purchase, or that the seller's title was infirm. In fact, open sale and transfer can be effected without the interposition of a Broker, but equally in fact the public prefer to forget that such a transfer is possible, and surrender their business with all its attendant details to the hands of the Brokers.

APPENDIX.

APPENDIX I.

PRINCIPAL JOINT STOCK BANKS OF ENGLAND, NUMBER OF THEIR BRANCHES, SUBSCRIBED CAPITAL, PAID-UP CAPITAL, AND AUTHORISED ISSUE.

Bank and Year Established.		No. of Branches.	Amount Subscribed.	Amount Paid-up.	Authorised Issue.
LONDON BANKS.			£	£	£
Alliance Bank (*Lim.*)	1862	3	2,000,000	800,000	...
Bank of England	1694	11	14,553,000	14,553,000	15,000,000
Central of London (*Lim.*)	1863	5	200,000	100,000	...
City Bank (*L.*) (*by Roy. Charter*)	1855	7	3,200,000	600,000	...
Consolidated Bank (*Lim.*)	1863	4	2,000,000	800,000	...
Imperial Bank (*Lim.*)	1862	2	2,250,000	675,000	...
London and Co. Bkg. Co. (*L.*)	1836	155	8,000,000	1,500,000	...
London Joint Stock Bank	1836	5	4,000,000	1,200,000	...
London and Provincial (*Lim.*)	1864	76	500,000	250,000	...
London and Sth-Western (*L.*)	1862	37	1,000,000	200,000	...
London & Westminster B. (*L.*)	1834	7	10,000,000	2,000,000	...
London and Yorkshire (*Lim.*)	1872	13	551,000	144,337	...
Merchant Bk. Co. of Lon. (*L.*)	1863	—	1,500,000	375,000	...
Midland Banking Co. (*Lim.*)	1863	40	1,380,000	255,000	...
National Provincial Bank of England (*Lim.*)	1833	147	12,037,500	1,890,000	...
Union Bank of London	1839	4	4,500,000	1,395,000	...
ENGLISH COUNTRY BANKS.					
Adelphi Bkg. Company (*Lim.*)	1861	1	260,220	130,110	...
Ashton, Stalybridge, Hyde and Glossop Bank	1836	—	125,000	50,000	...
Bank of Bolton (*Lim.*)	1836	4	989,000	353,040	...
Bank of Liverpool	1831	—	5,000,000	625,000	...
Bank of W'moreland (*Kendal*)	1833	1	214,000	25,680	12,225
Bank of Whitehaven (*Lim.*)	1837	5	295,590	98,530	32,681
Barnsley Banking Company	1832	1	294,800	47,168	9,563
Birmingham and Midland B. (*Lim.*)	1836	3	1,440,000	300,000	...
Birmingham Bank (*Lim.*)	1866	1	2,860,000	286,000	...
Birmingham Joint Stock Bank (*Lim.*)	1861	2	3,000,000	300,000	...

Appendix I.

English Country Banks—Cont.

Bank and Year Established.		No. of Branches.	Amount Subscribed. £	Amount Paid-up. £	Authorised Issue. £
Birmingham, Dudley & District Banking Co. (*Lim.*)	1836	7	1,425,000	285,000	...
Bradford Banking Co. (*Lim.*)	1827	—	1,360,000	408,000	49,292
Bradford Commercial B. C. (*L.*)	1833	—	1,116,000	279,000	20,084
Bradford District Bank (*L.*)	1862	1	851,100	297,885	...
Bradford Old Bank (*Lim.*)	1864	10	1,250,000	500,000	...
Bucks & Oxon Union B. (*L.*) (*Aylesbury*)	1866	8	400,000	80,000	...
Burton, Uttoxeter and Ashbourne Union Bank (*Lim.*)	1839	2	650,000	130,000	60,701
Bury Banking Co. (*Lim.*)	1836	—	750,000	150,000	...
Capital and Counties (*Lim.*)		53	1,750,000	350,000	...
Carlisle City & District B. (*L.*)	1837	5	400,000	80,000	19,972
Carlisle & Cumberland Bkg. Company (*Lim.*)	1836	6	400,000	100,000	25,610
Commercial Bank of Liverpool (*Lim.*)	1832	—	700,000	350,000	...
County of Gloucester Banking Co. (*Lim.*)	1836	11	800,000	181,100	144,352
County of Stafford		—	120,000	60,000	9,418
Coventry Union Banking Co.	1836	1	200,000	56,000	16,251
Craven Bank (*Lim.*)	1791	—	750,000	175,000	...
Crompton and Evans Union (*Lim.*)		7	1,000,000	200,000	...
Cumberland Union Banking Co. (*Lim.*) (*Workington*)	1829	21	600,000	250,000	35,395
Darlington District Bkg. Co.	1831	7	400,000	48,000	26,134
Derby & Derbyshire B. Co. (*L.*)	1833	4	250,000	62,500	20,093
Devon & Cornwall Bankg. Co. (*Plymouth*)	1832	22	400,000	160,000	...
Exchange & Discount (*Leeds*), (*Lim.*)		1	200,000	100,000	...
Glamorganshire Banking Co. (*Swansea*)	1836	6	351,900	300,000	...
Gloucestershire Banking Co. (*Gloucester*)	1831	36	1,000,000	450,000	155,920
Halifax Commercial Bkg. Co. (*Lim.*)	1836	3	300,000	150,000	13,733
Halifax Joint Stock Banking Co. (*Lim.*)	1829	2	500,000	200,000	18,534
Halifax & Huddersfield Union Banking Co.	1836	1	500,000	250,000	44,137
Huddersfield Banking Co.	1827	4	1,700,000	414,525	37,354
Hull Banking Co. (*Lim.*)	1833	3	693,000	121,275	29,333
Knaresborough & Claro Bkg. Company	1831	6	213,700	42,740	28,059
Lancashire and Yorkshire (*L.*)		16	600,000	300,000	...
Lancaster Banking Co.	1826	21	275,000	275,000	64,311

Appendix I.

Bank and Year Established.		No. of Branches.	Amount Subscribed.	Amount Paid-up.	Authorised Issue.
English Country Banks—*Cont.*			£	£	£
Leamington Priors & Warwickshire Bank (*Lim.*)	1835	3	200,000	40,000	13,875
Leeds & County Bank (*Lim.*)	1862	5	920,000	230,000	...
Leicestershire Banking Co. (*Lim.*) (*Leicester*)	1829	13	1,000,000	316,667	86,060
Lincoln and Lindsey Bank (*L.*)	1833	12	326,950	114,432	51,620
Lloyds' Banking Co. (*Lim.*) (*Birmingham*)	1865	43	3,000,000	480,000	
Manchester & County B. (*L.*)	1862	34	4,400,000	660,000	
Manchester & Salford Bank	1836	16	1,750,000	700,000	
Manchester & Liverpool District Banking Co. (*Lim.*)	1829	54	5,430,000	905,000	...
Manchester Joint Stock (*L.*)		1	341,000	102,300	...
Moore & Robinson's Nottinghamshire Banking Co. (*L.*)	1836	—	507,750	203,800	35,813
National B. of Liverpool (*L.*)	1863	4	600,000	300,000	...
National Bank of Wales (*L.*)		—	218,690	51,102	...
North Eastern (*Lim.*)	1858	26	806,500	255,950	...
Northamptonshire B. Co. (*L.*)	1836	4	466,925	93,385	20,401
Northamptonshire Union Bkg. Co. (*Lim.*)	1837	4	900,000	176,562	84,356
North and South Wales Bank (*Lim.*) (*Liverpool*)	1836	50	2,000,000	500,000	63,951
North-Western Bank (*Lim.*) (*Liverpool*)	1864	—	1,080,000	405,000	
Nottingham Joint Stock Bank (*Limited*)	1865	6	500,000	100,000	...
Nottingham & Notts Bkg. Co.	1834	8	407,000	203,500	29,477
Pares' Leicestershire B. Co.(*L.*)	1836	5	1,000,000	330,000	59,300
Parr's Banking Co. (*Lim.*)	1865	21	2,461,500	492,300	...
Preston Banking Co.	1844	10	100,000	100,000	...
Sheffield Union Banking Co.	1843	6	300,000	180,000	...
Sheffield & Rotherham B.C.(*L.*)	1836	5	1,200,000	192,000	52,496
Sheffield Banking Co. (*Lim.*)	1831	3	952,500	332,832	35,843
Sheffield & Hallamshire Bank	1836	—	840,000	210,000	23,524
Southport & West Lancashire (*Lim.*)		3	500,000	190,410	
Staffordshire Joint Stock Bk. (*Lim.*)	1864	11	875,000	175,000	
Stamford, Spalding & Boston Banking Co. (*Lim.*)	1832	19	825,000	275,000	55,721
Stuckeys' Banking Co.	1826	39	603,800	301,900	356,976
Swaledale & Wensleydale B. Co. (*Richmond*)	1836	4	400,000	63,000	54,372
Swansea (*Lim.*)		3	574,960	201,236	...
Three Towns Bkg. Co. (*Lim.*)		1	75,000	25,000	...
Union B. of Birmingham (*L.*)	1878	—	415,200	103,800	...
Union Bank of Liverpool	1835	1	600,000	600,000	...

Bank and Year Established.		No. of Branches.	Amount Subscribed.	Amount Paid-up.	Authorised Issue.
ENGLISH COUNTRY BANKS—*Cont.*			£	£	£
Union Bk. of Manchester (*L.*)	1836	29	1,000,000	440,000	...
Wakefield & Barnsley Union Bank...	1832	2	400,000	104,000	14,604
West Riding Union Banking Co. (*Huddersfield*)	1832	2	3,160,600	316,060	34,029
Whitehaven Joint Stock Bank	1829	5	300,000	45,000	31,916
Wilts and Dorset Banking Co. (*Salisbury*)	1835	64	450,000	300,000	76,162
Wolverhampton and Staffordshire Banking Co.	1832	—	500,000	100,000	35,378
Worcester City & County B. (*Lim.*)	1840	20	1,000,000	250,000	6,848
York City and County Bank	1830	23	698,000	174,500	94,695
Yorkshire Bkg. Co. (*L.*)(*Leeds*)	1843	24	1,500,000	250,000	122,532
York Union Banking Co. ...	1833	11	660,000	165,000	71,240

APPENDIX II.

A TABLE OF THE NUMBER OF DAYS FROM ANY DAY IN ONE MONTH TO THE SAME IN ANOTHER.

Months.	Jan.	Feb.	Mar.	April	May	June	July	Aug.	Sept.	Oct.	Nov.	Dec.
January	365	31	59	90	120	151	181	212	243	273	304	334
February	334	365	28	59	89	120	150	181	212	242	273	303
March	306	337	365	31	61	92	122	153	184	214	245	275
April	275	306	334	365	30	61	91	122	153	183	214	244
May	245	276	304	335	365	31	61	92	123	153	184	214
June	214	245	273	304	334	365	31	61	92	122	153	183
July	184	215	243	274	304	335	365	31	62	92	123	153
August	153	184	212	243	273	304	335	365	31	61	92	122
September	122	153	181	212	242	273	303	334	365	30	61	91
October	92	123	151	182	212	243	273	304	335	365	31	61
November	61	92	120	151	181	212	243	273	304	334	365	30
December	31	62	90	121	151	182	212	243	274	304	335	365

To calculate the days required, look along the *length* of this Table. Example: say from May 10th to October 15th, 153 days in the Table; add five, the difference in the dates from the 10th to the 15th = 158 the number required. In case of Leap Year, one more day to be added.

COMMISSION AND DISCOUNT TABLE.

At per Cent.

On			1		1¼		1½		2		2½		4		5		6		7		7½		10		12½		15		17½		20	
£	s.	d.	s.	d.	s.	d.	s.	d.	s.	d.	s.	d.	s.	d.	s.	d.	s.	d.	s.	d.	s.	d.	s.	d.	s.	d.	s.	d.	s.	d.	s.	d.
0	0	2	...		...		...		...		...		...		...		...		...		...		...		0	0¼	0	0¼	0	0¼	0	0¼
0	0	3	...		...		...		...		...		...		...		...		...		...		0	0¼	0	0¼	0	0¼	0	0½	0	0½
0	0	4	...		...		...		...		...		...		...		0	0¼	0	0¼	0	0¼	0	0¼	0	0½	0	0½	0	0½	0	0¾
0	0	5	...		...		...		...		...		...		0	0¼	0	0¼	0	0¼	0	0¼	0	0½	0	0½	0	0¾	0	0¾	0	1
0	0	6	...		...		...		...		...		0	0¼	0	0¼	0	0¼	0	0¼	0	0¼	0	0½	0	0¾	0	0¾	0	1	0	1¼
0	0	9	...		...		...		...		...		0	0¼	0	0¼	0	0½	0	0½	0	0½	0	0¾	0	1	0	1¼	0	1½	0	1¾
0	1	0	...		...		...		0	0¼	0	0¼	0	0¼	0	0½	0	0¾	0	0¾	0	0¾	0	1	0	1½	0	1¾	0	1¾	0	2¼
0	1	6	...		0	0¼	0	0¼	0	0¼	0	0¼	0	0½	0	0¾	0	1	0	1¼	0	1¼	0	1¾	0	2¼	0	2½	0	3	0	3½
0	2	0	0	0¼	0	0¼	0	0¼	0	0½	0	0½	0	0¾	0	1	0	1¼	0	1½	0	1¾	0	2¼	0	3	0	3½	0	4	0	4¾
0	2	6	0	0¼	0	0¼	0	0¼	0	0½	0	0¾	0	1	0	1½	0	1¾	0	2	0	2¼	0	3	0	3¾	0	4½	0	5¼	0	6
0	3	0	0	0¼	0	0¼	0	0½	0	0½	0	0¾	0	1¼	0	1¾	0	2	0	2½	0	2½	0	3½	0	4½	0	5¼	0	6¼	0	7
0	3	6	0	0¼	0	0½	0	0½	0	0¾	0	1	0	1½	0	2	0	2½	0	2¾	0	3	0	4	0	5¼	0	6¼	0	7¼	0	8¼
0	4	0	0	0½	0	0½	0	0½	0	0¾	0	1	0	1¾	0	2¼	0	2¾	0	3¼	0	3½	0	4¾	0	6	0	7	0	8¼	0	9½
0	5	0	0	0½	0	0¾	0	0¾	0	1	0	1½	0	2¼	0	3	0	3½	0	4	0	4½	0	6	0	7½	0	9	0	10½	1	0
0	7	6	0	0¾	0	1	0	1¼	0	1¾	0	2¼	0	3½	0	4½	0	5¼	0	6¼	0	6¾	0	9	0	11¼	1	1½	1	3¾	1	6
0	10	0	0	1	0	1½	0	1¾	0	2¼	0	3	0	4¾	0	6	0	7	0	8¼	0	9	1	0	1	3	1	6	1	9	2	0
0	12	6	0	1½	0	1¾	0	2¼	0	3	0	3¼	0	6	0	7½	0	9	0	10½	0	11¼	1	3	1	6½	1	10½	2	2¼	2	6
0	15	0	0	1¾	0	2¼	0	2½	0	3½	0	4½	0	7	0	9	0	10¾	1	0½	1	1½	1	6	1	10¾	2	3	2	7½	3	0
0	17	6	0	2	0	2½	0	3	0	4	0	5¼	0	8¼	0	10½	1	0½	1	2½	1	3¾	1	9	2	2¼	2	7½	3	0¾	3	6
1	0	0	0	2¼	0	3	0	3½	0	4¾	0	6	0	9½	1	0	1	2½	1	4¾	1	6	2	0	2	6	3	0	3	6	4	0
2	0	0	0	4¾	0	6	0	7	0	9½	1	0	1	7	2	0	2	4¾	2	9½	3	0	4	0	5	0	6	0	7	0	8	0
3	0	0	0	7	0	9	0	10¾	1	2¼	1	6	2	4¾	3	0	3	7	4	2¼	4	6	6	0	7	6	9	0	10	6	12	0
4	0	0	0	9½	1	0	1	2¼	1	7	2	0	3	2¼	4	0	4	9½	5	7	6	0	8	0	10	0	12	0	14	0	16	0
5	0	0	1	0	1	3	1	6	2	0	2	6	4	0	5	0	6	0	7	0	7	6	10	0	12	6	15	0	17	6	20	0
10	0	0	2	0	2	6	3	0	4	0	5	0	8	0	10	0	12	0	14	0	15	0	20	0	25	0	30	0	35	0	40	0

APPENDIX III.

MARRIED WOMAN'S ACCOUNT.—FORM OF LETTER OF AUTHORITY TO BANKER.

_____ 18

To the _____ Bank.

     I approve of my wife, Mrs. _____ having an account in her own Name in your Books, and I beg that you will, at all times, honour her Drafts and follow her directions in reference thereto, placing to her credit whatever sums may be remitted or paid to you by her or on her behalf; and that you will carry to her Account, the Dividends on any Stock or other Securities which may from time to time be standing in her name, following her sole directions as to such Stock or Securities, and as to any Boxes, Parcels, and other things she may deposit with you for safe Custody.

FORM OF INDEMNITY ON REPAYMENT OF LOST DEPOSIT RECEIPT, DRAFT, ETC.

To the _____ Bank.

_____ 188

GENTLEMEN,

     In consideration of your paying the amount [of Draft on Demand], [with interest accrued, of Deposit Receipt], issued at your _____ Office, on the _____ and Numbered _____, in favour of _____ for the sum of £_____, which [Draft] [Deposit Receipt] has been lost, stolen, or mislaid, _____ hereby indemnify The _____ Bank, Limited, and all or any of its officers, against all damages, losses or charges which they or any of them may incur, directly or indirectly, by reason of such payment, or in case of payment of said [Draft] [Deposit Receipt] by the Bank or its Officers, in error or through oversight; and having now received the amount of it, to wit, £_____ [with interest due, to wit, £_____] should the above-described [Draft] [Deposit Receipt] hereafter come into _____ possession, _____ hereby undertake to deliver it to the Bank.

                      Your obedient Servant,

Witness, _____

APPENDIX

TABLE IN TEN LANGUAGES OF CARDINAL NUMBERS AND

	English.	French.	German.	Spanish.	Italian.
1	One	Un	Ein	Uno	Uno
2	Two	Deux	Zwei	Dos	Due
3	Three	Trois	Drei	Tres	Tre
4	Four	Quatre	Vier	Cuatro	Quattro
5	Five	Cinq	Fünf	Cinco	Cinque
6	Six	Six	Sechs	Seis	Sei
7	Seven	Sept	Sieben	Siete	Sette
8	Eight	Huit	Acht	Ocho	Otto
9	Nine	Neuf	Neun	Nueve	Nove
10	Ten	Dix	Zehn	Diez	Dieci
11	Eleven	Onze	Elf	Once	Undici
12	Twelve	Douze	Zwölf	Doce	Dodici
13	Thirteen	Treize	Dreizehn	Trece	Tredici
14	Fourteen	Quatorze	Vierzehn	Catorce	Quattordici
15	Fifteen	Quinze	Fünfzehn	Quinze	Quindici
16	Sixteen	Seize	Sechzehn	Diez y seis	Sedici
17	Seventeen	Dix-sept	Siebzehn	Diez y siete	Diciassette
18	Eighteen	Dix-huit	Achtzehn	Diez y ocho	Diciotto
19	Nineteen	Dix-neuf	Neunzehn	Diez y nueve	Diciannove
20	Twenty	Vingt	Zwanzig	Viente	Venti
21	Twenty-one	Vingt-et-un	Ein und Zwanzig	Viente y uno	Vent'uno
30	Thirty	Trente	Dreiszig	Treinte	Trenta
40	Forty	Quarante	Vierzig	Cuarente	Quarenta
50	Fifty	Cinquante	Fünfzig	Cinquenta	Viaquanta.
60	Sixty	Soixante	Sechzig	Sesenta	Sessanta
70	Seventy	Soixante-dix	Siebenzig	Setenta	Settanta
80	Eighty	Quatre-vingt	Achtzig	Ochenta	Ottanta
90	Ninety	Quatre-vingt-dix	Neunzig	Noventa	Novanta
100	Hundred	Cent	Hundert	Cien	Cento
1000	Thousand	Mille	Tausend	Mil	Mille
	Day	Jour	Tag	Dia	Giorno
	Week	Semaine	Woche	Semana	Settimana
	Month	Mois	Monat	Més	Mese
	Year	Année	Jahr	Año	Anno
	On demand	À présentation	Nach sicht, or, bei Vorzeigung	À presentacion	A presentazione
	At sight	À vue	A vista	À la vista	A vista
	After sight	À jours de vue	Nachsicht	A..dias vista	Dopo vista
	After date	À jours de date	Nach dato, or nach heute	À ... dias fecha	Dopo data
	Pay to the order	Payez à l'ordre	Für mich, or uns an die ordre	À la órden	Pagate a l'ordine
	I promise to pay	Je payerai	Werde ich, or werden wir bezahlen	Pagaré	Pagare
	With interest	Avec intérêts	Mit zinsen	Con interés	Con interesse

IV.
COMMERCIAL TERMS USED IN BILLS OF EXCHANGE.

	Portuguese.	Dutch.	Russian.	Danish.	Swedish.
1	Hum, M. Huma, F.	Een	Odun	En	En
2	Doue, M. Duas, F.	Twee	Dba	To	Twa
3	Tres	Drie	Tza	Tre	Tre
4	Quatro	Vier	Tschetire	Fire	Fyra
5	Cinco	Vyf	Piat	Fem	Fem
6	Seis	Zes	Schest	Sex	Sex
7	Sete	Zeven	Sem	Syv	Sju
8	Outo	Acht	Votem	Otte	Atta
9	Nove	Negen	Deviat	Ni	Nio
10	Dez	Tien	Desat	Ti	Tio
11	Onze	Elf	Odinnatzat	Elleve	Elfva
12	Doze	Twaalf	Dvenzat	Tolo	Tolf
13	Treze	Dertien	Trenazat	Tretten	Tretton
14	Quatorze	Veertien	Cheterinazat	Fiorten	Fjorton
15	Quinze	Vyftien	Paznatzat	Femten	Femton
16	Dezaseis	Zestien	Schesnadzat	Sexten	Sexten
17	Dezasette	Zeventien	Semnatzat	Sytten	Sjutton
18	Dezocto	Achtien	Vosemnatzat	Atten	Aderton
19	Dezaneve	Negentien	Davetnazat	Nitten	Nitton
20	Vinte	Twintig	Dvatzat	Tyve	Tjugu
21	Vinte hum	Enen Twintig	Dvatzat - odnar	En og Tyve	Tjugu en
30	Trinta	Dertig	Trudzat	Tredive	Trettio
40	Quarenta	Veertig	Sorok	Fyrgetive	Fyrtio
50	Cincoenta	Vyftig	Piatdesat	Halvred sindative	Femtio
60	Secenta	Zestig	Schestdesat	Tredsindstyve	Sextio
70	Setenta	Zeventig	Semdesat	Halfierd indstyve	Sjuttio
80	Oitenta	Tachtig	Vosemdesat	Fürsindstyve	Attio
90	Noventa	Negentig	Devianosto	Halvemsindstyve	Nittio
100	Cem	Honderd	Sto	Hundredre	Ett hundra
1000	Mil	Duizend	Tizatz	Tusinde	Ett tusen
	Dia	Dag	Den	Dage	Dag
	Semana	Week	Nedela	Uger	Weeka
	Mez	Maanden	Mesatz	Maaned	Manad
	Anno	Jaar	God	Aar	Ar
	À presentação	Op vertoon	Po bziskam	Paa anforderierg	Pa anfordriug
	À vista	Op sight a vista	Po prediavieni	A vista	Vid sigt
	A...dias vista	Dagen na zigt	Po prediavieni	Efta sigt	Efter sigt
	A .. dias data	Dagen na dato	Gato	Efter dato	Fran dato
	Pagase à ordem	Voor my aan de order	Nlat it order	Behag at, betale til odre	Behagar att, betala til ordre
	Pagarei	Ik neem aan te betalen	Ia obetschai	Je forpligter mig at betale	Jag forpligtar mig att betala
	Com intereses	Met interest	Is prozentamu	Med reute	Med rauta

APPENDIX V.

Statutes.

THE BANKING COPARTNERSHIP REGULATION ACT, 1826. 7 GEO. 4, c. 46.
(The Act Authorising Joint Stock Banks.)

An Act for the better regulating Copartnerships of certain Bankers in England, and for amending so much of an Act of the Thirty-ninth and Fortieth Years of the Reign of His late Majesty King George the Third, intituled " An Act "for establishing an Agreement with the Governor and " Company of the Bank of England, for advancing the Sum "of Three Millions towards the Supply for the Service of "the Year 1800," as relates to the same. [26th May, 1826.]

WHEREAS an act was passed in the 39th and 40th years of the reign of his late Majesty King George the Third, intituled "An Act for establishing an agreement with the Governor "and Company of the Bank of England, for advancing the "sum of three millions towards the supply for the service of "the year 1800;" and whereas it was, to prevent doubts as to the privilege of the said governor and company, enacted and declared in the said recited act, that no other bank should be erected, established or allowed by Parliament; and that it should not be lawful for any body politic or corporate whatsoever, erected or to be erected, or for any other persons united or to be united in covenants or partnership, exceeding the number of six persons, in that part of Great Britain called England, to borrow, owe or take up any sum or sums of money on their bills or notes payable on demand, or at any less time than six months from the borrowing thereof, during the continuance of the said privilege to the said governor and company, who were thereby declared to be and remain a corporation, with the privilege of exclusive banking, as before recited; but subject nevertheless to redemption on the terms and conditions in the said act specified; and whereas the Governor and Company of the Bank of England have consented to relinquish so much of their exclusive privilege as

[margin: 39 and 40 Geo. 3, c. 28.]

prohibits any body politic or corporate, or any number of persons exceeding six, in England, acting in copartnership, from borrowing, owing or taking up any sum or sums of money on their bills or notes payable on demand, or at any less time than six months from the borrowing thereof; provided that such body politic or corporate, or persons united in covenants or partnerships, exceeding the number of six persons in each copartnership, shall have the whole of their banking establishments and carry on their business as bankers at any place or places in England exceeding the distance of 65 miles from London, and that all the individuals composing such corporations or copartnerships, carrying on such business, shall be liable to and responsible for the due payment of all bills and notes issued by such corporations or copartnerships respectively: be it therefore enacted, etc., that from and after the passing of this act it shall and may be lawful for any bodies politic or corporate erected for the purposes of banking, or for any number of persons united in covenants or copartnership, although such persons so united or carrying on business together shall consist of more than six in number, to carry on the trade or business of bankers in England, in like manner as copartnerships of bankers consisting of not more than six persons in number may lawfully do; and for such bodies politic or corporate, or such persons so united as aforesaid, to make and issue their bills or notes at any place or places in England exceeding the distance of 65 miles from London, payable on demand, or otherwise at some place or places specified upon such bills or notes exceeding the distance of 65 miles from London, and not elsewhere, and to borrow, owe or take up any sum or sums of money on their bills or notes so made and issued at any such place or places as aforesaid: provided always that such corporations or persons carrying on such trade or business of bankers in copartnership shall not have any house of business or establishment as bankers in London, or at any place or places not exceeding the distance of 65 miles from London; and that every member of any such corporation or copartnership shall be liable to and responsible for the due payment of all bills and notes which shall be issued, and for all sums of money which shall be borrowed, owed or taken up by the corporation or copartnership of which such persons shall be a member, such person being a member at the period of the date of the bills or notes, or becoming or being a member before or at the time of the bills or notes being payable, or

[margin: Copartnerships of more than six in number may carry on business as bankers in England, 65 miles from London, provided they have no establishment as bankers in London, and that every member shall be liable for the payment of all bills, &c.]

being such member at the time of the borrowing, owing or taking up of any sum or sums of money upon any bills or notes by the corporation or copartnership, or while any sum of money on any bills or notes is owing or unpaid, or at the time the same became due from the corporation or copartnership; any agreement, covenant or contract to the contrary notwithstanding.

<small>This act not to authorize copartnerships to issue, within the limits mentioned, any bills payable on demand; nor to draw bills upon any partner, &c., so resident, for less than £50;</small>

2. Provided always, that nothing in this act contained shall extend or be construed to extend to enable or authorise any such corporation, or copartnership exceeding the number of six persons, so carrying on the trade or business of bankers as aforesaid, either by any member of or person belonging to any such corporation or copartnership, or by any agent or agents, or any other person or persons on behalf of any such corporation or copartnership, to issue or re-issue in London, or at any place or places not exceeding the distance of 65 miles from London, any bill or note of such corporation or copartnership, which shall be payable to bearer on demand, or any bank post bill; nor to draw upon any partner or agent, or other person or persons who may be resident in London, or at any place or places not exceeding the distance of 65 miles from London, any bill of exchange which shall be payable on demand, or which shall be for a less amount than £50: provided also, that it shall be lawful, notwithstanding anything herein or in the said recited act contained, for any such corporation or copartnership to draw any bill of exchange for any sum of money amounting to the sum of £50 or upwards, payable either in London or elsewhere, at any period after date or after sight.

<small>nor to borrow money, or take up or issue bills of exchange, contrary to the provisions of the recited act, except as herein provided.</small>

3. Provided also, that nothing in this act contained shall extend or be construed to extend to enable or authorise any such corporation, or copartnership exceeding the number of six persons, so carrying on the trade or business of bankers in England as aforesaid, or any member, agent or agents of any such corporation or copartnership, to borrow, owe or take up in London, or at any place or places not exceeding the distance of 65 miles from London, any sum or sums of money on any bill or promissory note of any such corporation or copartnership payable on demand, or at any less time than six months from the borrowing thereof, nor to make or issue any bill or bills of exchange or promissory note or notes of such corporation or copartnership contrary to the provisions of the said recited act of the 39th and 40th years of King George the Third, save as provided by this act in that be-

half: provided also, that nothing herein contained shall extend, or be construed to extend, to prevent any such corporation or copartnership, by any agent or person authorised by them, from discounting in London or elsewhere any bill or bills of exchange not drawn by or upon such corporation or copartnership, or by or upon any person on their behalf.

4. That before any such corporation, or copartnership exceeding the number of six persons, in England, shall begin to issue any bills or notes, or borrow, owe or take up any money on their bills or notes, an account or return shall be made out, according to the form contained in the Schedule marked (A) to this acted annexed (*a*), wherein shall be set forth the true names, title or firm of such intended or existing *Such copartnerships shall, before issuing any notes, &c. deliver at the stamp office in London an account containing the name of the firm, &c.*

(*a*) SCHEDULE referred to by this Act.

Schedule (A).

RETURN or account to be entered at the Stamp Office in London, in pursuance of an Act passed in the seventh year of the reign of King George the Fourth, intituled [*here insert the title of this act*], viz.:

Firm or name of the banking corporation or copartnership, viz. [*set forth the firm or name*].

Names and places of abode of all the partners concerned or engaged in such corporation or copartnership, viz. [*set forth all the names and places of abode*].

Names and places of the bank or banks established by such corporation or copartnership, viz. [*set forth all the names and places*].

Names and descriptions of the public officers of the said banking corporation or copartnership, viz. [*set forth all the names and descriptions*].

Names of the several towns and places where the bills or notes of the said banking corporation or copartnership are to be issued by the said corporation or copartnership, or their agent or agents, viz. [*set forth the names of all the towns and places*].

A. B. of   secretary [*or other officer, describing the office*] of the above corporation or copartnership, maketh oath and saith, that the above doth contain the name, style, and firm of the above corporation or copartnership, and the names and places of the abode of the several members thereof, and of the banks established by the said corporation or copartnership, and the names, titles, and descriptions of the public officers of the said corporation or copartnership, and the names of the towns and places where the notes of the said corporation or copartnership are to be issued, as the same respectively appear in the books of the said corporation or copartnership, and also the names and places of abode of all the members of such corporation, or of all the partners concerned or engaged in such copartnership, as the same respectively shall appear on the books of such corporation or copartnership, and the name or firm of every bank or banks established or to be established by such corporation or copartnership, and also the names and places of abode of two or more persons being members of such corporation or copartnership, and being resident in England, who shall have been appointed public officers of such corporation or copartnership, together with the title of office or other description of every such public officer respectively, in the name of any one of whom such corporation shall sue and be sued as hereinafter provided, and also the name of every town and place where any of the bills or notes of such corporation or copartnership shall be issued by any such corporation, or by their agent or agents; and every such amount or return shall be delivered to the commissioners of stamps, at the stamp office in London, who shall cause the same to be filed and kept in the said stamp office, and an entry and registry thereof to be made in a book or books to be there kept for that purpose by some person or persons to be appointed by the said commissioners in that behalf, and which book or books any person or persons shall from time to time have liberty to search and inspect on payment of the sum of 1s. for every search.

Account to be verified by secretary.

5. That such account or return shall be made out by the secretary or other person, being one of the public officers appointed as aforesaid, and shall be verified by the oath of such secretary or other public officer, taken before any justice of the peace, and which oath any justice of the peace is hereby authorised and empowered to administer; and that such account or return shall, between the 28th day of February and the 25th day of March in every year, after such corporation or copartnership shall be formed, be in like manner delivered by such secretary or other public officer as aforesaid to the commissioners of stamps, to be filed and kept in the manner and for the purposes as hereinbefore mentioned.

corporation or copartnership, and to the best of the information, knowledge and belief of this deponent.
Sworn before me, the   day of   at in the county of

C. D. justice of the peace in and for the said county.

6. That a copy of any such account or return so filed or kept and registered at the stamp office, as by this act is directed, and which copy shall be certified to be a true copy under the hand or hands of one or more of the commissioners of stamps for the time being, upon proof made that such certificate has been signed with the handwriting of the person or persons making the same, and whom it shall not be necessary to prove to be a commissioner or commissioners, shall in all proceedings, civil or criminal, and in all cases whatsoever, be received in evidence as proof of the appointment and authority of the public officers named in such account or return, and also of the fact that all persons named therein as members of such corporation or copartnership were members thereof at the date of such account or return. *Certified copies of returns to be evidence of the appointment of the public officers, &c.*

7. That the said commissioners of stamps for the time being shall, and they are hereby required, upon application made to them by any person or persons requiring a copy certified according to this act, of any such account or return as aforesaid, in order that the same may be produced in evidence or for any other purpose, to deliver to the person or persons so applying for the same such certified copy, he, she, or they paying for the same the sum of 10s. and no more. *Commissioners of stamps to give certified copies of affidavits, on payment of 10s.*

8. Provided also, that the secretary or other officer of every such corporation or copartnership shall, and he is hereby required, from time to time, as often as occasion shall render it necessary, make out upon oath, in manner hereinbefore directed, and cause to be delivered to the commissioners of stamps as aforesaid, a further account or return according to the form contained in the schedule marked (B) to this act annexed (*a*), of the name or names of any person or persons *Account of new officers or members in the course of any year to be made.*

(*a*) SCHEDULE referred to by this act.

Schedule (B).

RETURN or account to be entered at the Stamp Office in London, on behalf of [*name the corporation or copartnership*] in pursuance of an act passed in the seventh year of the reign of King George the Fourth, intituled [*insert the title of this act*], viz.:

Names of any and every new or additional public officer of the said corporation or copartnership, viz.:

A. B. in the room of C. D. deceased or removed [*as the case may be*] [*set forth every name*].

Names of any and every person who may have ceased to be a member of such corporation or copartnership, viz. [*set forth every name*].

who shall have been nominated or appointed a new or additional public officer or public officers of such corporation or copartnership, and also of the name or names of any person or persons who shall have ceased to be members of such corporation or copartnership, and also of the name or names of any person or persons who shall have become a member or members of such corporation or copartnership, either in addition to or in the place or stead of any former member or members thereof, and of the name or names of any new or additional town or towns, place or places, where such bills or notes are or are intended to be issued, and where the same are to be made payable; and such further accounts or returns shall from time to time be filed and kept, and entered and registered at the stamp office in London, in like manner as is hereinbefore required with respect to the original or annual account or return hereinbefore directed to be made.

Copartnerships shall sue and be sued in the name of their public officers.

9. That all actions and suits, and also all petitions to found any commission of bankruptcy against any person or persons who may be at any time indebted to any such copartnership carrying on business under the provisions of this act, and all proceedings at law or in equity under any commission of bankruptcy, and all other proceedings at law or in equity to

---

Names of any and every person who may have become a new member of such corporation or copartnership [*set forth every name*].

Names of any additional towns or places where bills or notes are to be issued, and where the same are to be made payable.

 A. B. of   secretary [*or other officer*] of the above-named corporation or copartnership, maketh oath and saith, that the above doth contain the name and place of abode of any and every person who hath become or been appointed a public officer of the above corporation or copartnership, and also the name and place of abode of any and every person who hath ceased to be a member of the said corporation or copartnership, and of any and every person who hath become a member of the said copartnership since the registry of the said corporation or copartnership on the   day of   last, as the same respectively appear on the books of the said corporation or copartnership, and to the best of the information, knowledge, and belief of this deponent.

  Sworn before me, the   day of   at   in the county of

      C. D. justice of the peace in and for the said county.

be commenced or instituted for or on behalf of any such copartnership against any person or persons, bodies politic or corporate, or others, whether members of such copartnership or otherwise, for recovering any debts or enforcing any claims or demands due to such copartnership, or for any other matter relating to the concerns of such copartnership, shall, and lawfully may, from and after the passing of this act, be commenced or instituted and prosecuted in the name of any one of the public officers nominated as aforesaid for the time being of such copartnership, as the nominal plaintiff or petitioner for and on behalf of such copartnership; and that all actions or suits, and proceedings at law or in equity, to be commenced or instituted by any person or persons, bodies or corporate, or others, whether members of such copartnership or otherwise, against such copartnership, shall and lawfully may be commenced, instituted and prosecuted against any one or more of the public officers nominated as aforesaid for the time being of such copartnership, as the nominal defendant for and on behalf of such copartnership; and that all indictments, informations and prosecutions by or on behalf of such copartnership, for any stealing or embezzlement of any money, goods, effects, bills, notes, securities, or other property of or belonging to such copartnership, or for any fraud, forgery, crime, or offence committed against or with intent to injure or defraud such copartnership, shall and lawfully may be had, preferred and carried on in the name of any one of the public officers nominated as aforesaid for the time being of such copartnership; and that in all indictments and informations to be had or preferred by or on behalf of such copartnership against any person or persons whomsoever, notwithstanding such person or persons may happen to be a member or members of such copartnership, it shall be lawful and sufficient to state the money, goods, effects, bills, notes, securities, or other property of such copartnership, to be the money, goods, effects, bills, notes, securities, or other property of any one of the public officers nominated as aforesaid for the time being of such copartnership; and that any forgery, fraud, crime, or other offence committed against or with intent to injure or defraud any such copartnership, shall and lawfully may in such indictment or indictments, notwithstanding as aforesaid, be laid or stated to have been committed against or with intent to injure or defraud any one of the public officers nominated as aforesaid for the time being of such copartnership; and any offender or offenders may thereupon be lawfully convicted for any such forgery, fraud, crime or offence; and that in all other allegations, indictments, informations, or other proceedings of any kind whatsoever, in which it otherwise might or would have been necessary to state the names of the persons composing such copartnership, it shall and may be lawful and sufficient to state the name of any one of the public officers nominated as aforesaid for the time being of such copartnership; and the death, resignation, removal, or any act of such public officer, shall not abate or prejudice any such action, suit, indictment, information, prosecution or other proceeding commenced against or by or on behalf of such copartnership, but the same may be continued, prosecuted and carried on in the name of any other of the public officers of such copartnership for the time being.

Not more than one action for the recovery of one demand.

10. That no person or persons, or body or bodies politic or corporate, having or claiming to have any demand upon or against any such corporation or copartnership, shall bring more than one action or suit, in case the merits shall have been tried in such action or suit, in respect of such demand; and the proceedings in any action or suit, by or against any one of the public officers nominated as aforesaid for the time being of any such copartnership, may be pleaded in bar of any other action or actions, suit or suits, for the same demand, by or against any other of the public officers of such copartnership.

Decrees of a court of equity against the public officer to take effect against the copartnership.

11. That all and every decree or decrees, order or orders, made or pronounced in any suit or proceeding in any court of equity against any public officer of any such copartnership carrying on business under the provisions of this act, shall have the like effect and operation upon and against the property and funds of such copartnership, and upon and against the persons and property of every or any member or members thereof, as if every or any such members of such copartnership were parties members before the court to and in any such suit or proceeding; and that it shall and may be lawful for any court in which such order or decree shall have been made, to cause such order and decree to be enforced against every or any member of such copartnership, in like manner as if every member of such copartnership were parties before such court to and in such suit or proceeding, and although all such members are not before the court.

Judgments against such

12. That all and every judgment and judgments, decree or decrees, which shall at any time after the passing of this act

be had or recovered or entered up as aforesaid, in any action, suit, or proceedings in law or equity against any public officer of any such copartnership, shall have the like effect and operation upon and against the property of such copartnership, and upon and against the property of every such member thereof as aforesaid, as if such judgment or judgments had been recovered or obtained against such copartnership; and that the bankruptcy, insolvency, or stopping payment of any such public officer for the time being of such copartnership, in his individual character or capacity, shall not be nor be construed to be the bankruptcy, insolvency, or stopping payment, of such copartnership; and that such copartnership, and every member thereof, and the capital stock and effects of such copartnership, and the effects of every member of such copartnership, shall in all cases, notwithstanding the bankruptcy, insolvency, or stopping payment of any such public officer, be attached and attachable, and be in all respects liable to the lawful claims and demands of the creditor and creditors of such copartnership, or of any member or members thereof, as if no such bankruptcy, insolvency, or stopping payment of such public officer of such copartnership had happened or taken place. *public officer shall operate against the copartnership.*

13. That execution upon any judgment in any action obtained against any public officer for the time being of any such corporation or copartnership carrying on the business of banking under the provisions of this act, whether as plaintiff or defendant, may be issued against any member or members for the time being of such corporation or copartnership; and that in case any such execution against any member or members for the time being of any such corporation or copartnership shall be ineffectual for obtaining payment and satisfaction of the amount of such judgment, it shall be lawful for the party or parties so having obtained judgment against such public officer for the time being, to issue execution against any person or persons who was or were a member or members of such corporation or copartnership at the time when the contract or contracts or engagement or engagements in which such judgment may have been obtained was or were entered into, or became a member at any time before such contracts or engagements were executed, or was a member at the time of the judgment obtained : provided always, that no such execution as last mentioned shall be issued without leave first granted, on motion in open court, by the court in *Execution upon judgment may be issued against any member of the copartnership.*

which such judgment shall have been obtained, and when motion shall be made on notice to the person or persons sought to be charged, nor after the expiration of three years next after any such person or persons shall have ceased to be a member or members of such corporation or copartnership.

Officer, &c., in such cases indemnified.

14. Provided always, that every such public officer in whose name any such suit or action shall have been commenced, prosecuted, or defended, and every person or persons against whom execution upon any judgment obtained or entered up as aforesaid in any such action shall be issued as aforesaid, shall always be reimbursed and fully indemnified for all loss, damages, costs, and charges, without deduction, which any such officer or person may have incurred by reason of such execution, out of the funds of such copartnership, or in failure thereof, by contribution from the other members of such copartnership, as in the ordinary cases of copartnership.

Governor and Company of the Bank of England may empower agents to carry on banking business at any place in England.

15. And to prevent any doubts that might arise whether the said governor or company, under and by virtue of their charter, and the several acts of parliament which have been made and passed in relation to the affairs of the said governor and company, can lawfully carry on the trade or business of banking, otherwise than under the immediate order, management and direction of the court of directors of the said governor and company; be it therefore enacted, that it shall and may be lawful for the said governor and company to authorise and empower any committee or committees, agent or agents, to carry on the trade and business of banking, for and on behalf of the said governor and company, at any place or places in that part of the united kingdom called England, and for that purpose to invest such committee or committees, agent or agents, with such powers of management and superintendence, and such authority to appoint cashiers and other officers and servants as may be necessary or convenient for carrying on such trade and business as aforesaid; and for the same purpose to issue to such committee or committees, agent or agents, cashier or cashiers, or other officer or officers, servant or servants, cash, bills of exchange, bank post bills, bank notes, promissory notes, and other securities for payment of money; provided always, that all such acts of the said governor and company shall be done and exercised in such manner as may be appointed by any bye-laws, constitutions, orders, rules, and directions from time to time hereafter to be made by the general court of the said governor and company in that behalf, such bye-laws not being repugnant

to the laws of that part of the United Kingdom called England; and in all cases where such bye-laws, constitutions, orders, rules, or directions of the said general court shall be wanting, in such manner as the governor, deputy-governor, and directors, or the major part of them assembled, whereof the said governor or deputy-governor is always to be one, shall or may direct, such directions not being repugnant to the laws of that part of the United Kingdom called England; anything in the said charter or acts of parliament, or other law, usage, matter, or thing to the contrary thereof notwithstanding: provided always, that in any place where the trade and business of banking shall be carried on for and on behalf of the said governor and company of the Bank of England, any promissory note issued on their account in such place shall be made payable in coin in such place as well as in London.

16. That if any corporation or copartnership carrying on the trade or business of bankers under the authority of this act shall be desirous of issuing and re-issuing notes in the nature of bank notes, payable to the bearer on demand, without the same being stamped as by law is required, it shall be lawful for them so to do on giving security by bond to his Majesty, his heirs and successors, in which bond two of the directors, members, or partners of such corporation or copartnership, shall be the obligors, together with the cashier or cashiers, or accountant or accountants employed by such corporation or copartnership, as the said commissioners of stamps shall require; and such bonds shall be taken in such reasonable sums as the duties may amount unto during the period of one year, with condition to deliver to the said commissioners of stamps, within 14 days after the 5th day of January, the 5th day of April, the 5th day of July, and the 10th day of October, in every year, whilst the present stamp duties shall remain in force, a just and true account, verified upon the oaths or affirmations of two directors, members, or partners of such corporation or copartnership, and of the said cashier or cashiers, accountant or accountants, or such of them as the said commissioners of stamps shall require, such oaths or affirmations to be taken before any justice of the peace, and which oaths or affirmations any justice of the peace is hereby authorised and empowered to administer, of the amount or value of all their promissory notes in circulation on some given day in every week, for the space of one quarter of a year prior to the quarter day immediately

Copartnerships may issue unstamped notes on giving bond.

preceding the delivery of such account, together with the average amount of value thereof according to such account; and also to pay or cause to be paid into the hands of the receivers general of stamp duties in Great Britain, as a composition for the duties which would otherwise have been payable for such promissory notes issued within the space of one year, the sum of 7s. for every £100, and also for the fractional part of £100 of the said average amount or value of such notes in circulation, according to the true intent and meaning of this act; and on due performance thereof such bond shall be void; and it shall be lawful for the said commissioners to fix the time or times of making such payment, and to specify the same in the condition to every such bond; and every such bond may be required to be renewed from time to time, at the discretion of the said commissioners or the major part of them, and as often as the same shall be forfeited, or the party or parties to the same, or any of them, shall die, become bankrupt or insolvent, or reside in parts beyond the seas.

No corporation compelled to take out more than four licences.

17. Provided always, that no such corporation or co-partnership shall be obliged to take out more than four licences for the issuing of any promissory notes for money payable to the bearer on demand, allowed by law to be re-issued in all for any number of towns or places in England; and in case any such corporation or copartnership shall issue such promissory notes as aforesaid, by themselves or their agents, at more than four different towns or places in England, then after taking out three distinct licences for three of such towns or places, such corporation or copartnership, shall be entitled to have all the rest of such towns or places included in a fourth licence.

Penalty on copartnership neglecting to send returns, £500.

18. That if any such corporation or copartnership exceeding the number of six persons in England, shall begin to issue any bills or notes, or to borrow, owe, or take up any money on their bills or notes, without having caused such account or return as aforesaid to be made out and deliver in the manner and form directed by this act, or shall neglect or omit to cause such account or return to be renewed yearly and every year between the days or times hereinbefore appointed for that purpose, such corporation or copartnership so offending shall, for each and every week they shall so

Penalties for making false returns.

neglect to make such account and return, forfeit £500; and if any secretary or other officer of such corporation or copartnership shall make out or sign any false account or return or any account or return which shall not truly set forth all the several particulars by this act required to be contained or inserted in such account or return, the corporation or copartnership to which such secretary or other officer so offending shall belong shall for every such offence forfeit the sum of £500, and the said secretary or other officer so offending shall also for every such offence forfeit the sum of £100; and if any such secretary or other officer making out or signing any such account or return as aforesaid, shall knowingly or wilfully make a false oath of or concerning any of the matters to be therein specified and set forth, every such secretary or other officer so offending and being thereof lawfully convicted, shall be subject and liable to such pains and penalties as by any law now in force persons convicted of wilful and corrupt perjury are subject and liable to. False oath perjury.

19. That if any such corporation or copartnership exceeding the number of six persons, so carrying on the trade or business of bankers as aforesaid, shall, either by any member of or person belonging to any such corporation or copartnership, or by any agent or agents, or any other person or persons on behalf of any such corporation or copartnership, issue or re-issue in London, or at any place or places not exceeding the distance of 65 miles from London, any bill or note of such corporation or copartnership which shall be payable on demand; or shall draw upon any partner or agent or other person or persons who may be resident in London, or at any place or places not exceeding the distance of 65 miles from London, any bill of exchange which shall be payable on demand, or which shall be for a less amount than fifty pounds; or if any such corporation or copartnership exceeding the number of six persons, so carrying on the trade or business of bankers in England as aforesaid, or any member, agent or agents of any such corporation or copartnership, shall borrow, owe, or take up in London, or at any place or places not exceeding the distance of 65 miles from London, any sum or sums of money on any bill or promissory note of any such corporation or copartnership payable on demand, or at any less time than six months from the borrowing thereof, or shall make or issue any bill or bills of exchange or promissory note or notes of such corporation or copartnership contrary to the provisions of the said recited act of the 39th and 40th years of King George the Third, save as provided by this act, such corporation or Penalty on copartnership for issuing bills payable on demand; or drawing bills of exchange payable on demand, or for less than £50; borrowing or money on bills, except as herein provided.

copartnership so offending or on whose account or behalf any such offence as aforesaid shall be committed, shall for every such offence forfeit the sum of £50.

Not to affect the rights of Bank of England, except as herein specially altered.

20. Provided also, that nothing in this act contained shall extend or be construed to extend to prejudice, alter, or affect any of the rights, powers, or privileges of the said Governor and Company of the Bank of England; except as the said exclusive privilege of the said governor and company is by this act specially altered and varied.

Penalties, how recovered.

21. *That all pecuniary penalties and forfeitures imposed by this act shall and may be sued for and recovered in his Majesty's Court of Exchequer at Westminster, in the same manner as penalties incurred under any act or acts relating to stamp duties may be sued for and recovered in such court.* (Repealed by 36 & 37 Vict., c. 91).

THE COMPANIES ACT, 1862, SO FAR AS APPLICABLE TO BANKS. 25 & 26 Vict., c. 89.

An Act for the Incorporation, Regulation and Winding-up of Trading Companies and their Associations.

[7th August, 1862.]

Short title.

1. This act may be cited for all purposes as "The Companies Act, 1862."

Commencement of act.

2. This act . . . shall not come into operation until the 2nd day of November, 1862, and the time at which it comes into operation is referred to as the commencement of this act.

Prohibition of partnerships exceeding certain number.

4. No company, association or partnership consisting of more than 10 persons shall be formed, after the commencement of this act, for the purpose of carrying on the business of banking, unless it is registered as a company under this act, or is formed in pursuance of some other act of parliament, or of letter-patent.

Certain companies to publish statement entered in schedule.

44. Every limited banking company . . . shall, before it commences business, and also on the first Monday in February and first Monday in August in every year during which it carries on business, make a statement in the form marked (D) in the first schedule hereto (a), or as near thereto

---

(a) Form (D.) is as follows:—

The capital of the company is   , divided into   shares of   each.

as circumstances will admit, and a copy of such statement shall be put up in a conspicuous place in the registered office of the company, and in every branch office or place where the business of the company is carried on ; and if default is made in compliance with the provisions in this section, the company shall be liable to a penalty not exceeding £5 for every day during which such default continues, and every director and manager of the company who shall knowingly and wilfully authorise or permit such default shall incur the like penalty. Every member, and every creditor of the company, shall be entitled to a copy of the above-mentioned statement on payment of a sum not exceeding 6d.

205. After the commencement of this act there shall be repealed the several acts specified in the first part of the third schedule hereto, with this qualification, that so much of the said acts as is set forth in the second part of the said third schedule shall be hereby re-enacted and continued in force as if unrepealed. *Repeal of acts.*

SALE AND PURCHASE OF SHARES IN JOINT STOCK BANKING COMPANIES. 30 VICT., C. 29.
(LEEMAN'S ACT.)

An Act to amend the Law in respect of the Sale and Purchase of Shares in Joint Stock Banking Companies.

[17th June, 1867.]

WHEREAS it is expedient to make provision for the prevention of contracts for the sale and purchase of shares and stock in joint stock banking companies of which the sellers are not possessed or over which they have no control : be it enacted, etc.

The number of shares issued is
Calls to the amount of   pounds per share have been made.
    under which the sum of   pounds has been received.
The liabilities of the company on the first day of January (or July) were—
    Debts owing to sundry persons by the company—
        On judgment, £
        On specialty, £
        On notes or bills, £
        On simple contracts, £
        On estimated liabilities, £
The assets of the company on that day were :—
    Government securities [*stating them*], £
    Bills of exchange and promissory notes, £
    Cash at the Bankers, £
    Other securities, £

328   Appendix V.

Contracts for sale, &c., of shares to be void unless the numbers by which such shares are distinguished are set forth in contract.

1. That all contracts, agreements, and tokens of sale and purchase which shall, from and after the 1st day of July, 1867, be made or entered into for the sale or transfer, or purporting to be for the sale or transfer, of any share or shares, or of any stock or other interest, in any joint stock banking company in the United Kingdom of Great Britain and Ireland constituted under or regulated by the provisions of any act of parliament, royal charter, or letters patent, issuing shares or stock transferable by any deed or written instrument, shall be null and void to all intents and purposes whatsoever, unless such contract, agreement, or other token shall set forth and designate in writing such shares, stock, or interest by the respective numbers by which the same are distinguished at the making of such contract, agreement, or token on the register or books of such banking company as aforesaid, or where there is no such register of shares or stock by distinguishing numbers, then unless such contract, agreement, or other token shall set forth the person or persons in whose name or names such shares, stock, or interest shall at the time of making such contract stand as the registered proprietor thereof in the books of such banking company; and every person, whether principal, broker, or agent who shall wilfully insert in any such contract, agreement, or other token any false entry of such numbers, or any name or names other than that of the person or persons in whose name such shares, stock, or interest shall stand as aforesaid, shall be guilty of a misdemeanor, and be punished accordingly, and, if in Scotland, shall be guilty of an offence punishable by fine or imprisonment.

Registered shareholders may see lists.

2. Joint stock banking companies shall be bound to show their list of shareholders to any registered shareholder during business hours, from ten of the clock to four of the clock.

Extent of act limited.

3. This act shall not extend to shares or stock in the Bank of England or the Bank of Ireland.

COMPANIES ACTS AMENDMENT. 40 & 41 VICT. c. 26.
(REDUCTION OF CAPITAL.)
An Act to amend the Companies Act of 1862 and 1867.

[23rd July, 1877.]

30 and 31 Vic. c. 131.

WHEREAS doubts have been entertained whether the power given by the Companies Act, 1867, to a company of reducing its capital extends to paid-up capital, and it is expedient to remove such doubts:

Be it enacted by the Queen's most Excellent Majesty, by and with the advice and consent of the Lords Spiritual and Temporal, and Commons, in this present Parliament assembled, and by the authority of the same, as follows:

1. This Act may be cited for all purposes as the Companies Act, 1867. *Short title.*

2. This Act shall, so far as is consistent with the tenor thereof, be construed as one with the Companies Acts, 1862 and 1867, and the said Acts and this Act may be referred to as "The Companies Acts, 1862, 1867, and 1877." *Construction of Act. 25 and 26 Vic. c. 89. 30 and 31 Vic. c. 131.*

3. The word "capital" as used in the Companies Acts, 1867, shall include paid-up capital; and the power to reduce capital conferred by that Act shall include a power to cancel any lost capital, or any capital unrepresented by available assets, or to pay off any capital which may be in excess of the wants of the company; and paid-up capital may be reduced either with or without extinguishing or reducing the liability (if any) remaining on the shares of the company, and to the extent to which such liability is not extinguished or reduced it shall be deemed to be preserved, notwithstanding anything contained in the Companies Act, 1867. *Construction of "capital" and powers to reduce capital contained in 30 and 31 Vic. c. 131.*

4. The provisions of the Companies Act, 1867, as amended by this Act, shall apply to any company reducing its capital in pursuance of this Act and of the Companies Act, 1867, as amended by this Act: *Application of provisions of 30 and 31 Vic. c. 131.*

Provided that where the reduction of the capital of a company does not involve either the diminution of any liability in respect of unpaid capital or the payment to any shareholder of any paid-up capital.

(1.) The creditors of the company shall not, unless the Court otherwise direct, be entitled to object or required to consent to the reduction; and

(2.) It shall not be necessary before the presentation of the petition for confirming the reduction to add, and the Court may, if it thinks it expedient so to do, dispense altogether with the addition of, the words "and reduced," as mentioned in the Companies Act, 1867.

In any case that the Court thinks fit so to do, it may require the company to publish in such manner as it thinks fit the reasons for the reduction of its capital or such other information in regard to the reduction of its capital as the Court may think expedient with a view to give proper information to the public in relation to the reduction of its capital *30 and 31 Vic. c. 131.*

by a company, and, if the Court thinks fit, the causes which led to such reduction.

The minute required to be registered in the case of reduction of capital shall show, in addition to the other particulars required by law, the amount (if any) at the date of the registration of the minute proposed to be deemed to have been paid up on each share.

<small>Power to reduce capital by the cancellation of unissued shares.</small>

5. Any company limited by shares may so far modify the conditions contained in its memorandum of association, if authorized so to do by its regulations as originally framed or as altered by special resolution, as to reduce its capital by cancelling any shares which, at the date of the passing of such resolution, have not been taken or agreed to be taken by any person; and the provisions of "The Companies Act, 1867," shall not apply to any reduction of capital made in pursuance of this section.

<small>Reception of certified copies of documents as legal evidence. 25 and 26 Vic. c. 89. 30 and 31 Vic. c. 131. 40 and 41 Vic. c. 26.</small>

6. And whereas it is expedient to make provision for the reception as legal evidence of certificates of incorporation other than the original certificates, and of certified copies of or extracts from any documents filed and registered under the Companies Act, 1862 to 1877: Be it enacted, that any certificate of the incorporation of any company given by the registrar or by any assistant registrar for the time being shall be received in evidence as if it were the original certificate; and any copy of or extract from any of the documents or part of the documents kept and registered at any of the offices for the registration of joint stock companies in England, Scotland, or Ireland, if duly certified to be a true copy under the hand of the registrar or one of the assistant registrars for the time being, and whom it shall not be necessary to prove to be the registrar or assistant registrar, shall, in all legal proceedings, civil or criminal, and in all cases whatsoever, be received in evidence as of equal validity with the original document.

BANKING AND JOINT STOCK COMPANIES BILL (1879).

A BILL intituled an Act to amend the Law with respect to the Liability of Members of Banking and other Joint Stock Companies; and for other purposes :—

Be it enacted by the Queen's most excellent Majesty, by and with the advice and consent of the Lords Spiritual and

Temporal, and Commons, in this present Parliament assembled, and by the authority of the same as follows:—

1. This Act may be cited as the Companies Act, 1879. *Short title.*

2. This Act shall not apply to the Bank of England.

3. This Act shall, so far as is consistent with the tenor thereof, be construed as one with the Companies Acts, 1862, 1867, and 1877, and those Acts together with this Act may be referred to as the Companies Acts, 1862 to 1879. *Construction of Act.*

4. Subject as in this Act mentioned, any company registered before or after the passing of this Act as an unlimited company may register under the Companies Acts, 1862 to 1879, as a limited company, or any company already registered as a limited company, may re-register under the provisions of this Act. *Registration anew of unlimited company as limited company.*

The registration of an unlimited company as a limited company in pursuance of this Act shall not affect or prejudice any debts, liabilities, obligations, or contracts incurred or entered into by, to, with, or on behalf of such company prior to registration, and such debts, liabilities, contracts, and obligations may be enforced in manner provided by Part VII. of the Companies Act, 1862, in the case of a company registering in pursuance of that Part.

5. An unlimited company may, by the resolution passed by the members when assenting to registration as a limited company under the Companies Acts, 1862 to 1879, and for the purpose of such registration or otherwise, increase the nominal amount of its capital by increasing the nominal amount of each of its shares. *Capital of unlimited company assenting to register as a limited company.*

Provided always, that no part of such increased capital shall be capable of being called up, except in the event of and for the purpose of the company being wound up.

And, in cases where no such increase of nominal capital may be resolved upon, an unlimited company may, by such resolution as aforesaid, provide that a portion of its uncalled capital shall not be capable of being called up, except in the event of and for the purpose of the company being wound up.

A limited company may by a special resolution declare that any portion of its capital which has not been already called up shall not be capable of being called up, except in the event of and for the purpose of the company being wound up; and thereupon such portion of capital shall not be capable of being called up, except in the event of, and for the purposes of the company being wound up.

Unlimited liability of Bank of Issue in respect of Notes.

6. Section one hundred and eighty-two of the Companies Act, 1862, is hereby repealed, and in place thereof it is enacted as follows :—A bank of issue registered as a limited company, either before or after the passing of this Act, shall not be entitled to limited liability in respect of its notes ; and the members thereof shall continue liable in respect of its notes in the same manner as if it had been registered as an unlimited company ; but in case the general assets of the company are, in the event of the company being wound up, insufficient to satisfy the claims of both the noteholders and the general creditors, then the members, after satisfying the remaining demands of the noteholders, shall be liable to contribute towards payment of the debts of the general creditors, a sum equal to the amount received by the noteholders out of the general assets of the company.

For the purposes of this section the expression "the general assets of the company" means the funds available for payment of the general creditor as well as the noteholder.

It shall be lawful for any bank of issue registered as a limited company, to make a statement on its notes to the effect that the limited liability does not extend to its notes, and that the members of the company continue liable in respect of its notes in the same manner as if it had been registered as an unlimited company.

Audit of accounts of Banking companies.

7. (1.) Once at the least in every year the accounts of every banking company registered after the passing of this Act as a limited company, shall be examined by the auditor or auditors who shall be elected annually by the company in general meeting.

(2.) A director or officer of the company shall not be capable of being elected auditor of such company.

(3.) An auditor on quitting office shall be re-eligible.

(4.) If any casual vacancy occurs in the office of any auditor the surviving auditor or auditors (if any) may act, but if there is no surviving auditor, the directors shall forthwith call an extraordinary general meeting for the purpose of supplying the vacancy or vacancies in the auditorship.

(5.) Every auditor shall have a list delivered to him of all books kept by the company, and shall at all reasonable times have access to the books and accounts of the company ; and any auditor may, in relation to such books and accounts, examine the directors or any other officer of the company, provided that if a banking company has branch banks beyond the limits of Europe, it shall be sufficient if the auditor is allowed access to such copies of and extracts from the books and accounts of any such branch as may have been transmitted to the head office of the banking company in the United Kingdom.

(6.) The auditor or auditors shall make a report to the members on the accounts examined by him or them, and on every balance sheet laid before the company in general meeting during his or their tenure of office; and in every such report shall state whether, in his or their opinion, the balance sheet referred to in the report is a full and fair balance sheet properly drawn up, so as to exhibit a true and correct view of the state of the company's affairs, as shown by the books of the company; and such report shall be read before the company in general meeting.

(7.) The remuneration of the auditor or auditors shall be fixed by the general meeting appointing such auditor or auditors, and shall be paid by the company.

8. Every balance sheet submitted to the annual or other meeting of the members of every banking company registered after the passing of this Act as a limited company shall be signed by the auditor or auditors, and by the secretary or manager (if any), and by the directors of the company, or three of such directors at least. *Signature of balance sheet*

9. On the registration, in pursuance of this Act, of a company which has been already registered the registrar shall make provision for closing the former registration of the company and may dispense with the delivery to him of copies of any documents with copies of which he was furnished on the occasion of the original registration of the company; but, save as aforesaid, the registration of such a company shall take place in the same manner and have the same effect as if it were the first registration of that company under the Companies Acts, 1862 to 1879, and as if the provisions of the Acts under which the company was previously registered and regulated had been contained in different Acts of Parliament from those under which the company is registered as a limited company.

10. A company authorised to register under this Act may register thereunder and avail itself of the privileges conferred by this Act, notwithstanding any provisions contained in any Act of Parliament, Royal charter, deed of settlement, contract of co-partnery, cost book, regulations, letters patent, or other instrument constituting or regulating the company. *Privileges of Act available notwithstanding constitution of company.*

CROSS-WRITTEN DRAFTS OR CHEQUES.

19 & 20 VICT. C. 25.

An Act to amend the Law relating to Drafts on Bankers.

[23rd June, 1856.]

WHEREAS doubts have arisen as to the obligations of bankers with respect to cross-written drafts; and whereas it would conduce to the ease of commerce, the security of property, and the prevention of crime, if drawers or holders of drafts on bankers payable to bearer or to order on demand were enabled effectually to direct the payment of the same to be made only to or through some banker; be it therefore enacted, &c.

Draft crossed with Banker's name, &c., to be payable only to or through some Banker.

1. In every case where a draft on any banker, made payable to bearer or to order on demand, bears across its face an addition, in written or stamped letters, of the name of any banker or of the words "and company," in full or abbreviated, either of such additions shall have the force of a direction to the bankers upon whom such draft is made, that the same is to be paid only to or through some banker, and the same shall be payable only to or through some banker.

Construction.

2. In the construction of this act the word "banker" shall include any person or persons, or corporation, or joint stock or other company acting as a banker or bankers.

CROSSING CHEQUES OR DRAFTS ON BANKERS

21 & 22 VICT. C. 79.

An Act to amend the Law relating to Cheques or Drafts on Bankers.

[2nd August, 1858.]

WHEREAS it is expedient to amend the law relating to cheques on bankers, be it therefore enacted as follows :—

The crossing to be deemed a material part of a cheque or draft, &c.

1. Whenever a cheque or draft on any banker, payable to bearer or to order on demand, shall be issued, crossed with the name of a banker, or with two transverse lines with the words "and company," or any abbreviation thereof, such crossing shall be deemed a material part of the cheque or draft, and except as hereafter mentioned, shall not be obliterated or added to or altered by any person whomsoever after the issuing thereof; and the banker upon whom such cheque or draft shall be drawn shall not pay such cheque or draft to any other than the banker with whose name such cheque or

draft shall be so crossed, or if the same be crossed as aforesaid without a banker's name, to any other than a banker.

2. Whenever any such cheque or draft has been issued uncrossed, or shall be crossed with the words "and company," or any abbreviation thereof, and without the name of any banker, any lawful holder of such cheque or draft, while the same remains so uncrossed, or crossed with the words "and company," or any abbreviation thereof, without the name of any banker, may cross the same with the name of a banker; and whenever any such cheque or draft shall be uncrossed, any such lawful holder may cross the same with the words "and company," or any abbreviation thereof, with or without the name of a banker; and any such crossing as in this section mentioned shall be deemed a material part of the cheque or draft, and shall not be obliterated or added to or altered by any person whomsoever after the making thereof, and the banker upon whom such cheque or draft shall be drawn shall not pay such cheque or draft to any other than the banker with whose name such cheque or draft shall be so crossed as last foresaid. *The lawful holder of a cheque uncrossed, or crossed "and company," may cross the same with the name of banker.*

3. (*a*).

4. Provided always, that a banker paying a cheque or draft which does not, at the time when it is presented for payment, plainly appear to be or to have been crossed as aforesaid, or to have been obliterated, added to or altered as aforesaid, shall not be in any way responsible or incur liability, nor shall such payment be questioned by reason of such cheque having been so crossed as aforesaid, or having been obliterated, added to or altered as aforesaid, and of his having paid the *Banker not to be responsible for paying a cheque which does not plainly appear to have been crossed or altered.*

(*a*) Section 3 is repealed by 24 & 25 Vict. c. 95, and the following section is substituted by 24 & 25 Vict. c. 98 :—

25. Whenever any cheque or draft on any banker shall be crossed with the name of a banker, or with two transverse lines with the words "and company," or any abbreviation thereof, whosoever shall obliterate, add to, or alter any such crossing, or shall offer, utter, dispose of, or put off any cheque or draft whereon any such obliteration addition or alteration has been made, knowing the same to have been made, with the intent, in any of the cases aforesaid, to defraud, shall be guilty of felony, and being convicted thereof shall be liable at the discretion of the court to be kept in penal servitude for life, or for any term not less than five years (27 & 28 Vict. c. 47, s. 2), or to be imprisoned for any term nor exceeding two years, with or without hard labour, and with or without solitary confinement. *Obliterating crossings on cheques.*

same to a person other than a banker, or than the banker with whose name such cheque or draft shall have been so crossed, unless the banker shall have acted malâ fide, or been guilty of negligence in so paying such cheque.

Interpretation of the word "banker."
5. In the construction of this Act the word "banker" shall include any person or persons, or corporation, or joint stock company, acting as a banker or bankers.

THE CROSSED CHEQUES ACT.

An Act for amending the Law relating to Crossed Cheques.
[15th August, 1876.]

BE it enacted by the Queen's most Excellent Majesty, by and with the advice and consent of the Lords Spiritual and Temporal, and Commons, in this present Parliament assembled, and by the authority of the same, as follows:

Short title.
1. This Act may be cited as The Crossed Cheques Act, 1876.

Repeal of Acts in schedule.
2. The Acts described in the schedule to this Act are hereby repealed, but this repeal shall not effect any right, interest or liability acquired or accrued before the passing of this Act.

3. In this Act—

Interpretation.
"Cheque" means a draft or order on a banker payable to bearer or to order on demand, and includes a warrant for payment of dividend on stock sent by post by the Governor and Company of the Bank of England or of Ireland, under the authority of any Act of Parliament for the time being in force:

"Banker" includes persons or corporation or company acting as bankers.

General and special crossing.
4. Where a cheque bears across its face an addition of the words "and company," or any abbreviation thereof, between two parallel transverse lines, or of two parallel transverse lines simply, and either with or without the words "not negotiable," that addition shall be deemed a crossing, and the cheque shall be deemed to be crossed generally.

Where a cheque bears across its face an addition of the name of a banker, either with or without the words "not negotiable," that addition shall be deemed a crossing, and the cheque shall be deemed to be crossed specially, and to be crossed to that banker.

Crossing after issue.
5. Where a cheque is uncrossed, a lawful holder may cross it generally or specially.

Where a cheque is crossed generally, a lawful holder may cross it specially.

Where a cheque is crossed generally or specially, a lawful holder may add the words "not negotiable."

Where a cheque is crossed specially, the banker to whom it is crossed may again cross it specially to another banker, his agent for collection.

6. A crossing authorised by this Act shall be deemed a material part of the cheque, and it shall not be lawful for any person to obliterate or, except as authorised by this Act, to add to or alter the crossing. *Crossing material part of cheque.*

7. Where a cheque is crossed generally, the banker on whom it is drawn shall not pay it otherwise than to a banker. *Payment to banker only.*

Where a cheque is crossed specially, the banker on whom it is drawn shall not pay it otherwise than to the banker to whom it is crossed, or to his agent for collection.

8. Where a cheque is crossed specially to more than one banker, except when crossed to an agent for the purpose of collection, the banker on whom it is drawn shall refuse payment thereof. *Cheque crossed specially more than once not to be paid.*

9. Where the banker on whom a crossed cheque is drawn has in good faith and without negligence paid such cheque, if crossed generally to a banker, and if crossed specially to the banker to whom it is crossed, or his agent for collection being a banker, the banker paying the cheque and (in case such cheque has come to the hands of the payee) the drawer thereof shall respectively be entitled to the same rights, and be placed in the same position in all respects, as they would respectively have been entitled to and have been placed in if the amount of the cheque had been paid to and received by the true owner thereof. *Protection of banker and drawer where cheque crossed specially.*

10. Any banker paying a cheque crossed generally otherwise than to a banker, or a cheque crossed specially otherwise than to the banker to whom the same shall be crossed, or his agent for collection, being a banker, shall be liable to the true owner of the cheque for any loss he may sustain owing to the cheque having been so paid. *Banker paying cheque contrary to provisions of Act to be liable to lawful owner.*

11. Where a cheque is presented for payment, which does not at the time of presentation appear to be crossed, or to have had a crossing which has been obliterated, or to have been added to or altered otherwise than authorised by this Act, a banker paying the cheque, in good faith and without negligence, shall not be responsible or incur any liability, nor shall the payment be questioned, by reason of the cheque *Relief of banker from responsibility in some cases.*

having been crossed, or of the crossing having been obliterated or having been added to or altered otherwise than as authorised by this Act, and of payment being made otherwise than to a banker or the bankers to whom the cheque is or was crossed, or to his agent for collection being a banker (as the case may be).

<small>Title of holder of cheque crossed specially.</small>

12. A person taking a cheque crossed generally or specially, bearing in either case the words "not negotiable," shall not have and shall not be capable of giving a better title to the cheque than that which the person from whom he took it had.

But a banker who has in good faith and without negligence received payment for a customer of a cheque crossed generally or specially to himself shall not, in case the title to the cheque proves defective, incur any liability to the true owner of the cheque by reason only of having received such payment.

BANK NOTES AND BILLS COMPOSITION STAMP DUTIES.

9 GEO. 4, C. 23.

An Act to enable Bankers in England to issue certain unstamped Promissory Notes and Bills of Exchange, upon Payment of a Composition in lieu of the Stamp Duties thereon (a).

[19th June, 1828.]

<small>Certain bankers may issue unstamped promissory notes and bills of exchange, subject to the regulations herein mentioned.</small>

WHEREAS it is expedient to permit all persons carrying on the business of bankers in England (except within the city of London or within three miles thereof), to issue their promissory notes payable to bearer on demand, or to order within a limited period after sight, and to draw bills of exchange payable to order on demand, or within a limited period after sight or date, on unstamped paper, upon payment of a composition in lieu of the stamp duties which would otherwise be payable upon such notes and bills respectively, and subject to the regulations hereinafter mentioned; be it therefore enacted, etc., that from and after the 1st day of July, 1828, it shall be lawful for any person or persons carrying on the business of a banker or bankers in England (except within the city of London, or within three miles thereof), having first duly obtained a licence for that purpose, and given

---

(*a*) By the Statute Law Revision Act, 1873, 36 & 37 Vict., c. 91, ss. 16 and 17 are repealed.

security by bond in manner hereinafter mentioned, to issue, on unstamped paper, promissory notes for any sum of money amounting to £5 or upwards, expressed to be payable to the bearer on demand, or to order, at any period not exceeding seven days after sight; and also to draw and issue, on unstamped paper, bills of exchange, expressed to be payable to order on demand, or at any period not exceeding seven days after sight, or twenty-one days after the date thereof; provided such bills of exchange be drawn upon a person or persons carrying on the business of a banker or bankers in London, Westminster, or the borough of Southwark, or provided such bills of exchange be drawn by any banker or bankers at a town or place where he or they shall be duly licensed to issue unstamped notes and bills under the authority of this act, upon himself or themselves, or his or their co-partner or co-partners, payable at any other town or place where such banker or bankers shall also be duly licensed to issue such notes and bills as aforesaid.

2. That it shall be lawful for any two or more of the commissioners of stamps to grant to all persons carrying on the business of bankers in England (except as aforesaid), who shall require the same, licences authorising such persons to issue such promissory notes and to draw and issue such bills of exchange as aforesaid, on unstamped paper; which said licences shall be and are hereby respectively charged with a stamp duty of £30 for every such licence. *Commissioners of stamps may grant licences to issue unstamped notes and bills.*

3. That a separate licence shall be taken out in respect of every town or place where any such unstamped promissory notes or bills of exchange as aforesaid shall be issued or drawn; provided always, that no person or persons shall be obliged to take out more than four licences in all for any number of towns or places in England; and in case any person or persons shall issue or draw such unstamped notes or bills as aforesaid, at more than four different towns or places, then, after taking out three distinct licences for three of such towns, or places, such person or persons shall be entitled to have all the rest of such towns or places included in a fourth licence. *A separate licence to be taken out for every place where such notes or bills shall be issued, but not to exceed four licences for any number of such places.*

4. That every licence granted under the authority of this act shall specify all the particulars required by law to be specified in licences to be taken out by persons issuing promissory notes payable to bearer on demand, and allowed to be re-issued; and every such licence which shall be granted between the 10th day of October and the 11th day *Regulations respecting licences.*

of November in any year shall be dated on the 11th day of October, and every such licence which shall be granted at any other time shall be dated on the day on which the same shall be granted; and every such licence shall (notwithstanding any alteration which may take place in any copartnership of persons to whom the same shall be granted) have effect and continue in force from the day of the date thereof until the 10th day of October then next following, both inclusive, and no longer.

<small>Commissioners may cancel licences already taken out, and grant licences under this act in lieu thereof.</small>

5. Provided always, that where any banker or bankers shall have obtained the licence required by law for issuing promissory notes payable to bearer on demand, at any town or place in England, and during the continuance of such licence shall be desirous of taking out a licence to issue at the same town or place unstamped promissory notes and bills of exchange under the provisions of this act, it shall be lawful for the commissioners of stamps to cancel and allow as spoiled the stamp upon the said first-mentioned licence, and in lieu thereof to grant to such banker or bankers a licence under the authority of this act; and every such last-mentioned licence shall also authorise the issuing and reissuing of all promissory notes payable to the bearer on demand, which such banker or bankers may by law continue to issue or re-issue at the same town or place, on paper duly stamped.

<small>Bankers while licensed under this act shall not issue, for the first time, notes on stamped paper.</small>

6. Provided always, that if any banker or bankers, who shall take out a licence under the authority of this act, shall issue, under the authority of either this or any other act, any unstamped promissory notes for payment of money to the bearer on demand, such banker or bankers shall, so long as he or they shall continue licensed as aforesaid, make and issue on unstamped paper all his or their promissory notes for payment of money to the bearer on demand, of whatever amount such notes may be; and it shall not be lawful for such banker or bankers, during the period aforesaid, to issue for the first time any such promissory note as aforesaid, on stamped paper.

<small>Bankers licence to issue unstamped notes or bills shall give security by bond, for the due performance of the conditions herein contained.</small>

7. That before any licence shall be granted to any person or persons to issue or draw any unstamped promissory notes or bills of exchange under the authority of this act, such person or persons shall give security, by bond, to his Majesty, his heirs and successors, with a condition, that if such person or persons do and shall from time to time enter or cause to be entered in a book or books to be kept for that purpose, an

account of all such unstamped promissory notes and bills of exchange as he or they shall so as aforesaid issue or draw, specifying the amount or value thereof respectively, and the several dates of the issuing thereof; and in like manner also, a similar account of all such promissory notes as having been issued as aforesaid, shall have been cancelled, and the dates of the cancelling thereof, and all such bills of exchange as, having been drawn or issued as aforesaid, shall have been paid, and the dates of the payment thereof; and do and shall from time to time, when thereunto requested, produce and show such accounts to, and permit the same to be examined and inspected by, the said commissioners of stamps, or any officer of stamps appointed under the hands and seals of the said commissioners for that purpose ; and also do and shall deliver to the said commissioners of stamps half-yearly, (that is to say,) within fourteen days after the 1st day of January and the 1st day of July in every year, a just and true account in writing, verified upon the oaths or affirmations, (which any justice of the peace is hereby empowered to administer,) to the best of the knowledge and belief of such person or persons, and of his or their cashier, accountant, or chief clerk (*a*), or of such of them as the said commissioners shall require, of the amount or value of all unstamped promissory notes and bills of exchange, issued under the provisions of this or any former act in circulation within the meaning of this act on a given day, (that is to say,) on Saturday in every week, for the space of half a year prior to the half-yearly day immediately preceding the delivery of such account, together with the average amount or value of such notes and bills so in circulation, according to such account ; and also do and shall pay or cause to be paid to the receiver-general of stamp duties in Great Britain, or some other person duly authorised by the commissioners of stamps to receive the same, as a composition for the duties which would otherwise have been payable for such promissory notes and bills of exchange issued or in circulation during the past half year, the sum of three shillings and sixpence for every one hundred pounds, and also for the fractional part of one hundred pounds, of the said average amount or value of such notes and bills in circulation, according to the true intent and meaning of this

---

(*a*) The manager of the bank may make the affidavit. *Reg.* v. *Greenland*, 1 L. R., C.C. 65 ; 36 L. J., M. C. 37.

act; and on due performance thereof such bonds shall be void, but otherwise the same shall be and remain in full force and virtue.

<small>For what period notes and bills are to be deemed in circulation.</small>

8. That every such unstamped promissory note payable to the bearer on demand, issued under the provisions of this act, shall, for the purpose of payment of duty, be deemed to be in circulation from the day of the issuing to the day of the cancelling thereof, both days inclusive, excepting nevertheless the period during which such note shall be in the hands of the banker or bankers who first issued the same, or by whom the same shall be expressed to be payable: and that every unstamped promissory note payable to order, and every unstamped bill of exchange so as aforesaid issued, shall for the purpose aforesaid be deemed to be in circulation from the day of the issuing to the day of the payment thereof, both days inclusive: provided always, that every such promissory note payable to order, and bill of exchange as aforesaid, which shall be paid in less than seven days from the issuing thereof, shall, for the purpose aforesaid be included in the account of notes and bills in circulation on the Saturday next after the day of the issuing thereof, as if the same were then actually in circulation.

<small>Regulations respecting the bonds to be given pursuant to this act.</small>

9. That in every bond to be given pursuant to the directions of this act the person or persons intending to issue or draw any such unstamped promissory notes and bills of exchange as aforesaid, or such and so many of the said persons as the commissioners of stamps shall require, shall be the obligors; and every such bond shall be taken in the sum of one hundred pounds, or in such larger sums as the said commissioners of stamps may judge to be the probable amount of the composition or duties that will be payable from such person or persons, under or by virtue of this act, during the period of one year; and it shall be lawful for the said commissioners to fix the time or times of payment of the said composition or duties, and to specify the same in the condition of every such bond; and every such bond may be required to be renewed from time to time, at the discretion of the said commissioners, and as often as the same shall be forfeited, or the parties to the same, or any of them, shall die, become bankrupt or insolvent, or reside in the parts beyond the seas.

<small>Fresh bonds to be given on alterations of copartnership.</small>

10. That if any alteration shall be made in any copartnership of persons who shall have given any such security by bond as by this act is directed, whether such alteration shall

be caused by the death or retirement of one or more of the partners of the firm, or by the accession of any additional or new partner or partners, a fresh bond shall be given by the remaining partner or partners, or the persons composing the new copartnership, as the case may be, which bond shall be taken as a security for the duties which may be due and owing, or may become due and owing, in respect of the unstamped notes and bills which shall have been issued by the persons composing the old copartnership, and which shall be in circulation at the time of such alteration, as well as for duties which shall or may be or become due or owing in respect of the unstamped notes and bills issued or to be issued by the persons composing the new copartnership; provided that no such fresh bond shall be rendered necessary by any such alteration as aforesaid in any copartnership of persons exceeding six in number, but that the bonds to be given by such last mentioned copartnerships shall be taken as securities for all the duties they may incur so long as they shall exist, or the persons composing the same, or any of them, shall carry on business in copartnership together, or with any other person or persons, notwithstanding any alteration in such copartnership; saving always the power of the said commissioners of stamps to require a new bond in any case where they shall deem it necessary for better securing the payment of the said duties.

11. That if any person or persons who shall have given security, by bond, to his Majesty, in the manner hereinbefore directed, shall refuse or neglect to renew such bond when forfeited, and as often as the same is by this act required to be renewed, such person or persons so offending shall for every such offence forfeit and pay the sum of £100. *Penalty on bankers neglecting to renew their bonds.*

12. That if any person or persons who shall be licensed under the provisions of this act shall draw or issue, or cause to be drawn or issued, upon unstamped paper, any promissory note payable to order, or any bill of exchange which shall bear date subsequent to the day on which it shall be issued, the person or persons so offending shall, for every such note or bill so drawn or issued, forfeit the sum of £100. *Penalty for post-dating unstamped notes or bills.*

13. That nothing in this act contained shall extend or be construed to extend to exempt or relieve from the forfeitures or penalties imposed by any act or acts now in force, upon persons issuing promissory notes or bills of exchange not duly stamped as the law requires, any person or persons who under any colour or pretence whatsoever shall issue any un- *This act not to exempt from penalties any persons issuing unstamped notes or bills not in accordance herewith.*

stamped promissory note or bill of exchange, unless such person or persons shall be duly licensed to issue such note or bill under the provisions of this act; and such note or bill shall be drawn and issued in strict accordance with the regulations and restrictions herein contained.

Recovery of penalties.

14. That all pecuniary forfeitures and penalties which may be incurred under any of the provisions of this act shall be recovered for the use of his Majesty, his heirs and successors, in his Majesty's Court of Exchequer at Westminster, by action of debt, bill, plaint or information, in the name of his Majesty's attorney or solicitor-general in England.

Not to affect the privileges of the Bank of England.

15. Provided always, that nothing in this act contained shall extend or be construed to extend to prejudice, alter or affect any of the rights, powers or privileges of the Governor and Company of the Bank of England.

16. [Where any bankers taking out licenses under this act shall have stamps in their possession which will become useless, the commissioners may cancel such stamps, and make allowance for the same, if application be made within six calendar months next after the passing of the act.]

STAMP DUTIES ON BILLS, NOTES, CHEQUES, PROTESTS AND RECEIPTS, AND THE CANCELLATION OF ADHESIVE STAMPS.

33 & 34 VICT. C. 97.

An Act for granting certain Stamp Duties in lieu of Duties of the same kind now payable under various Acts, and consolidating and amending Provisions relating thereto.

(For provisions relating to Bills of Exchange, see *ante*, page 181.)

[10th August, 1870.]

Short title, and commencement of act.

1. This Act may be cited as "The Stamp Act, 1870," and shall come into operation on the 1st day of January, 1871, which date is hereinafter referred to as at the commencement of this Act.

All duties to be paid according to the regulations of this act, and the schedule to be read as part of this act.

6. (1.) All stamp duties which may from time to time be chargeable by law upon any instruments are to be paid and denoted according to the general and special regulations in this Act contained.

(2.) The said schedule, and everything therein contained, is to be read and construed as part of this Act.

16. (1.) Upon the production of an instrument chargeable with any duty as evidence in any court of civil judicature in any part of the United Kingdom, the officer whose duty it is to read the instrument shall call the attention of the judge to any omission or insufficiency of the stamp thereon, and if the instrument is one which may legally be stamped after the execution thereof, it may, on payment to the officer of the amount of the unpaid duty, and the penalty payable by law on stamping the same as aforesaid, and of a further sum of £1, be received in evidence, saving all just exceptions on other grounds. *(Terms upon which unstamped or insufficiently stamped instruments may be received in evidence in any court.)*

25. Any person who— *(Penalty for frauds in relation to adhesive stamps, or to any duty, £50.)*

(1.) Fraudulently removes or causes to be removed from any instrument any adhesive stamp, or affixes any adhesive stamp which has been so removed to any other instrument with intent that such stamp may be used again.

(2.) Sells or offers for sale, or utters, any adhesive stamp which has been so removed, or utters any instrument having thereon any adhesive stamp which has to his knowledge been so removed as aforesaid;

(3.) Practises or is concerned in any fraudulent act, contrivance, or device not specially provided for, with intent to defraud her Majesty, her heirs or successors of any duty,

shall forfeit, over and above any other penalty to which he may be liable, the sum of £50.

[An unauthorised defacement of adhesive stamps subjects a person to a penalty of £5. By the Stamp Duties Management Act, 1870, 33 & 34 Vict. c. 98, s. 25, every person who by any writing in any manner defaces any adhesive stamp *before it is used* shall forfeit the sum of £5: provided that any person may, with the express sanction of the commissioners, and in the manner and in conformity with the conditions which they may prescribe, write upon an adhesive stamp before it is used for the purpose of identification thereof.] *(As to defacement of adhesive stamps.)*

PAYMENT OF BILLS AND NOTES PAYABLE AT SIGHT, AND STAMP DUTY.

33 & 35 VICT. C. 74.

An Act to abolish Days of Grace in the case of Bills of Ex-

change and Promissory Notes payable at Sight or on Presentation.

[14th August, 1871.]

WHEREAS doubts have arisen whether by the custom of merchants a bill of exchange or promissory note purporting to be payable at sight or on presentation is payable until the expiration of a certain number of "days of grace :"

And whereas it is expedient that such bills of exchange and promissory notes should bear the same stamp and should be payable in the same manner as bills of exchange and promissory notes purporting to be payable on demand :

Be it enacted, &c., as follows :

Short title.
1. This act may be cited as "The Bills of Exchange Act, "1871."

Bills payable at sight or on presentation to be payable on demand.
2. Every bill of exchange or promissory note, drawn after this act comes into operation and purporting to be payable at sight or on presentation, should bear the same stamp and shall, for all purposes, whatsoever, be deemed to be a bill of exchange or promissory note payable on demand, any law or custom to the contrary notwithstanding.

Definition of terms.
3. For the purposes of this act, the terms "bill of exchange" and "promissory note" shall have the same meanings as are given to them in "The Stamp Act, 1870."

Admissibility in evidence of past bills.
4. A bill of exchange purporting to be payable at sight and drawn at any time between the 1st day of January, 1871, and the day of the passing of this act, both inclusive, and stamped as a bill of exchange payable on demand, shall be admissible in evidence on payment of the difference between the amount of stamp duty paid on such bill and the amount which would have been payable if this act had not passed.

COMPOSITIONS FOR STAMP DUTY ON BANK POST BILLS OF £5 AND UPWARDS.

27 & 28 VICT. C. 86.

An Act to permit for a Limited Period Compositions for Stamp Duty on Bank Post Bills of £5 and upwards in Ireland.

[29th July, 1864.]

16 and 17 Vic., c. 63.
WHEREAS by an act passed in the 16th and 17th years of her Majesty's reign, chapter 63, the commissioners of her Majesty's treasury are authorized and empowered to compound and agree with all or any bankers in Scotland or elsewhere for a composition in lieu of the stamp duties payable on the bills of exchange of such bankers : and whereas it is ex-

pedient to permit bankers in Ireland for a limited period to compound for the stamp duties payable on their bank post bills as well as on their bills of exchange : be it enacted, &c., as follows :

1. It shall be lawful for the commissioners of her Majesty's treasury and they are hereby authorized and empowered to compound and agree with any banker in Ireland for a composition in lieu of the stamp duties payable on the bank post bills to be made or drawn by such banker at any time during the period of three years from the passing of this act, for any sum of money amounting to £5 or upwards, and such composition shall be made on the like terms and conditions and with such security as the said commissioners are by the said act empowered to require in the case of compounding for the stamp duties on bills of exchange ; and upon such composition being entered into by such banker it shall be lawful for him, during the period aforesaid, to make, draw, and issue all such bank post bills, for which composition shall have been made, on unstamped paper, anything in any act contained to the contrary notwithstanding. *Power to treasury to compound with bankers in Ireland for the stamp duty on bank post bills for a period of three years.*

COMPOSITIONS FOR STAMP DUTY ON BANK POST BILLS OF £5 AND UPWARDS.

30 & 31 VICT. c. 89.

An Act to render perpetual an Act passed in the Session holden in the 27th and 28th Years of her present Majesty, intituled " An Act to permit for a limited Period Compositions " for Stamp Duty on Bank Post Bills of £5 and upwards " in Ireland."

[12th August, 1867.]

WHEREAS by an act passed in the session holden in the 27th and 28th years of the reign of her present Majesty, chapter 86, intituled " An Act to permit for a limited period com- " positions for stamp duty on bank post bills of £5 and " upwards in Ireland," the commissioners of her Majesty's treasury are empowered to compound and agree, in manner therein mentioned, with any banker in Ireland for a composition in lieu of the stamp duties payable on the bank post bills to be made or drawn by such banker at any time during the period of three years from the passing of the said act for any sum of money amounting to £5 and upwards : and *27 and 28 Vic., c. 86.*

whereas it is expedient to make perpetual the powers conferred by the said act: be it enacted, &c., as follows:

Powers of 27 and 28 Vic., c. 86, made perpetual.

1. The powers conferred by the said act of the session of the 27th and 28th years of the reign of her present Majesty shall be perpetual, and the said act shall be construed as if the words "during the period of three years from the passing of this act" had been omitted therefrom.

Short title.

2. This act may be cited for all purposes as "The Stamp Duty Commission (Ireland) Act, 1867."

VALIDITY OF CHEQUES OR DRAFTS FOR LESS THAN 20s.

23 & 24 VICT. C. III.

An Act for granting to her Majesty certain Duties on Stamps, and to amend the Laws relating to the Stamp Duties (a).

[28th August, 1860.]

Section 18 of 55 Geo. 3, c. 184, prohibiting the issuing of bankers' notes with printed dates, repealed.

19. Whereas by s. 18 of the 55 Geo. 3, c. 184, the issuing of promissory notes payable to bearer on demand with printed dates therein is prohibited, and such prohibition is an unnecessary restriction; *be it enacted*, that the said section shall be and is hereby repealed: provided always, that, notwithstanding anything in any act of parliament contained to the contrary, it shall be lawful for any person to draw upon his banker, who shall bonâ fide hold money to or for his use, any draft or order for the payment to the bearer or to order on demand, of any sum of money less than 20s.

Drafts on bankers for less than 20s. to be lawful.

SPIRITUAL PERSONS PROHIBITED BEING MEMBERS OF JOINT STOCK BANKS.

4 VICT. C. 14.

An Act to make good certain Contracts which have been or may be entered into by certain Banking and other Copartnerships (b).

[18th May, 1841.]

WHEREAS divers associations and copartnerships, consisting

(a) 33 & 34 Vict. c. 99, repeals sects. 1 to 18, both inclusive, and the schedule.

(b.) This statute is a re-enactment of 1 Vict. c. 10, originally temporary and limited in operation, and repealed by the Statute Law Revision Act, 1861, 24 & 25 Vict. c. 101.

of more than six members or shareholders, have from time to time been formed for the purpose of being engaged in and carrying on the business of banking and divers other trades and dealings for gain and profit, and have accordingly for some time past been and are now engaged in carrying on the same by means of boards of directors or managers, committees or other officers, acting on behalf of all the members or shareholders of or persons otherwise interested in such associations or copartnerships: and whereas divers spiritual persons, having or holding dignities, prebends, canonries, benefices, stipendiary curacies, or lectureships, have been and are members or shareholders of or otherwise interested in divers of such associations and copartnerships: and whereas it is expedient to render legal and valid all contracts entered into by such associations or copartnerships, although the same may now be void by reason of such spiritual persons being or having been such members or shareholders or otherwise interested as aforesaid; be it therefore enacted, &c., that no such association or copartnership already formed or which may be hereafter formed, nor any contract either as between the members, partners, or shareholders composing such association or copartnership for the purpose thereof, or as between such association or copartnership and other persons, heretofore entered into, or which shall be entered into by any such association or copartnership already formed or hereafter to be formed, shall be deemed or taken to be illegal or void, or to occasion any forfeiture, whatsoever, by reason only of any such spiritual person as aforesaid being or having been a member, partner, or shareholder of or otherwise interested in the same, but all such associations and copartnerships shall have the same validity and all such contracts shall and may be enforced in the same manner to all intents and purposes as if no such spiritual person had been or was a member, partner, shareholder of or interested in such association or copartnership; provided always, that it shall not be lawful for any spiritual person holding any cathedral preferment, benefice, curacy, or lectureship, or who shall be licensed or allowed to perform the duties of any ecclesiastical office, to act as a director or managing partner, or to carry on such trade or dealing as aforesaid in person.

No association or copartnership, or contract entered into by any of them to be illegal or void by reason only of spiritual persons being members thereof.

No spiritual person beneficed or performing ecclesiastical duty to act as director.

BANK HOLIDAYS.
34 VICT. C. 17.

An Act to make provision for Bank Holidays, and respecting Obligations to make Payments and do other Acts on such Bank Holidays.

[25th May, 1871.]

WHEREAS it is expedient to make provision for rendering the day after Christmas Day, and also certain other days bank holidays, and for enabling bank holidays to be appointed by royal proclamation :

Be it enacted, &c., as follows :

Bills due on bank holidays to be due on the following day.

1. After the passing of this act, the several days in the schedule to this act mentioned (a) and which days are in this act hereinafter referred to as bank holidays, shall be kept as close holidays in all banks in England and Ireland and Scotland respectively, and all bills of exchange and promissory notes which are due and payable on any such bank holiday shall be payable, and in case of non-payment may be noted and protested, on the next following day, and not on such bank holiday ; and any such noting or protest shall be as valid as if made on the day on which the bill or note was made due and payable ; and for all the purposes of this act the day next following a bank holiday shall mean the next following day on which a bill of exchange may be lawfully noted or protested.

Provision as to notice of dishonour and presentation for honour.

2. When the day on which any notice of dishonour of an unpaid bill of exchange or promissory note should be given, or when the day on which a bill of exchange or promissory note should be presented or received for acceptance, or accepted or forwarded to any referee or referees, is a bank holiday,

---

(a) SCHEDULE.

Bank Holidays in England and Ireland.
Easter Monday.
The Monday in Whitsun week.
The first Monday in August.
The 26th day of December, if a week day.

Bank Holidays in Scotland.
New Year's Day.
Christmas Day.
  If either of the above days fall on a Sunday the next following Monday shall be a bank holiday.
Good Friday.
The first Monday of May.
The first Monday of August.

such notice of dishonour shall be given and such bill of exchange or promissory note shall be presented or forwarded on the day next following such bank holiday.

3. No person shall be compellable to make any payment or to do any act upon such bank holidays which he would not be compellable to do or make on Christmas Day or Good Friday; and the obligation to make such payment and do such act shall apply to the day following such bank holiday; and the making of such payment and doing such act on such following day shall be equivalent to payment of the money or performance of the act on the holiday. *As to any payments on bank holidays.*

4. It shall be lawful for her Majesty, from time to time as to her Majesty may seem fit, by proclamation, in the manner in which solemn fasts or days of public thanksgiving may be appointed, to appoint a special day to be observed as a bank holiday, either throughout the United Kingdom or in any part thereof, or in any county, city, borough or district therein, and any day so appointed shall be kept as a close holiday in all banks within the locality mentioned in such proclamation, and shall, as regards bills of exchange and promissory notes payable in such locality, be deemed to be a bank holiday for all the purposes of this act. *Appointment of special bank holidays by royal proclamation.*

5. It shall be lawful for her Majesty in like manner, from time to time, when it is made to appear to her Majesty in council in any special case that in any year it is inexpedient that a day by this act appointed for a bank holiday should be a bank holiday, to declare that such day shall not in such year be a bank holiday, and to appoint such other day as to her Majesty in council may seem fit to be a bank holiday instead of such day; and thereupon the day so appointed shall in such year be substituted for the day so appointed by this act. *Day appointed for bank holiday may be altered by order in council.*

6. The powers conferred by sections 3 and 4 of this act on her Majesty may be exercised in Ireland, so far as relates to that part of the United Kingdom, by the Lord Lieutenant of Ireland in Council. *Exercise of powers conferred by sections 4 and 5 in Ireland by Lord Lieutenant (a).*

7. This act may be cited for all purposes as "The Bank Holidays Act, 1871." *Short title.*

(a) The exercise of the powers conferred by sects. 4 and 5 will render unnecessary the passing of a special act of parliament, as in the case of the public funeral of the Duke of Wellington, 16 & 17 Vict., c. 1, and on the occasion of the entry of the Princess Alexandrina of Denmark into London, 26 & 27 Vict., c. 2.

HOLIDAYS EXTENSION ACT (1875).

When 26th Dec. falls on a Sunday, Monday to be the holiday.

2. Whenever the twenty-sixth day of December shall fall on a Sunday, the Monday immediately next following, that is to say, the twenty-seventh day of December, shall be a Holiday under this Act, and also under the Holidays Act of 1871.

BANKERS' BOOKS EVIDENCE ACT (1878).

A Bill to amend the Law of Evidence with respect to Bankers' Books.

Be it enacted by the Queen's most Excellent Majesty, by and with the advice and consent of the Lords Spiritual and Temporal, and Commons, in this present Parliament assembled, and by the authority of the same, as follows:

Short title.

1. This Act may be cited as the Bankers' Books Evidence Act, 1878.

Repeal of Act.

2. The Bankers Books Evidence Act, 1876, shall be repealed as from the *passing of this Act*, but such repeal shall not affect anything which has been done or happened before such repeal takes effect.

Mode of proof of entries in bankers' books.

3. Subject to the provisions of this Act, a copy of any entry in a banker's book shall in all legal proceedings be received as *primâ facie* evidence of such entry, and of the matters, transactions, and accounts therein recorded, and a bank or any officer thereof shall not in any legal proceeding be compellable to produce any of the books of the bank except by order of a court or judge.

Provided that in any proceeding to which the bank is a party such a copy shall not be received in evidence in favour of the bank under this Act except by consent or by order of a court or judge, and on such terms, if any, as the court or judge thinks just.

Proof that book is a banker's book.

4. A copy of an entry in a banker's book shall not be received in evidence under this Act unless it be first proved that the book was at the time of the making of the entry one of the ordinary books of the bank, and that the entry was made in the usual and ordinary course of business, and that the book is in the custody or control of the bank.

Such proof may be given by one of the partners or officers of the bank, and may be given orally or by an affidavit sworn before any commissioner or person authorised to take affidavits.

5. A copy of an entry in a banker's book shall not be received in evidence under this Act unless it be further proved that the copy has been examined with the original entry and is correct.

Verification of copy.

Such proof shall be given by some person who has examined the copy with the original entry, and may be given either orally or by an affidavit sworn before any commissioner or person authorised to take affidavits.

6. A banker or officer of a bank shall not, in any legal proceeding to which the bank is not a party, be compellable to produce in evidence any banker's book the contents of which can be proved under this Act, unless by order of a judge made for special cause; and no summons or other process shall issue or be enforced against a banker or officer of a bank to compel such production without such an order in a legal proceeding to which the bank is not a party; and default by a party to the proceeding in giving the notices required by this Act shall not be deemed to be special cause for such an order.

Evidence shall be given under this Act except where otherwise ordered, and except where the bank is a party.

7. On the application of any party to a legal proceeding a court or judge may order that such party be at liberty to inspect and take copies of any entries in a banker's book for any of the purposes of such proceedings. An order under this section may be made either with or without summoning the bank or any other party, and shall be served on the bank three clear days before the same is to be obeyed, unless the court or judge otherwise directs.

Court or judge may order inspection, &c.

8. The costs of any application to a court or judge under or for the purposes of this Act, and the costs of anything done or to be done under an order of a court or judge made under or for the purposes of this Act shall be in the discretion of the court or judge who may order the same or any part thereof to be paid to any party by the bank, where the same have been occasioned by any default or delay on the part of the bank. Any such order against a bank may be enforced as if the bank were a party to the proceeding.

Costs.

9. In this Act the expressions "bank" and "banker" means any person, persons, partnership, or company carrying on the business of bankers and having duly made a return to the Commissioners of Inland Revenue, and also any savings bank certified under the Acts relating to savings banks.

Interpretation of "bank" and "bankers' books."

It shall not be necessary to prove that a bank has made a return, or that a savings bank has been certified, as in this section mentioned, unless such proof is required by written notice by the party against whom the evidence is proposed to be given under this Act. Such written notice must be given to the other party *two* clear days before the day on which the evidence is proposed to be given. Where such proof is required, it may be given in the case of a savings bank by an office or examined copy of its certificate, and in the case of any other bank by production of a copy of its return verified by the affidavit of a partner or officer of the bank, or by the production of a copy of a newspaper purporting to contain a copy of such return published by the Commissioners of Inland Revenue.

Expressions in this Act relating to "bankers' books" include ledgers, day books, cash books, account books, and all other books used in the ordinary business of the bank.

Interpretation of "legal proceeding," "court," "judge."

10. In this Act—

The expression "legal proceeding" means any civil or criminal proceeding or inquiry in which evidence is or may be given, and includes an arbitration ;

The expression "the court" means the court, judge, arbitrator, persons, or person before whom a legal proceeding is held or taken ;

The expression "a judge" means with respect to England a judge of the High Court of Justice, and with respect to Scotland a lord ordinary of the Outer House of the Court of Session, and with respect to Ireland a judge of the High Court of Justice in Ireland ;

The judge of a county court may with respect to any action in such court exercise the powers of a judge under this Act.

Computation of time.

11. Sunday, Christmas Day, Good Friday, and any bank holiday shall be excluded from the computation of time under this Act.

INDEX.

INDEX.

	PAGE
Abercorn, The Earl of: His project for an Irish Bank	88
Aberdeen, Bank of	72, 74
Acceptance—	183, 189
"Differing"	191
For gambling debt	185
For illegal or immoral purposes	185
For stock-jobbing debt	185
"For honour" of drawee	222
"General"	189
On blank stamp	191
"Particular"	189, 219
Presentation for	216
"Qualified" or "conditional"	192
"Special"	189
Suing on	189
"Supra protest"	222
What it admits	193
Words of acceptance now unnecessary	191
Acceptor—When his liability is discharged	220
Not discharged by non-presentation	219
Not entitled to notice of dishonour	222
Primarily liable	220
Accommodation Bill	187
"Account Day" on Stock Exchange	297
Administrator's current account	145
Endorsement	149
"After Sight"	216, 217
Agent—Cannot bind his principal in bill	197
Cannot overdraw principal's current account	177
Endorsement by	150
Agricultural Bank (Ireland)	111

	PAGE
Alexander the Great, Coinage of	20
Alexander's Bank (Dublin)	94
Alexanders & Co. (Ipswich)	66
Alien Enemy as party to a bill	200
Allan, Alexander & Co. (Edinburgh)	72
Allen, Robert & Co. (Edinburgh)	72
Allonge	214
Alteration in bill	235
in cheque	140
Amades, a Goldsmith, lends to Henry VIII.	41
"And Company" Crossing, Origin of	151
Anderson's Bank (Ireland)	100
Arbroath Banking Co.	74
Argentarii, Ancient Roman Bankers	24
Aryandis, the Satrap of Egypt, First who struck coins	16
Ashley, Lord—His plan to close the Exchequer	43
Assent by a Banker, Consequences of	179
Assignee's Current Account	145
Assignment of Policy	247
Assimilation of English and Scotch Coinages	83
Assyria, Ancient Banking in	17
"At Sight"	143, 193, 194
Attorney-Partnership in Respect to Bills	197
Attributiones, Ancient Roman Cheques	24
"Authorised Clerk" on Stock Exchange	289
Babylonia, Ancient Banking in	17
"Backwardation"	298
Backwell, Edward—A London Goldsmith	46
Balance Sheets, False	278
Ball & Co.'s Bank (Dublin)	98
Bank, Derivation of the word	28, 29, 114
Functions of a	115
Bank Holidays	162
Bank Notes	187, 253
Acts regulating issues of	253
Antiquity of	15
Do not lapse	265
Invented in Europe	32
Forged or worthless	264, 267
For 30s. and £2	260
Scotch and Irish Issues of	257
Differ from English	76, 260
Profits on	262, 263

	PAGE
Bank Notes *(Continued)*	
Halved	265
Lost	265
Protested	83, 263
Stopping payment of	264
Under £1, abolished	260
Bank of Amsterdam	31
Barcelona	31
Berlin	32
Copenhagen	32
Bank of England	59
Authorised issue of	61, 62
Banking department of	62
Dates when various notes were issued	61
Differs from other Banks	65
Directors' qualifications	64
Founded	59
Garden of	61
Government debt to	61
Issue Department	62
Notes issued by	60, *et seq.*
Notes not legal tender in Ireland	163
Opens branches	61
Panics affecting	63
Post Bills	61, 216, 238
" Reserve "	64
Suspends payment	60, 66
Bank of France	33
Geneva	31
Genoa	31
Hamburg	32
Ireland	102, *et seq.*
the Netherlands	32
Rotterdam	32
Scotland	70
St. George	31
St. Petersburg	32
Stockholm	32
Venice	29
Bank Post Bills	61, 216, 238
Bank Post Bills under £5	238
Banker and Customer, relations between	123
Bankers' Bills	216

	PAGE
Bankers' Books as Evidence	174
Bankers' Drafts	238
Bankers' License	254
Bankers Plundered by Charles II.	43
Banking, Antiquity of	11, *et seq.*
in Ireland	84
in Scotland	70
Reference to in New Testament	14
Science of, invented by Romans	23
Banking Act of 1879 (See Appendix)	273, 280
Bankruptcy, derivation of the word	115
Bankruptcy of Acceptor of Bill	218, 227
of Drawer of cheque	170
of Party to Bill	227
Banks of Issue	117
Barclay, Bevan & Co.	56
Barnetts, Hoares & Co.	52
Barons & Bishops in England as Coiners	36
Barton, Bernard—a bank clerk	67
"Bear" on Stock Exchange	298
"Bearer," cheques payable to	141
Beckett & Co. (Leeds)	67
Belfast Bank	99, 100
Belfast Discount Co.	99
Bellamy *v.* Majoribanks, what it decided	153
Beresford, John Claudius & Co.'s Bank (Dublin)	97
Billon, a Scotch coin	82
Bills of Exchange (see also **Acceptance**)	181
Acceptor on	183
Accommodation Bills	187
Advantages of	182
Alteration in	235
Amount in	194
Can be taken out of Statute of Limitations	236
Compulsory signing of	235
Constituent features of	194
Date on	194
Definition of	183
"Differing" acceptance	191
Differ from Cheques	183
Discount	229
Dishonour of	222
Do not require a *consideration*	185

Index. 361

Bills of Exchange *(Continued).*

	PAGE
Drawee	195
Drawer	195
Drawn in sets	237
Early	26, 28, 181
Endorsement on	184, 214
Foreign	212, 237
In foreign Languages, tables of translations	310
Introduced into commerce	181
Introduced into England	39
Left for acceptance	46
Liability on, how avoided	214
order of	219
Loan on	230
Lodged for collection	233
Lost Bill	236
Need not be on paper	193
Need not be written in ink	193
Non-endorsement of	215
Notice of Dishonour of	220
Origin of	26, 181
Payable at Acceptor's Bankers	190
Payable at Bank where acceptor has no account	190
Payee	194
Payment and part payment of	215, 219
Persons incapacitated to be parties to	197
Place where payable	195
Post Bills	238
Post-dated Bill	194
Presentation for acceptance	216
payment	217
Re-issue of	212
Several Drawees on	191
Special means of recovering on	195
Specially payable	213
Stamp duties on	202
Suing on	190, 195
Time when payable	194
Transfer of	213
Usual form of	188
"Value received;" the words	195
When dishonoured	219

	PAGE
Bills of Lading	217
As security	248
Bills of Sale, when required by Banker	250
Bill Stamp, exhausted by one transaction	212
Blackstone quoted	29
his illustration of utility of Bills of Exchange	182
Bonnet-piece, a Scotch coin	82
Boyle, Low, Murray & Co. (Dublin)	98
Brahmans, Banking amongst the ancient	14
Brass Money, coined in Dublin	79, 80
England	34
Britain (Ancient)	34
Greece (Ancient)	20
Rome (Ancient)	22
British Linen Company's Bank	71, 74
Britannia, on English coins	37
Britons, Coinage of Ancient	34
Brokers (partners) position of in respect to Bills	197
(See Stockbroker)	
Brutus, reference to	25
"**Bull**" on Stock Exchange	299
Burton and Falkener's Bank (Dublin)	89
Cæsar quoted	34
Cairnes, Sir Alexander, a Banker	55
Caisse D'Escompte (France)	32
"**Cannot Pay**," Insufficient answer of dishonour	168
Capital	271
"Paid up"	272
"Subscribed"	272
Carlin v. *Ireland*	159
Carrick & Co. (Glasgow)	71, 74
"**Cash Credit**"	74
"**Cash Notes**"	41
Cash Order	188
Cato, referred to as a usurer	25
Certificate of Shares	274
Pledging	274
Do by Stockbroker	275
Charles I. seizes the Goldsmiths' Moneys	41
Charles II. robs the Exchequer	43
Tin coined by	35
Cheque Bank, The	171

	PAGE
Cheques	135
Alteration in	139, 140
Amount in	138
Are not money	166
Criminal offences by means of	172
Crossed	151
Date on	137
Death of Drawer of	170
Delay in presentation of	162
Dishonour of	167, 169
Drawee	136
Drawer's signature	143
Drawn by Administrator	145
Assignees in Bankruptcy	145
Company	145
Corporation	145
Directors	145
Drunken man	144
Executors	145
Firm	145
Idiot	144
Infant	143
Joint account holders	144
Lunatic	144
Marksman	143
Married Woman	144
Partners	145
Trustees	144
Essential constituents of	136
Forgery of	139
Form of	136
Free gift of	179
For illegal or immoral purposes	170
Known by ancient Grecian bankers	22
Roman bankers	24
In lodgment	165
In payment of Bill of Exchange	166, 218
Initialing for payment	165
Lost	172
Mutilated	
"Not negotiable"	159
On engraved forms	165
Originate in England	42

24—2

Cheques *(Continued).*
        Payable to "Bearer" . . . 141
                  "Order" . . . 141
        Part payment of . . . 167
        Payee 141
        Payment of . . . 163
        Post dated . . . 137
        Presentation of . . . 161
        Right to sue on . . . 179
        "Specially Payable" . . . 142
        "Stale" . . . 162
        Stamp on . . . 137
        Stopping payment of . . . 166
        Under £1 . . . 136
        When paid . . . 173, 178
        Which are incapable of Dishonour . . 171
        Wrongful dishonour of . . . 169
Child & Co. 49
China, Ancient banking in . . . 15
Cicero, reference to . . . 24, 29
Circular Notes 240
Circulation 253
        Of Irish Banks . . . 259
        Of Scotch Banks . . . 260
        Profits of . . . 262
City of Glasgow Bank . . . 73
"Clearing House" . . . 268
        Method of working . . . 268
        Returns 1867 to 1881 . . 270
Clergymen, Cannot be Directors of Bank . . 276
Clifford, Sir Thomas, referred to . . 43
Clipping Coin 37, 38, 39
Cochrane v. O'Brien . . . 130
Cocks, Biddulph & Co. . . . 57
Coin, Current and manufactured (1840—1878) . 38
        Made *Sterling* . . . 36
        To be held against note issues . . 257
Coinage, Ancient Chinese . . . 15
       ,,   Egyptian . . . 16
       ,,   Grecian . . . 19
       ,,   Jewish . . . 12
       ,,   Lydian . . . 19
       ,,   Roman . . . 22
        Early English . . . 34

Coinage—*(Continued).*
    Early Irish 77
    ,, Scotch 82
Colchester, Roman mint at 35
Collateral Securities 246
        Policies of assurance . . 246
        Shares and Stocks . . 247
        Bills of Lading . . . 248
        Dock Warrants . . . 248
        Title Deeds . . . 249
        Goods 249
Colebrooke, Sir George & Co.'s Bank (Dublin) . 97
Collier, John, a London Banker . . . 49
Colville, John, a London Banker . . . 49
Commercial Bank (Aberdeen) . . . 74
    (Belfast) 99
    of Scotland 74
Company, Cheques Drawn by . . . 145
    Endorsement by . . . 150
    As party to a Bill of Exchange . . 201
Composition Duties on Notes . . . 255
Compulsory Signing of Bill 235
Conditional Acceptance 192
Conditional Endorsement 192
Confidential Reports by Bankers . . . 242
Consideration, not necessary to Bill of Exchange . 185
    not requisite in Guaranty . . 245
"**Contango**" 298
Contract by Banking Company . . . 277
Convicted Felons, as parties to Bill of Exchange . 200
Copper Coined by Servius Tullius . . . 22
    in England 35, 37
Corporations, Cheques drawn by . . . 145
    Endorsement by . . . 150
    As parties to Bill of Exchange . 201
Cotter & Co.'s Bank (Cork) 100
Counterfeit Coin, payment in . . . 163
Coutts & Co. 52
Credit, Letters of 239
    Marginal 240
Criminal Offences, by means of Cheques . . 172
Criminal Offences by Directors . . . 279, 292
    Stock Brokers . . 292
"**Crockards**" a base Irish coin . . . 79

	PAGE
Cromwell, Banking under	41
Coinage under	37
Crowns and Half-Crowns Coined	37
Crossed Cheques	151
Origin of	151
"Generally"	151
"Specially"	151
"Not negotiable"	159
Current Account	42, 125, 135
Differs from deposit account	135
Interest on	176
Overdrawn	177
Compound interest on overdraft	178
At two branches of same bank	178
Date on Cheque	137
on Bill	194
Dawson's Bank (Dublin)	94
Days of Grace	183, 212, 217
Death of Acceptor	227
of Drawer of Cheque	170
of Endorser	170
Debts, Early Roman law as to transfer of	26
Deed of Transfer	235
Deeds as Securities	249
Delacour's Bank (Ireland)	100
Delay in Presentation of Cheque	162
Demar or Damer, a Dublin usurer	86
Dempster & Co., John (Fife Bank)	73
Demosthenes, reference to	21
Denarius	22
Deposit for safe custody	12, 41, 251
Letter of	247
of goods	249
of securities	246
Depositor, as guarantor or security	131
Deposit Receipt	41, 125, 127
Case of double liability of bank under a.	131
Exempt from stamp duty	133
In joint names	128
In name of Infant	129
Married Woman	129
Spinster	129

	PAGE
Deposit Receipt—*continued.*	
In several names	128
Lost	134
Not transferable	130
Deposits of Money, originate in England	41
Ireland	84
Dillon's Bank (Dublin)	94
Directors of joint stock companies and their powers	271, 277
Acceptance by	201
Bill drawn by	201
Cheque drawn by	145
Traffic in Shares by	279
Clergymen cannot be	276
Criminal offences by	279, 292
Duties and qualifications of	277, 283
False or fraudulent representations by	278
Disclosure of Customer's Account	168
Discount	229
Principle of, known in Ancient Greece	22
,, ,, ,, Rome	25
Dishonour of acceptance	190
Notice of	220, 222
Remedy for	227
of cheque	167, 169
"Cannot pay"	168
"No account"	168
"No funds"	168
"N. S.," or "not sufficient funds"	168
"Present again"	168
"Refer to Drawer"	168
Notice of	169
Remedy for	179
Wrongful	169
Dividend, Payment of unearned	278
Dock Warrants as Security	248
Documents with Bills, Duty of Banker in regard to	217
Douglas, Heron & Co.	72
Drafts, Bankers'	238
Known by ancient Babylonian Bankers	18
,, Grecian Bankers	21
,, Roman ,,	26, 28
Drawee's Name on Bill of Exchange	191, 195
on Cheque	134

	PAGE
Drawer of Cheque, who can be	143
Drawer's Signature on Bill of Exchange	195
on Cheque	143
Drummond's Bank	56
Drunkenness of party to Bill of Exchange	200
Dublin Bankers, Early	84
Dublin Mints, Old	78
Duncombe & Kent's Bank	51
Dundee Bank	73
Edinburgh and Glasgow Bank	73
Edinburgh and Leith Bank	73
Edward I. banishes Jews from England	40
Egibi & Co., the great Babylonian Bankers	17
Egypt, Ancient banking in	16
Endorsement, What it is	146
By administrator	149
By agent	150
By companies and corporations	150
By executor	149
By two or more payees	150
By way of acknowledgment	150
"Esquire" in an	148
For the payee	148
In pencil	147
"Lodge," or "lodged to account," in an	149
On cheque payable to "Messrs."	149
,, "Mr." or "Mrs."	148
,, "Senior" or "Junior"	149
On bill	184, 214
Per procuration	148
Restrictive	214
When regular and irregular	146
Endorser, on Bill of Exchange, liability of	214, 219
As surety	220
England, Bank of	
(See **Bank of England**)	
English and Irish Bank, The	109
Enquiries, Confidential	242
Entry in Bank Pass Book	176
False	176
Erasure of Crossing on Cheque	154
European Bank (Dublin)	109

Index. 369

	PAGE
Evelyn quoted	30, 38, 43, 51, 59, 182
Exchange, Bill of (See **Bills of Exchange**)	
Exchequer closed by Charles II.	43
Executors' Current Account	145
Executors, Endorsement by	149
Fade & Co.'s Bank (Dublin)	89, 93
Failure to Present Bill of Exchange	218, 219
False Entries :—	
Pass Book	176
in Bank Balance Sheet	278
Farthings, First coined in Dublin	78
Felons as parties to Bill of Exchange	200
Ffrench's Bank (Dublin and Tuam)	98
Fife Bank	73
Finlay's Bank (Dublin)	94
Firm, Cheques drawn by	145
Florence, Banks of	27
Florins	36
Forbes' (Lord), Bank project (Ireland)	88
Sir William & Co.'s Bank	71, 74
Foreign Bills	212, 237
Stamp on	212
Protest of	222
Translation of Terms used in	310
Foreign Letters of Credit in Ancient Greece	21
Rome	26
Forged Bank Notes	264
Passed to banker	264
Forged Endorsement	147, 173, 190
Forgery of Cheque	173
of Bank-notes	267
of Drafts drawn under letter of Credit	240
of Transfer of Shares	276
Fourpenny Pieces first coined	38
Fraudulent Purpose, Cheque for	172
Fuller, Banbury & Co.	56
Furfidius, A Roman Money-lender	25
Gambling Debt, Acceptance for	185
Garfit & Co. (Boston)	67
"General Acceptance"	189

	PAGE
Gift of Cheque	179
"Giving Time"	244
Glasgow Banking Co.	74
Glasgow Bank, City of	73
Glasgow Joint Stock Bank	73
Glasgow Union Bank	74
Gleadowe & Co.'s Bank (Dublin)	92
Glyn, Mills, & Co.	55
Godfrey, Michael, A founder of Bank of England	59
Gold and Silver Coin held against note issues	259, etc.
Gold Coins, First English	36
Gold in Ancient Ireland	77
"Golden Bottle," sign of Hoare's Bank	50
Goldsmiths, Early Dublin	84
Early London	39, 52
London, in Elizabeth's reign	41
Plundered by Charles I.	41
,, Charles II.	43
Goldsmith's Notes	41, 84, 185, 253
Goods, As securities	249
Goslings and Sharpe	50
Grace, Days of	183, 212, 217
Grammont quoted	45
Greece, Banking and Coinage of Ancient	19
Gresham, Sir Thomas	52
Guaranties by third parties	243
Guarantie, Definition of	243
Consideration not necessary	245
General	244
Giving time under	244
Limit of by Guarantor	244
Specific	244
Verbal	243
When invalidated	244
Withdrawal of	244
Guarantor of Bill	227
Release of	244
Guineas first coined	37
Punishment for "sweating"	82
Guinness, Mahon & Co. (Dublin)	98
Half Notes	265
Harp of Ireland, first quartered on coinage	37

Index.   371

	PAGE
Henry's (Hugh) Bank (Dublin)	89
Henry VIII. a borrower from a goldsmith	41
Herries, Farquhar & Co.	56
Hibernian Bank	106
Hoare's Bank	50
Holidays, Bank	162
on Stock Exchange	297
Homer's reference to Brass money	20
Horace, His character of Furfidius the money-lender	25
Horneby, Joseph	47
Houblon, Sir John, First governor of Bank of England	60
Hunters & Co. (Ayr)	71, 74
Humbug, derivation of word	80
I. O. U.	267
Does not require stamp duty	268
Is not transferable	268
Idiot, Cheque drawn by	144
As party to a Bill of Exchange	199
Illegal or Fraudulent Purpose, Acceptance for	185
Cheque for	170
Indemnity, Letter of, for lost instrument	309
Infant, As Depositor	129
As Drawer of Cheque	143
As Endorser on Bill of Exchange	198
As party to Bills of Exchange	198
As agent	199
Initialing Cheque for future payment	160, 165, 170
Instalments, Promissory Note payable by	187
Interest allowed by early Goldsmiths	41
on Current Accounts	176
Deposit Receipts	128
Charged on overdue Bills	234
Irish Banks, Early	84
Irish Banks of Issue, Law regulating	257
Irish Coinage, Early	77
Irish Joint Stock Banks	102, 110
Failed	111
Irish Money assimilated to English	38, 82
Iron used for money	34
James II., his Brass Money	80

	PAGE
Jews, Banished by Edward I.	40
Banished by Elizabeth	27, 40
Banking amongst the Ancient	12
Established Banking Houses in Europe	27
Examples of usurious practices of	40
Lombard	27, 40
Only Bankers in England	39
Persecution and plundering of	40
Sent to England by Pope Gregory IX.	40
Johnston, Lawson & Co. (Dumfries)	72
Joint and Several Promissory Note	186, 201
Joint Current Account, Cheques drawn on	144
Joint Names in Deposit Receipt	128
Joint Promissory Note	186
Joint Stock Banks in England	67
Ireland	102
Joint Stock Company, as party to Bill	201
Definition of	271
Acts of, 1856 and 1857	273
Julius Cæsar's Coinage	23
"**Junior**" in an Endorsement	149
Justinian's regulation of rates of discount	26
Kane (a Dublin Banker)	89
Kinnear & Sons (Edinburgh)	72
Knox, Sir John, Patent for Irish coining granted to	80
Lamb, Samuel—A London Banker	41
La Touche's Bank (Dublin)	88, 89
Law Regulating Irish Note Issues	257
Laws to regulate Banking in Ancient Rome	24, 26
Leases as Securities	249
Leather Money in Ancient China	15
"**Leeman's Act**"	275
Legal Tender	163
Leith Bank	73
Lennox's Bank (Dublin)	93
Leofstan, a London Goldsmith	39
Letters of Credit	239
Known in Ancient Babylon	18
,, ,, Greece	21
,, ,, Rome	26

		PAGE
Liability, Endorser can divest himself of		214
on Promissory Notes		220
order of, on Bill of Exchange		219
of Bank Shareholders		274
of Bankers for conduct of Agents and Correspondents		242
for false reports on customers		242
for goods deposited for safe custody		251
under forged or worthless Bank Notes		264
License, Banker's		254
Licensed Houses, Lease of, as security		249
Lien, what it is		240
General		240
How extinguished		241
On Bills lodged for collection		233
On policy of Assurance		246
Specific		240
Where a Banker has no lien		241
On shares		275
On Dividends		277
Lighton, Needham & Shaw's Bank (Dublin)		98
Limitations, Statute of		235
Limited Companies		272
As parties to Bills of Exchange		201
Limited Liability		272, 281
List of Shareholders, must be exhibited		273
Litteræ Bancales		28
Litteræ Cambitoriæ		28
Livy, reference to		24
Loan on Bills of Exchange		230
"Lodge" and "Lodged to Account" in an Endorsement		149
Lodgment with Banker, two descriptions of		123
for special purpose		178
Lombard Jews sent to England		27, 40
Lombard Street		27, 41
London and County Bank		69
London and Dublin Bank		111
London and Westminster Bank		69
London Bankers, Early		39
London Joint Stock Bank		69
Loss or Destruction of Bills lodged for collection		233
of goods deposited for safe custody		251
Lost Bank Notes		265
Lost Bill of Exchange		236

	PAGE
Lost Cheque	172
(See also Appendix for form of Letter of Indemnity.)	
Lunatic, as party to a Bill	199
Cheque drawn by	144
Lydians, The inventors of coinage	19
Lyndsay, John, a London Banker	49
Macaulay quoted	28
Malone & Clement's Bank (Dublin)	93
Marginal Letters of Credit	240
Marks, coined in Dublin	78
Marksman as drawer of Cheque	143
Married Woman as Depositor	129
as drawer of Cheque	144
as party to a Bill	199
as Shareholder	276
(See also Appendix.)	
Martin & Co. (London)	51
Martin v. Boure	181
"Marygolde," sign of Child's Bank	49
Matthiesson and An. v. London and County Bank	157
Maturity of a Bill of Exchange, How computed	217
Maunsell's Bank (Limerick)	100
McAdam, John & Co. (Ayr)	72
Meade and Curtis's Bank (Dublin)	89
Mensarii, Ancient Roman Bankers	24
Merchant Banking Co. of Glasgow	72
"Messrs.," Endorsement of Cheque payable to	149
Miles, Cave, Baillie & Co. (Bristol)	67
"Milling" on coins first introduced	37
Mints, Dublin	78
Grecian	20
Early Irish	78
Roman, in England	35
Royal and other English	35
Saxon	35
Misrepresentations by Directors	278
by Banker to Guarantor	245
Mitchell and Macarell's Bank (Dublin)	94
"Moneyers"	35
Money in payment of Bill	218
Money-Lending among the Jews	12
Monti, the early Italian Loan Banks	29

	PAGE
Montrose Bank	73
Moses, Laws of, against usury	13
"Mr." or "Mrs.," in an Endorsement	148
Munster Bank	108
Mutilated Cheque	169
"Name Day," on Stock Exchange	297
National Bank (of Ireland)	107
National Debt, First European	29
National Land Bank of England	66
Necessaries, Infant's acceptance for	198
Negociatores, Ancient Roman Bankers	24
Newcomen's Bank (Dublin)	92
Newenham's Bank (Cork)	100
Newport & Co.'s Bank (Waterford)	99
"No Account"	168
"No Funds"	168
Nobles Coined	36
Non-Acceptance, Notice of	216
Non Compos Mentis, Party to a Bill of Exchange	199
Non-endorsement of Bill by Transferor	215
Non-Presentation, When it relieves Acceptor	219
Northern Bank (Belfast)	99, 109
"Not Negotiable," Crossing	156
What it means	159
"Not Sufficient Funds"	168
Note, Promissory (see Promissory Note)	186
Note (Bank), Definition of	253
Note-issue, A source of profit	262
Difference between English, Scotch, and Irish	76, 260
Note-issues of Irish Banks	259
of Scotch Banks	260
Note of Hand (see Promissory Note)	186
"Notes," for threepence (Ireland)	100
Notes burned by populace (Ireland)	98
Notice of Dishonour of Bill of Exchange	220
Examples of sufficient	224
,, insufficient	223
Byles' form of	226
of non-acceptance	226
of withdrawal of Deposits	228
to acceptor	226
to Drawer and Endorsers	102, 220, 222

	PAGE
Notice to guarantor on Bill	227
Noting	221
Nummularii, Ancient Roman Bankers	24
Nuttall & McGuire's Bank (Dublin)	89
Obligations of Banker to his Customer	125
Obliteration of crossing on a Cheque	154
O'Connell (Daniel), Founder of National Bank of Ireland	107
" **Options** " on Stock Exchange	298
" **Order,** " Cheque payable to	141, 146
" **Ordinary Care** " of safe custody deposits	251
O'Reyley's Money (Ireland)	79
Origin of Crossed Cheques	151
Ostensible Partners	198
Otto, The first English Goldsmith	39
Overdrawn Current Account	177
Overdue Bills	228
Interest on	234
Over-payment by Banker	164
Paid Bill of Exchange	215
Paid Cheques	173
Surrender of	173, 178
" **Paid-up** " **Capital**	272
Paisley Bank	74
Paisley Union Bank	74
Paper Money, in Ancient China	15
Modern	187, 253
" **Par** "	298
Part Payment of Bill of Exchange	215, 219
of cheque	167
Particular Acceptance	189, 219
Partners, Ostensible	198
Powers of, in respect to Bills of Exchange	197
Secret	198
Partnership Current Account	145
Pasion, The great Grecian Banker	21
Pass Book	175
Effect of Entry in	176
Past Due Bills, Interest upon	234
Patent for Irish Coinage, Granted by Charles II.	79
Granted to Wood	81
Paterson, William—Founder of Bank of England	59

	PAGE
Paul, Sir John Dean, failure of his Bank	48
Payee of Bill	194
of Cheque	141
Payment of Bill, Presentation for	217
by money	218
by cheque	218
Payment of Cheques	163
Cannot be recalled	164
Stopping	166
in Bank Notes	163
in forged, or worthless notes	163
in legal tender	163
in spurious coin	163
Pease's Bank (Hull)	67
Pecunia, Derivation of	22
Pencil, Bill of Exchange written in	193
Endorsement in	147
Pennies, Copper, first coined	38
Silver	35
first coined in Ireland	78
Pepys (Samuel), quoted	45, 46, 49, 50, 52
"Per Procuration," Bills drawn	193
Cheques endorsed	148
Persons incapacitated to be parties to Bills of Exchange	197
Perth Bank	73
"Pieces of Silver," Jewish	12
Pike's Bank (Cork)	100
Pistoles coined in Scotland	82
Place where payable, on Bill of Exchange	195
Plack, a Scotch coin	82
Policy of Assurance as Collateral Security	246
Form for assignment of	247
"Pollards"—a base Irish coin	79
Pompey—a usurer	25
Portman, John	49
Portraits of Kings on coins	23
Post Bills	238
Post dated Bill of Exchange	194
Post dated Cheque	137
Praed's Bank	56
Præscriptiones	24
Premium on shares	273

	PAGE
Presentation of Bills of Exchange :—	
For acceptance	216
For payment	217
Presentation of Cheques :	
Delay in	162
Time of	161
Presentation of Promissory Notes	219
"**Present again,**" insufficient answer of dishonour	168
Prescott, Grote & Co.	56
Price's (Mr. Hilton) Book on London Bankers	39
Private Bankers	
Dublin (early)	84
,, (present)	98
English	67
,, issues of	68
London (early)	43
,, (present)	49
in Scotland	71
Private Enquiries	242
"**Privity**"	123, 179
Profits from Scotch and Irish note circulation	262
Project to establish a National Irish Bank (1720)	88
Promissory Notes	185
Definition of	186
Joint	186
Joint and several	187
Order of liability on	220
Origin of	185
Payable by instalments	187
Presentation of	219
To one's self	187
Specially payable	213
When not enforceable	220
Usual form of	186
Protesting	221
" For better security "	222
Registered Protest	221
Provident Bank of Ireland	111
Provincial Bank	105
Qualified or Conditional Acceptance	192
Railway Company as party to a Bill of Exchange	201
Ramsay, Bonar & Co. (Edinburgh)	72

Ransom, Bouverie & Co.	56
Rate of Discount	229
Actual rate charged is in excess of apparent rate	229
Rate of Interest Charged in Ancient Greece	21
in Ancient Rome	26
by Ancient Brahmans	14
Early legal regulations (Ireland)	84
Ratification by Principal of Agent's Act	197
of acts done while drunk	200
of Infants' contracts	198
Realisation of Securities	177, 241, 250
Rebate on Bills	230
How a Banker should compute it for his yearly Balance Sheet	231
Redmond's Bank (Wexford)	100
"Refer to Drawer"	168
Refusal to Accept	192
Refusal to Transfer Shares	276
Relations between Banker and Customer	123
Release of Guarantor	244
Remedy for Dishonour of Bill of Exchange	227
of Cheque	179
Renfrewshire Bank	73
Reports on Customers, Banker's	242
Restrictive Endorsement on Bill of Exchange	214
Richard I. massacres Jews	40
Rider, a Scotch Coin	82
Right to Sue on Bill of Exchange	184, 189, 220
on Cheque	179
Robarts, Lubbock & Co.	56
Roberts & Co.'s Bank (Cork)	100
Roche's Bank (Cork)	100
Rogers, Samuel, referred to	57
Roman Coinage, Ancient	22
Rome, Bankers in Ancient	22
Royal Bank of Ireland	108
Royal British Bank	73
Rowe, Thomas, a London Goldsmith	49
"Running Account," origin of	42
Sadlier, John, M.P. (The Tipperary Bank)	111
"Safe Custody"	251

	PAGE
Sans Frais	222
Sans Protet	222
Sans Recours	214
Scotch Banking, Differs from English and Irish	74
Scotch Banks, Table of existing	76
Law regulating Issues of	259
Scotch Coinage, Early	77
Scotland, Banking in	70
Bank of	70
Royal Bank of	71
Private Banking in	71
Scott, Sir Samuel & Co.	57
Scrip	297
Scrupulum	22
Scully's Bank (Ireland)	100
Secret Partners	198
Securities, Deposits of	246
Realisation of by Banker	177, 241, 250
"Senior," in an Endorsement	149
Separate Estate, a married woman's	144
Sets, Bills of Exchange drawn in	237
Several Drawees on Bill of Exchange	191
Severus', constitution of, in reference to transfer of debts	26
Shares and Shareholders	271
and Stock, Deposit of	247
Transfer of	273
Definition of	285
Shares (Bank) Forgery of transfer	276
Held by married woman	276
Held jointly	276
Lien on	276
Purchase of by Bank itself	277
Refusal to Transfer	276
Traffic in by Directors	278
Are personal property	274
Broker's contract for purchase of	275
Liability of seller of	274
Shareholders, Liability of	274
Lists of	273
Shaw (Sir Robert) & Co. (Dublin)	98
Shekel, Jewish	12
Shetland Bank	73
Shillings first coined	38

"Short Bills"	234
Sight, At	143, 194
After	194
Signature of Drawer of Bill	195
of Cheque	143
Signing on Compulsion	235
Silver Coinage for Ireland, the Patent to Vyner	44
Silver Pennies	35
Simmonds v. *Taylor*	195
Sceatta and Styca—Early British Coins	35
Skill, want of, in transacting customer's business	126
Smith and Co. (Samuel), Nottingham	67
Smith, Donald & Co. (Edinburgh)	72
Smith, Payne and Smiths	57
Smith v. *Union Bank of London*	154
Snell, George	47
Snow, Jeremiah	47
Societies, as parties to Bills of Exchange	201
Southern Bank of Ireland	111
Scotland	73
Southwell, James—A Dublin usurer	86
Sovereigns first coined	38
Special Acceptance	189
Special Lodgment	178
"Specially Payable"	142
Specific Lien	240
Spinster as a Depositor	129
Spurious Coinage by Ancient Britons	34
Irish	78
in William III.'s reign	37
Spurious Notes, payment in	163
Squirrels (Three), Sign of Gosling's Bank	50
St. Patrick coins money	78
"Stale Cheque"	162
Stamp Act, 1870	202
Stamp Duties	202
Instruments Exempt from	211
On Bank Notes	255
On Foreign Bills	237
Paid by early Irish Private Bankers	101
Statute of Limitations	235
Does not apply to Bank Notes	265
Sterling, coins first styled	36

Stirling Bank	73
"Stock," definition of	285
Stock-jobbing Debt, acceptance for	185
Stopping Payment—of Bank Notes	264
of Cheques	166
Stock Broker	285, 289
Frauds by	292
Qualifications of	288, 296
Stock Exchange (London):—	
History of	286
Constitution of	288
Mode of dealing on	289, 294
Stock Exchange (Dublin)	295
Stock-Jobbers	289
Strahan, Paul & Bates	48
"Subscribed" Capital	272
Sue on a Bill, right to	184, 189, 220
Cheque, right to	179
Surrender of Bills of Lading	217
Stow quoted	40
"Sweating" the Coin, punishment in Ireland for	82
Swift & Co's Bank (Dublin)	89, 92
Swift, Dean, his attacks on Wood's halfpence	81
Elegy on John Damer	86
Lines on Snow, the Banker	48
A Banking Experience of	54
On the Irish Coinage	81
On the Irish Bankers (1727)	87
"Sworn Broker"	291
Testoons coined in Dublin	79
Thistle Bank (Glasgow)	74
Thomson, A. G. & A. (Glasgow)	72
Threepenny Pieces first coined	38
Tin, coinages of	35
Tipperary Joint Stock Bank	111
Time when payable, of Bill of Exchange	194
Title Deeds as securities	249
"Tokens" in Ireland	80
Transfer of Bank Shares	273, 275, 276
Trapezitæ—The Bankers of Ancient Greece	21
Travers, Sheares and Travers (Cork)	100
Trusts not recognised in shareholdings	276

Index.

	PAGE
Trustees, Cheques drawn by	144
Turner, Bernard	47
Tuscany, Banking in the Middle Ages in	27
Two Current Accounts kept by one person	178
Ulster Bank	110
Undated Cheque	137
Undue Influence, Bill or note given under	200
Unicorn, a Scotch coin	82
Union Bank of Ireland	111
London	69
Scotland	72, 74
Unfilled Stamp, Acceptance on	191
Unlimited Companies	272
Unlimited Liability	272, 281
Unstamped Bill of Exchange	211
Usury, derivation of word	24(*n*.)
Usury Laws Abolished	235
Usury, Laws Against :—	
English	234
Early Irish	84
Mosaic	13
Roman (Ancient)	24, 25, 26
"Value Received"	195
Vyner, Sir Robert	44
Sir Thomas	44
Welstead, Robert, a London Goldsmith	49
Western Bank of Scotland	73
Whitehall, Gilbert, a London Goldsmith	47
Wicklow Goldmines	77
Williams and Finn, Dublin Bankers	98
Williams, Deacon & Co.	57
Winchester, Mint at	35
Wood's Bank (Gloucester)	67
Wood's Halfpence (Ireland)	81
Words of Acceptance on Bill of Exchange	191
Worthless Bank Notes, Liability under	264
Wright & Co. (Nottingham)	67
Wrongful Dishonour of Bill	190
of Cheque	169

STATUTES.

	PAGE
The Banking Copartnerships Regulation Act (1826)	312
(The Act Authorising Joint Stock Banks)	
The Companies Act (1862)	326
Sale and Purchase of Shares in Joint Stock Banking Companies ("Leeman's Act")	327
The Companies Acts Amendment Act (1877)	328
The Banking and Joint Stock Companies Bill (1879)	330
Act relating to Crossed Cheques (1856)	334
Do. (1858)	334
Do. (1876)	336
Bank Notes and Bills Composition Stamp Duties (1828)	338
Stamp Duties (1870)	344
An Act to abolish "Days of Grace" on Bills *at Sight* (1871)	345
Compositions for Stamp Duty on Bank Post Bills (1864)	346
Do. (1867)	347
Validity of Cheques or Drafts for less than £1 (1860)	348
Clergymen as Members of Joint Stock Banks (1841)	348
Bank Holidays Act (1871)	350
Holidays Extension Act (1875)	352
Bankers' Books (Evidence)	352

THE END.

JAMES CORNISH AND SONS, 297, HIGH HOLBORN, W.C.

www.ingramcontent.com/pod-product-compliance
Lightning Source LLC
Chambersburg PA
CBHW030359230426
43664CB00007BB/662